Terrorism and the
Psychoanalytic Space

Terrorism and the Psychoanalytic Space

International Perspectives from Ground Zero

EDITED BY

Joseph A. Cancelmo, Psy.D.
Isaac Tylim, Psy.D.
Joan Hoffenberg, Ph.D.
Hattie Myers, Ph.D.

New York
Pace University Press
2003

ISBN 0-944473-63-6 (pbk: alk.ppr.)

Library of Congress Cataloging-in-Publication Data

Terrorism and the psychoanalytic space : international perspectives from
Ground Zero / edited by Joseph A. Cancelmo . . . [et al.].
 p. cm.
Includes index.
 ISBN 0-944473-63-6 (alk. paper)
 1. Terrorism—Psychological aspects—Congresses. 2. September 11
Terrorist Attacks, 2001—Psychological aspects—Congresses. 3. Victims
of terrorism—Psychological aspects--Congresses. 4. Post-traumatic
stress disorder—Patients—Rehabilitation—Congresses. I. Cancelmo,
Joseph A.
 RC552.P67T478 2003
 616.85 ' 2103—dc21

Contents

Preface

IN THE AFTERMATH OF SEPTEMBER 11th, MANY OF us whose life's work is helping others found ourselves in conflict over how best to contribute to the city's needs. At IPTAR (The Institute for Psychoanalytic Training and Research), some analysts chose to go to Ground Zero and work with survivors and their families, or with the rescue teams, while others felt they needed to maintain the therapeutic frame for their patients, or be with their own families. Whatever choice was made, no one felt they had done enough. At an IPTAR community meeting soon after the terrorist attacks, members made it clear that we were all working under conditions that were virtually unknown to us. There was a general agreement that individually many of us needed to develop skills in working with the victims of the attacks and that as a psychoanalytic society we needed to coordinate our efforts to help the community in this crisis. The IPTAR Society designated the IPTAR Clinical Center (ICC) to spearhead these efforts.

In the early days following the destruction of the Twin Towers, members and candidates at IPTAR volunteered to work *pro bono* with anyone who called the ICC referral line for help. With the help of Mr. Anthony Woods, the Clinical Center submitted a grant proposal to the Ittleson Foundation. Additional funds were needed to support the treatment of patients who were suddenly in financial need, to provide for additional training in working with crisis victims, and for in-service training. The idea for an international conference came from our recognition that the clinical territory we were in was new to us but, sadly, not new to many analysts in other countries. Our awareness that we needed new kinds of support suggested to us that other mental health practitioners in New York might also benefit from IPTAR's affiliation with the International Psychoanalytical Association.

We are grateful to Anthony Woods, the Executive Director of the Ittleson Foundation, who met with us and helped us take stock of both our international and analytic resources and our immediate clinical concerns. We are particularly appreciative of Henry Ittleson's generous financial support, without which this conference could not have happened. We would also like to express our appreciation to Dr. Herbert Krauss, Chair of the Psychology Department at Pace University, for co-sponsoring this conference.

Dr. Joseph A. Cancelmo, who was director of the Adult Division at the IPTAR Clinical Center, and Dr. Isaac Tylim, who was Program Chair of the IPTAR Society, graciously took on the task of co-chairing the conference. In less than half a year, under their remarkable leadership, both our own needs for greater clinical expertise, and our wish as an analytic community to contribute meaningfully toward the rebuilding of our devastated city have begun to be realized. We would also like to acknowledge the invaluable help of our conference committee that included Drs. Phyllis Beren (who was President of the IPTAR Society), Leon Anisfeld, Carolyn Ellman, Beth Hart, Ruth Stein, and Florence Williams, MA.

This conference, "Terrorism and the Psychoanalytic Space: International Perspectives from Ground Zero," was held on May 3-4, 2002, at Pace University, in the former shadows of the World Trade Center. The conference was an extraordinary experience for the hundreds of mental health professionals attending, who felt they learned a great deal personally and professionally from the papers and workshops presented by our international panelists and our IPTAR colleagues. We hope this book, which is essentially a record of these papers and workshops, will help other mental health professionals expand their clinical possibilities as we continue to respond to the changing needs of our community.

Joan Hoffenberg, PhD
Hattie Myers, PhD
Co-Directors, IPTAR Clinical Center (ICC)

Conference Participants

Abby Adams-Silvan, PhD - NY Freudian Society; IPTAR.

Lord John Alderdice, FRCPsych MLA - Speaker of the Northern Ireland Assembly, Member of the House of Lords (Westminster); Consultant Psychiatrist, Medical Psychotherapist.

Leon Anisfeld, DSW - IPTAR; Assistant Clinical Professor Of Psychiatry, Mount Sinai School of Medicine.

Donna Bassin, PhD – Faculty, IPTAR.

Mordechai Benyakar, MD - Argentine Psychoanalytic Society; VP, President Elect, World Psychiatric Association, Secretary On Military Psychiatry and Disaster.

Phyllis Beren, PhD - President, IPTAR.

Maria Bergmann, PhD - NY Freudian Society; IPTAR.

Avram Bornstein, PhD – Assistant Professor Of Anthropology, John Jay College of Criminal Justice, CUNY.

Martha Bragin, PhD - Psychosocial Advisor, UNICEF (Afghanistan); IPTAR.

Joseph Cancelmo, PsyD - Director ICC Adult Division; IPTAR.

Anne Early, MSW - Private Practice, Oklahoma City; Psychoanalytic Institute of N. California.

Shmuel Erlich, PhD - President, Israel Psychoanalytic Society; Chair, Freud Center, Hebrew University.

Mira Erlich-Ginor, MA - Israel Psychoanalytic Society.

K. William Fried, PhD - Former Associate Director, Residency Program, Maimonides Hospital, NY; IPTAR.

Myrna Gannagé, PhD - Professor Of Clinical Psychology, St. Joseph's University, Beruit; Director Of the Psychological Center For the Welfare of War Children and their Families.

Caroline Garland, PhD - Consultant Clinical Psychologist, Psychoanalyst, Tavistock Clinic; Founder and Head, Unit for the Study of Trauma and its Aftermath: British Health Service.

Alan Grey, PhD - Professor Emeritus of Psychology, Fordham Univ.; William Alanson White Institute.

Deena Harris, MD - Assistant Clinical Professor Of Psychiatry, Columbia Presbyterian Center.

Beth Hart, PhD - Professor Of Psychology, Pace University; IPTAR.

Elizabeth Hegeman, PhD - Professor Of Anthropology, John Jay College of Criminal Justice, CUNY; Training Analyst, William Alanson White Institute.

Paulina Kernberg, MD - Professor Of Psychiatry, Weill Medical College, Cornell University; Director Of Training, Child-Adolescent Residency Program, NY Presbyterian Hospital - Westchester.

Laura Kleinerman, MS - Director Child and Adolescent Program, IPTAR; Infant and Child Program, Columbia University.

Danielle Knafo, PhD - IPTAR, Assistant Professor Of Psychology, Long Island University.

Karen Komisar-Proner, MA - IPTAR; Tavistock Clinic.

Herbert Krauss, PhD - Chair, Psychology Department, Pace University, NYC.

Naama Kushnir-Barash, PhD - IPTAR; Israel Psychoanalytic Society.

Kay Ludwig, MSW - Private Practice, Oklahoma City; Psychoanalytic Institute of N. California.

Gilead Nachmani, PhD - William Alanson White Institute.

Richard Neugebauer, PhD, MPH - Department of Epidemiology of Developmental Brain Disorders, NYS Psychiatric Institute; Faculty of Medicine, College of Physicians and Surgeons, Columbia University.

Corliss Parker, PhD - IPTAR.

Maribeth Rourke, MSW - Director ICC Child - Adolescent Division; IPTAR; Faculty, IPTAR Child-Adolescent Program.

Edith Schwartz, PhD - IPTAR.

Ruth Stein, PhD - IPTAR; Israel Psychoanalytic Society.

Irving Steingart, PhD - IPTAR; NY Freudian Society.

Isaac Tylim, PsyD - Chair, IPTAR Program Committee; Department of Psychiatry, Maimonides Hospital, NY.

Sverre Varvin, MD - VP International Psychoanalytical Association; Senior. Consultant, Psychosocial Center For Refugees, University of Oslo.

Marcelo Vinar, MD - Uruguay Psychoanalytic Society; Former Director Of Department of Medical Education, University Of Uruguay School of Medicine.

Valentina Vrtikapa, MD - Formerly of General Hospital Trebinje, Bosnia and Herzegovina; Maimonides Hospital, NY.

Conference Commitee: Joseph Cancelmo & Isaac Tylim, Co-Chairs; Leon Anisfeld, Phyllis Beren, Carolyn Ellman, Beth Hart, Joan Hoffenberg, Hattie Myers, Ruth Stein, Florence Williams.

Introduction: Terrorism and the Psychoanalytic Space International Perspectives from Ground Zero
Conceptual Crossroads—Clinical Challenges

JOSEPH A. CANCELMO, ISAAC TYLIM

JOAN HOFFENBERG & HATTIE MYERS

THIS GLOBAL, COLLABORATIVE EFFORT THAT CULMINATED in our groundbreaking conference was meant to be a resource for New York City clinicians faced with an unprecedented demand for services at a moment of great urgency and distress. While attempting to help others, we were also coping with our own reactions to September 11. It was the intensity of these dual obligations that encouraged us to turn to our colleagues from around the world who had long been living and working under conditions of terror and stress. Under these difficult circumstances, mental health clinicians from North America, South America, the Middle East, Eastern Europe, England and Northern Ireland came together to discuss the conceptual and practical consequences of terrorism and continuing trauma on ourselves, on our patients, and our analytic paradigms.

We hoped that the conference would be a springboard toward deeper reflection on the meaning of this violation of our sense of safety in the psychoanalytic space. We designed the conference with these things in mind—starting with our choice of location. It seemed incomprehensible to us to have this conference anywhere else but at *Ground Zero,* and yet this was a difficult decision to make. New Yorkers were still numb and disoriented (not yet thinking about professional conferences), and also anxious navigating around the wounded city. Pace University, the site of our conference, was in the shadow of the former towers, and hit hard that magnificent and now infamous late summer day as students began morning classes.

We began there on Friday evening with an introductory panel and moved Saturday morning into smaller, more intimate experiential settings to facilitate dialogue and shared reflection for all who attended. We ended with a luncheon panel at South Street Seaport's Bridgewaters, a soaring space with views of New York Harbor and the Brooklyn Bridge, offering us a protective and inspirational space to hear more from our colleagues, and then to discuss their ideas in roundtable dialogue.

The conference was well attended and feedback was extremely positive, including a groundswell of interest in seeing the panel and workshop presentations in print. Our international participants, in particular, were enthusiastic about this long-awaited opportunity to share expertise and adaptation forged in their own struggles with state sponsored terror, man-made and natural disasters, and war here at "ground zero." This book contains our collaborative vision for the conference through an edited collection of papers from three main panels: Conceptual Crossroads: The Altered Psychoanalytic Space; Clinical Challenges: Navigating the Altered

Psychoanalytic Space; and a Symposium: Developmental Effects on Children and Adolescents, as well as workshop papers on related topics that capture the range of responses demanded of psychoanalysts faced with these challenges.

The first panel, entitled "Conceptual Crossroads: The Altered Psychoanalytic Space," was designed with the intention of highlighting both differences and similarities in the conceptualization of dramatic disruptions or attacks on the psychoanalytic frame. Each of the papers brings to the fore a unique perspective on the imperative demand to question our own theoretical and technical positions when faced with the impact of the immediate effects and ongoing threats of terrorism.

Three internationally prominent psychoanalysts shared their direct and vivid experiences in their clinical and consultative practices with traumatic events and ongoing threats of terrorism in conflict areas of the world where such events continue to be daily occurrences. Lord John Alderdice, Speaker of the Northern Ireland Assembly, Member of the House of Lords (Westminster) and Consultant Psychiatrist, Medical Psychotherapist, discussed his extensive experience in the area of community conflicts between Protestants and Catholics in Northern Ireland. A politician and clinician, Lord Alderdice's work may be classified as one of applied psychoanalysis to larger groups. Shmuel Erlich, Psychoanalyst and Psychologist, President, Israel Psychoanalytic Society and Chair, Freud Center, Hebrew University, invited us to enter into the privacy of the psychoanalyst's consulting room and to confront the immediate impact of terror from the street in the analytic space. Marcello Vinar, Psychiatrist and Psychoanalyst, Uruguay Psychoanalytic Society, and Former Director of Medical Education, University of Uruguay School of Medicine, outlined his understanding of violence and trauma based on his own experience with state sponsored terror in South America. The papers clearly illustrated the complex issues at hand while offering moving accounts of the meetings between analyst and patient as partners sharing a common traumatic reality.

The workshops which were presented during the Saturday morning session integrated many of the broader themes presented by the panelists—a melding of the conceptual crossroads and the clinical challenges for the psychoanalytic space. These presentations, "Clinical Crossroads: Psychoanalysts' Response to Terrorism and the Expansion of the Psychoanalytic Space," allowed for more intimate discussion and focus on nuances of experience. The goal of these workshops was to help us understand how we might find solid ground when assumptions about physical safety and predictability are shattered. These workshops addressed more specifically *what* happens and *to whom* in cases of acute trauma and ongoing terrorism: The direct effects of trauma and terrorism on our patients (Benyakar), whether they be tortured refugees (Varvin) or a retired British policeman in Northern Ireland (Alderdice); the reverberations between patient and analyst trying to work in the midst of instability in Israel (Kushner-Barash; Erlich-Ginor) and in New York (Bergmann); the ruptures in the parent-child bond in Oklahoma City (Ludwig & Early) and New York (Beren & Parker); how terror casts a shadow over entire generations past, present, and future (Bornstein & Hegeman, et. al.), from the aftermath of surviving the Holocausts (Harris; Vrtikapa & An i s f e l d) to the effects on adolescents watching the towers collapse from classroom windows (Hart & Krauss) to workers at ground zero (Fried; Adams-Silvan), and the attempts to preserve the memory of what was destroyed (Bassin & Neugebauer). On a more conceptual yet personal note, Marcello Vinar presented a moving account of how extreme torture affects and distorts our subjectivity.

The conference continued with a Symposium of two panels devoted to the effects of living under conditions of terror for adolescents and children: "A Child-Adolescent Panel and Symposium: Developmental Effects on Children and Adolescents." The first of these panels expanded on the developmental and educational aspects of the experience of terrorism on children and adolescents. Shmuel Erlich joined us again to discuss the creation of terrorists. Using two theoretical models, he developed an understanding of the need that becoming a terrorist might play for adolescents. Myrna Gannagé, Professor of Clinical Psychology at St. Joseph's University in Beirut, Lebanon, was unable to attend the conference due to political circumstances. Her paper was read by Yasmine Saad, psychology extern at IPTAR and a doctoral student at Adelphi University. Gannagé reported research she had completed on differences among children living in Lebanon during the war years, children living in Paris whose parents had lived in Lebanon during the war, and Parisian children. Paulina Kernberg, Professor of Psychiatry, Weill Medical College, Cornell University, and Director of Training, Child-Adolescent Psychiatry Residency Program, New York Presbyterian Hospital—Westchester, was also on this panel. (Unfortunately, she was unable to contribute her presentation in the form of a paper for this book.) In her presentation, she tried to elucidate the current lives of Arabic children and the possible implications of aspects of their education for their participation in and views on terrorism. Finally, Irving Steingart, a Child and Adult Psychoanalyst and Psychologist, Fellow of IPTAR and the New York Freudian Society, discussed these wide ranging papers.

The second part of the morning's program dealt more specifically with the clinical implications of terror in the lives of children—that is, trauma-born failure to symbolize and mourn and its impact on identity formation. Martha Bragin, a candidate at IPTAR and a psychosocial advisor for UNICEF in Afghanistan, began by talking of what happens when what should remain fantasy is enacted in life. Through examples of her work in Afghanistan, she described how these enactments of violent fantasy material in our lives have a disorganizing effect on children, therapists and society as a whole. Following her, Karen Proner, Psychoanalyst and member of IPTAR and the Tavistock Clinic, presented very evocative clinical material from a young girl she treated soon after September 11. Proner, drawing her theoretical frame from the theories of Meltzer and Bion, noted how new ideas can often have a disastrous effect as they force one to reorganize all previously held ideas. Finally, Laura Kleinerman, Child and Adult Psychoanalyst, Director of the Child and Adolescent Psychotherapy Program at IPTAR and Fellow and faculty member at IPTAR, presented her work with a young girl whose earlier life traumas were reawakened by the events of September 11. Kleinerman evokes the child's efforts to grapple with and defend against the recent trauma and the reactivated earlier difficulties.

3

In the afternoon, over 250 people walked the short distance to Bridgewaters at South Street Seaport to share a meal and to discuss their experiences. Following lunch, the afternoon panel, "Clinical Challenges: Navigating the Altered Psychoanalytic Space," focused on boundaries between analysts and their patients in times of terror.

Caroline Garland, Consultant Clinical Psychologist and Psychoanalyst at the Tavistock Clinic, London, and the founder and head of the unit for the Study of Trauma and its Aftermath, British Health Service, described, from a Kleinian perspective, ways in which the analytic space can be used to reflect upon and contain universal aspects of human destructiveness. She did so through the poignant, clinically familiar case of her patient's massive childhood trauma. Mordechai Benyakar, Psychologist, Psychiatrist and Psychoanalyst, and President Elect of the World Psychiatric Association's Section on Military Psychiatry and Disaster, presented his overview of the psychic impact of what he calls the "violent irruptions" of the traumatic. He described the impact of these psychically disruptive situations such as acute trauma, disasters (whether natural or manmade), and terrorism. Through clinical examples, he differentiated these personal events from psychically disruptive environments, whether they are from ongoing terrorist threats or rapidly deteriorating social structure. Sverre Varvin, Psychiatrist and Psychoanalyst, and Senior Consultant for the Psychosocial Center for Refugees, University of Oslo, and VP, International Psychoanalytical Association, described his view of how the experience of terror may affect the mind along several dimensions: through isolation and inability to use others for emotional regulation and support, to isolation from the group, affecting identity and self-image, and through isolation from culture as a containing resource and anchor for meaning and shared reality. Through the lens of his treatment of a traumatized refugee who endured unthinkable torture in her homeland, he described how this terror impacted the analyst and the metasetting, in terms of his patient's lack of symbolization and mentalization of affective states and experiences.

The chapters in this book follow the flow of the panel presentations. The workshop reports are presented last. We begin this book with the Opening Address to the conference, written just months after 9/11, on the heels of the tragic plane crash in Far Rockaway, and with New York still anxious over anthrax, and the daily terrorist alerts and bomb threats.

Opening Address

I RECALL WHEN THE KERNEL OF AN IDEA FOR THIS conference first occurred to me: it was the evening of 9/11. A frantic e-mail from an out-of-town relative ended with a question: "I hear they're asking New York Mental Health Professionals to volunteer downtown. Don't you all need some help from *outside*?"

Of course, there was so much the New York mental health community *could* do and *did* do to help those directly traumatized in those first hours and days, and, since then, as the dust has settled, to also assist those in need with mourning and their struggle to cope with the painful reactivation of earlier trauma and loss.

But we gather here this weekend to get some "help" from "outside"—from colleagues from around the world, and from Oklahoma City; colleagues who have grappled in their own lands with the reverberation of terrorism and trauma in the analytic space. We, in turn, can offer our help to them, since our experience is also unique.

September 11 has narrowed the distance between consultation room and street. It seems, at times, that the boundaries between the two have blurred. The shared reality of this horrific attack on the Twin Towers, the traumatic loss of thousands who perished in the wake of their collapse, the anguish of those left behind, the specter of future terrorism, but also, the resilience of the human spirit and the depth of empathy, altruism and national unity, have clearly altered our internal experiences in profound ways, both as citizens of the world and as analysts and therapists.

But our work also remains familiar, reassuringly so; like an asteroid temporarily knocked from orbit by some catastrophic event, there is still the gravitational pull of our analytic frame which keeps us on course. Yet somehow, everything seems changed, transformed, perhaps still evolving on a path of its own unknown trajectory.

Our patients' anxieties about flying, about nuclear, biological and chemical warfare, and even here, about human bombs, are one moment conscious, and the next, subtly woven into psychic fabric. But these are our anxieties as well—not just located in our patients—something the "other" has experienced. These anxieties are rooted in the objective reality of events that did, unthinkably, happen, and now, unthinkably, could happen, for we have seen the unspeakable unfold before our eyes, for many, burned into hard drive memory, capable of instant retrieval when a siren sounds; subjectively, at a deeper knowing level, they may echo previous trauma and loss, and for all, evoke the earliest anxieties that form the bedrock of our human condition.

As mental health professionals we gather enormous strength from our attempts to understand the trauma and terror of others, to help them with the protracted process of mourning when loss is sudden and traumatic. We know we are vulnerable to the secondary traumatization that comes from such work. And we also know that we are particularly vulnerable to our patients' traumatic experiences when they find a home in our internal world.

The shared reality of 9/11 is of another order. We cannot grasp this impact yet we live with it, each in our own ways, day to day. Comprehension fails us—as we ponder "ground zero" do we see hallowed ground? a construction site? a place where less than nine months ago, great and powerful buildings soared, teeming with lives in progress? These impossible structures, illusive in their comings and goings in clouds and mist, now, like phantom limbs, make their past presence felt through their painful absence and the absence of thousands of lost souls.

So, analyst and patient now coexist in a shared world where trauma is both objective and subjective, both common and unique, located out there in the "other," and within ourselves.

Our recovery—our adjustment to base line—has been referred to as the "New Normal," an adaptive yet disquieting re-alignment of our sense of security. A new space where we manage to compartmentalize our unease yet, paradoxically, a space whose very necessity belies our vulnerability. Our previous reliance on our ability to provide a safe and constant analytic space no longer feels a given and only adds to these feelings of vulnerability. We meet this weekend as citizens of the world to attempt some comprehension of this unleashing of aggression, and its impact on our internal worlds.

And we meet this weekend as psychoanalysts and therapists to reflect in this shared space upon the conceptual and practical consequences of terrorism and continuing trauma on ourselves, on the children, adolescents and adults that we treat, and on our paradigms. We will talk about nuances of these experiences in our workshops. And we will end the conference with an unprecedented opportunity to share a meal and intimate dialogue with our colleagues, and, soon, new friends from other parts of the United States, from South America, The Middle East, Northern Ireland and England.

As I wrote these thoughts, I recalled a comment by the pilot on a flight I recently took—my first since 9/11; consciously I was anxious, but of course, like a good analyst (at least I hope), I was able to put it in objective and subjective context for myself. Then the doors of the plane slammed shut—once familiar sounds now potential harbingers of peril. The tension was palpable—was it only my reaction, a projection, a shared experience?

The pilot interrupted my reverie—he introduced himself, and then said: "Now please take a moment and introduce *yourself* to the person next to you. For the duration of this flight, we're all family here—all in this place together."

PART I

Conceptual Crossroads: The Altered Psychoanalytic Space

Reflections on the fate of unsymbolized trauma and the interplay of objective and subjective experience

Introduction

ISAAC TYLIM

SEVEN MONTHS AFTER THE TERRORIST ATTACK ON THE World Trade Center, an international community of psychoanalytically informed theoreticians and clinicians gathered blocks away from Ground Zero. The purpose of this special event was to delve into the effects of terrorism on the psychoanalytic space.

The September 11 terrorist attacks in downtown Manhattan exerted a profound impact on psychoanalysts' practices. Unpredictable intrusions in the analytic space seem to have challenged psychoanalysts' capacity to maintain an optimal therapeutic distance from their analysands. More than ever before in the history of American psychoanalysis, the morning after that infamous Tuesday, impingements from without underscore the interplay between internal and external reality, between process and disrupted frame, foreground and background.

Shrouded in a new unexpected feeling of vulnerability, analyst and analysand jointly visited unexplored islands of psychic despair. They were forced to face together that which is capable of arousing the unknown known in our psyche, a terror that is akin to the internal state of the infant when the protective shield breaks down.

The stability of the analytic frame allows the process to unfold. A relatively unperturbed frame with its background immutability helps to contain the most primitive and regressive pockets of the psyche. Conversely, a frame which is shaken up by violent disruptions may be more likely to move into the foreground of the analytic domain. The result is a major alteration in the frame caused by the opening of deep fissures that color the analysis with intimations of catastrophe and doom.

How do analysts conceptualize experiences of terror? Terror has the potential to induce, in both partners of the analytic dyad, primitive affective states. Under these circumstances we enter the land of the uncanny. The plasticity of our mental apparatus seems to re-establish what in psychodynamic terms is referred to as the "imperishable," those early developmental stages which co-exist with more advanced ones despite subsequent developmental achievements. These affective states which disorganize and disorient our ego capacities connote the uncanny.

Uncanny in the original German text is 'unheimlich,' the opposite of 'heimisch'—homely, domestic, native, concealed. Freud reminds us of the ambivalence inherent in the word 'umheimlich' which may be also used as the contrary of what is familiar, "for this uncanny is in reality nothing new or alien, but something which is familiar and old established in the mind and which has become alienated from it through the process of repression" (Freud, 1919, p. 220).

Moreover, geography, ideologies, and circumstances may highlight differences and similarities in our ability to conceptualize terrorism. In June 1939 a Spanish physician, Dr. Mira, read a paper before the British Psychoanalytic Society in which he gave a gruesome account of his experiences in Madrid during the civil war. He was particularly impressed with the severity of certain acute shock conditions such as mutism, emotional paralysis and even death among the patients he treated. Jones observed that those conditions were uncommon during the London Blitz, wondering whether differences in national psychology had to be considered to explain this striking contrast.

Back in 1939 London, English analysts were eager to compare notes with Spanish colleagues; today in New York, 2002, American analysts invited the international analytic community to join them in a renewed effort to conceptualize the unspeakable

The new generation of American psychoanalysts has been spared from having to deal with the psychological effects of terrorism in their own backyards. This panel aimed at establishing a dialogue between American psychoanalysts and international colleagues who had had years of direct exposure to the effect of terrorism on their respective psychoanalytic practices. Whether in Northern Ireland, Israel, or Uruguay, whether in English, Hebrew, or Spanish, each of the panelists had at one historical juncture or another attempted to name, to put words to that which subverts representation and attacks *logos*.

Lord Alderdice from Northern Ireland, Dr. Erlich from Israel, and Dr. Vinar from Uruguay are welcome messengers who deliver moving and thought provoking reflections on disruptive analytic spaces. Their work becomes an important tool in the arduous process of elaborating the most pressing theoretical and clinical challenge post-September 11 American psychoanalysts have been called to confront. These three prominent analysts were, and continue to be, witness to unnamed, unsymbolized cruelty that in today's global order seems to stretch our analytic frames and test the limits of our discourse.

Lord Alderdice's paper reveals the unusual work of a politician and clinician who is well versed in psychoanalytic thinking. He elegantly illustrates the application of psychoanalytic conceptualization to the area of inter- and intra-communal conflict in Northern Ireland. As a Speaker's chair in the Northern Ireland Assembly, he displays a capacity to listen and reflect not unlike an analyst would in his or her consulting room. The worlds of individuals transport him into the world of the community they represent. In this vein Lord Alderdice studies the phenomenon of terrorism at the systemic level of the regional community where he believes the need to contain powerful affects is most needed.

Lord Alderdice assumes a realistic and practical position, being fully aware of the limitations of his method. He does recognize the inevitability of acting out when a divided community such as Northern Ireland attempts to resolve long lasting conflicts. Reflecting on "the motivation of those who have acted with extreme violence and positive engagement," Lord Alderdice insists that the same respect with which the analyst treats his or her patients must be extended to those who hold different ideological positions. Only in an atmosphere of mutual respect may opposite groups within a community enhance their capacity to contain feelings and responses.

Dr. Vinar's paper stresses the need for analysts to pay attention to the new challenges brought about by patients' stories of violence and terror. He reflects on the analyst's attempt to sustain alive the analytic function in front of those stories since the destructive work of the death instinct tends to render useless the capacity for symbolization or representation. He addresses the problem of preserving the analytic frame and the inherent difficulties in dealing with those social catastrophic situations that disorganize the social link and disarticulate the ordinary ways of psychic functioning.

Delving into the connections between group psychology and culture, he refers to the lack of objective account for the reality of extreme violence. The analyst must deal with the tension generated by the need to remember and the need to forget. In Dr. Vinar's words, the analyst working with victims of terror and violence must "recognize the power of testimony and the strength of negation and denial."

Dr. Erlich delivers a personal and vivid account of his daily experience as a psychoanalyst and psychotherapist in Israel under siege of recurrent terrorist attacks. He focuses on his work with individuals who although not directly affected by an actual terrorist attack, come to their regular sessions with a curious mixture of "active passivity." These patients suffer from a state that is characterized by a restriction of movement, worrying about themselves and their significant relationships, and frequently unable to concentrate at work.

After expanding on the nature of the psychoanalytic space, the differentiation between the psychoanalytic space and the psychoanalytic situation, and the links between psychic reality and physical or external reality, Dr. Erlich offers three thought provoking clinical vignettes that share a common background of horror and terror despite their different ways of dealing with the impact of external reality. With sensitivity and respect, Dr. Erlich elaborates on the ethical dilemma one faces when the external conditions may dent the safety of the psychoanalytic space. He raises important questions regarding the analyst's responsibility towards his or her patient's welfare when terror seems to take over the streets, and traveling to and from sessions may endanger patients.

Acts of terrorism evoke associations of psychological catastrophe, ideas of doom, or apocalyptic fantasies. Acts that defy symbolization seem to place hope on hold and may lead to a de-idealization of psychoanalysis. The following papers are three distinctive and unique psychoanalytic voices that in the sea of terror have opened doors to meaning.

REFERENCES

Jones, E. (1948). Psychology and war conditions. In *Papers on Psychoanalysis* (pp. 173-190). Baltimore: The Williams and Wilkins Company.
Freud, S. (1919). The 'Uncanny'. *Standard Edition*. 17, 219-253.

Terrorism and the Psychoanalytic Space

LORD JOHN ALDERDICE

FOR SOME MONTHS I TREATED A MAN WHO HAD been involved in a loyalist terrorist gang well known for having committed some of the most gruesome murders of the whole period of "the Troubles" in Northern Ireland. He had left paramilitary activity behind some years before, had married and settled down and was seeking help for episodes of anxiety of recent onset. The source of the anxiety quickly became apparent. From time to time he would become angry with his wife and he, connecting with his powerful feelings of aggression, panicked that he would violently attack his wife, as he had in the past participated in the savage murder of Catholic people.

This revelation led to him talking about his own past. He had been the illegitimate son of a young unmarried Protestant woman who had an affair with a Catholic man but was deserted by him when she became pregnant. She bore the child but her life was blighted by the affair. The patient harbored a profound and bitter resentment about the humiliation that he and his mother had suffered during his childhood, living in a hard-line Protestant ghetto and known to be the illegitimate son of a Catholic. It was not difficult for me, or indeed him, to make a connection between his hatred of Catholics in general and his own shaming experience. The result was a positive one in that he became able to manage his anger with his wife without the terror that it would lead to him killing the one he loved.

It would be possible to explore this individual story further, addressing ambivalent feelings about his mother, the relationship with his grandmother, dream material that connected various parts of his life and so on, and it is an interesting case because it is not common for terrorists or former terrorists to seek psychotherapeutic help. The individual psychoanalytic approach created for this man a space where his feelings were contained, and in which it became more possible to reflect on what was going on at various levels in his mind, to make connections, to achieve some mastery over his emotions, and find some resolution. Without doubt this work was made easier by the distance in time between his paramilitary activities and the period in therapy.

My own particular interest over the years, however, has been in whether it is possible to translate this psychoanalytical approach beyond the arena of individual intrapsychic conflict and into the field of intra- and inter-communal conflict. Politics has been for some fifteen years the place where I spend most of my life, and politics is now more than ever dominated by the pressure to act rather than to think. Even words in political life are more often than not "twenty second sound-bite" actions rather than expressions of thought. Statements are often reactions to events rather than the communication of reflections. One of the values to me of my analytic background is its facilitation of the capacity to reflect. Previously during the Talks

Process and now in the Speaker's chair in the Northern Ireland Assembly, this professional discipline helps me think about why a member is saying the things he is saying. How far are they a reflection of his/her personal background or current circumstances? How far is it an expression of the mood of the House at that moment? It will without doubt be, and be claimed as, an expression of the view of the community he or she represents, but what does it say about that community, and the much wider world community of which we are all a part? Just as important is the psychoanalytic imperative to contain and reflect upon one's own thoughts, feelings and reactions and to try to become clear how far they are a response to the other and to external reality, and how far they are an expression of one's own "assumptive world."

I have come to the view that the psychoanalytic approach can create a space for reflection too valuable to be restricted to work with individuals and small groups. I believe that this is particularly true when political discourse in our community is overtaken by powerful emotions, as is the case during times of crisis like now. The violence of domestic and international terrorism, which has been experienced by more than half of the countries in the world, provokes particularly strong feelings and I should like to describe how we in Northern Ireland have tried to understand and address terrorism.

In the late 1960's there were civil rights marches in the United States, Britain, Germany, France, Japan, and in Northern Ireland. In each context they addressed the particular concerns of that community and in Northern Ireland it was discrimination against Catholics which was center stage. The mainly Catholic protestors were joined by a significant number of Protestants who shared their concerns about injustice in Northern Ireland, but other Protestants were opposed to the civil rights movement, staging counter-demonstrations which resulted in violence. Vigilante groups emerged in both communities and the situation deteriorated with the appearance of gun and bomb attacks. Terrorism, which had a long history in Ireland, had reappeared. As the situation began to spiral out of control the reaction of the government was predictable and understandable. These were criminal acts and must be met by the full force of the law, first by police intervention, then the army called in as back-up, and by 1971 due process set aside and hundreds of republicans and loyalists interned by executive order, without trial. However natural this response, the result was not stabilization but further deterioration. Soon it became necessary to reflect more carefully on the nature of the terrorism we were facing.

Unlike other "isms" such as nationalism, communism, liberalism or socialism, terrorism is not a belief system but a tactic. It may be used by the left or the right, or by more populist and nationalist extremists. It involves the premeditated use of violence to create a climate of fear, but is aimed at a wider target than the immediate victims of the violence. Count Mikhail Bakunin, the Russian anarchist, called this the "propaganda of the deed"—the target is the audience, not the immediate victims The victims are often civilians and while arbitrarily chosen, they have symbolic significance; but the real target is the responsible authority. The organizationally weak terrorist group aims to provoke organizationally strong authorities into substantial response and preferably an over-reaction that will damage its standing and moral authority both domestically and internationally. To this end the violence is not only intentionally criminal in terms of the domestic law but also of any human code such that by violating the social norms it provokes outrage and can not be ignored. What is perhaps most difficult for people from a stable law-abiding community to comprehend is that those who engage in terrorism believe themselves to be entirely justified. They see themselves as righting some terrible wrong, some humiliation, some deep disrespect that has been done them, their community or their nation and they in their weakness are, with great courage and risk to themselves, embarked on the heroic task of righting that wrong. One thing at least is common to both the terrorists and those who are combating terrorism—that is the belief that to kill off the "evil thing" is good, and should one die in the attempt it is not only a good and courageous act it also confirms the evil of the enemy. I must here point out that I do make a differentiation between terrorism, whose purpose is to bring about radical change in a polity, and the tactics of terror used by some dictatorial states to maintain the status quo. I am not making any judgments about moral equivalence or otherwise, but I am differentiating between the two because without some clarity of definition it is hard to come to an understanding of the different mechanisms by which violence is used in the political field.

Reflection by the authorities in Northern Ireland led to the adoption of a number of principles in addressing terrorism in Northern Ireland. First, the recognition that the purpose of policing is first and foremost the maintenance of the human rights of everyone in the community, and that all actions must be measured against this indicator of success. As a result all legislation against terrorism needs to approximate as closely as possible to ordinary criminal law and procedure and must conform to international law and conventions. It is crucial to observe due process and maintain scrutiny and control by civil authorities subject to democratic accountability. Any additional offences and powers must be necessary, proportionate, and balance security needs and civil rights and liberties. If it begins to appear to the civilian population that the liberal democratic nature of the society is being damaged by the reaction of the government, it is the authorities that will be blamed in the long-term, not the terrorists. If there is a resort to general repression the government may be unable to demonstrate that it is taking proportionate and properly directed measures only against terrorists and their active collaborators. Soon the terrorists are able to present themselves, to at least some sections of the community, as the protectors of civil society against an oppressive regime—exactly the view the terrorists set out to demonstrate and address.

It is of course relatively easy to describe such an approach in the cool climate of a psychoanalytic conference. It is quite another matter to promulgate it in the raging heat of a community torn apart by violence and death, but it is at precisely this level that I believe the creation of psychoanalytical space is most needed. There are many levels on which one could explore the issue of terrorism. One can address it at the individual level as I have briefly described in the case of one patient. One can study it at the macro level of world systems theory where it can be interpreted as an expression of the international instability and overt conflict that appears in semi-peripheral regimes during periods of hegemonic transition or decline. I choose to apply it at the systemic level of the regional community not least because this is where the psychoanalytical capacity to contain powerful emotions is most needed.

Returning to Northern Ireland, the application of these principles helped stabilize the situation but it did not resolve it. A stalemate developed where neither side could win militarily. This led to a serious exploration of the political dimension. Initially many different solutions were suggested with the unstated assumption that if the "right plan" could be invented everyone would suddenly grasp it with relief and implement it. Of course this was an illusion. It is not the content of a solution that is critical but the process of achieving it. We know in our own work that merely telling the patient where their problem lies, or giving them an analytic text to read, is rarely a healing intervention. It is taking the patient through the analytic process which is transformational.

The political transformation began outside Northern Ireland. We know that when parents bring us a child with symptoms we must address not just the child but also the parental relationship if we are not to have our therapeutic efforts founder. In the same way Northern Ireland had no prospect of peace without the British and Irish Governments working together, just as, one might say, Cyprus will not see a resolution unless Greece and Turkey work together. Joining the European Community on the same day in 1973 gave the United Kingdom and the Republic of Ireland a foundation that was then greatly strengthened by the 1985 Anglo-Irish Agreement. This was not in itself a solution but an institutional framework which ensured that officials from the two countries met regularly to address political, economic and security issues, whatever the current state of relationships on the ground. It then took two more years to persuade the parties to engage in "talks about talks" and another four years of these "talks about talks" until in 1991 agreement was reached on the framework for substantive negotiations. This was an equivalent to the South African "Memorandum of Understanding" which provided the structure for their negotiations much in the way that the structure of our regular psychoanalytical sessions contains the patient and therapist through the storms of the treatment. The Northern Ireland Talks began when the leader of the Fianna Fail party, Albert Reynolds, was Irish Taosieach and Conservative leader John Major was British Prime Minister. Albert Reynolds was succeeded by Fine Gael Taosieach John Bruton, and he by the current Fianna Fail leader Bertie Aherne, while John Major was replaced by Labour Prime Minister Tony Blair. Not just the governments but even the Northern Ireland participating parties changed. Prior to the paramilitary cease-fires the governments and the other parties would not talk with Sinn Fein and the loyalist parties, but when after the cease-fires on both sides they were welcomed into the Talks, Dr. Paisley and many of the other unionist parties walked out. Whatever the turbulent state of relations it was of crucial importance that the Process was robust enough to survive. In passing I would note that there was never a time when all the parties were around the table, but they were all afforded the possibility of being there, and all were there at some point.

In our work we are aware not only that that there will be acting out which needs to be explored but also that it will often take a long time for change to take place. It is also important that there are not any "No-Go Areas," things that cannot be spoken about. Our psychoanalytic work must be, in the current political parlance, "inclusive." In the same way it was a characteristic of our process and of the South African process that the parties involved were not just the large parties, but all the parties, and that everything was open to be spoken about, without commitment. This is a notable difference from what is proposed for the Middle East.

The role of Senator George Mitchell was crucial in this part of the Process. While in the Middle East he has been asked to produce a Plan, his great strength in our Talks was his capacity to conduct the Process. I was often reminded of the psychoanalytic process during his chairmanship. On one occasion a party leader spoke for seven hours, interrupted only by the overnight recess. Month after month Senator Mitchell listened, clarified and facilitated. Everyone was given the dignity of explaining their concerns and perspectives, the history of their community, its grievances and vision of the future. Everyone was also required to listen to their traditional enemies speak of these things, and given the opportunity to explore them together. As a result, when much later Senator Mitchell intervened no one accused him of not understanding, for everyone knew that he did understand, both intellectually and emotionally. His use of an agreed deadline, also a lesson from South Africa, was carefully crafted with all the parties in the Fall of 1997, and was achieved with the Agreement on Good Friday. He had given some five months notice to enable us to work towards closure—a model of good analytic practice.

One of the few clear messages from research in international conflict resolution is that the most successful outcomes are those where there is long-term follow-up and support for the process, after the achievement of an agreement. I should like to say just a few words about this implementation phase. The central feature is the establishment of an Assembly where the elected representatives of all sections of the community meet to pass legislation and govern on a power-sharing basis. Of course they still do not agree on the fundamental political principles, but politics is not about such agreement. It is about how we disagree without killing each other. That is what happens when democratic politics fails. What can be done is to agree on the institutions and to work together on the practical issues. The structure of the Assembly is entirely proportionate. A party with 10% of the popular vote will have 10% of the Assembly Members, 10% of the Committee places 10% of the Chairmanships and Deputy Chairmanships and, most unusual of all, 10% of the Ministers in the Government. If the Ministers refuse to meet, as some do, then the work is carried out by written procedure. Votes on contentious issues require not just a majority of the House, but also a majority of unionist members and a majority of nationalist members. In this way everyone has a say in how things run.

Dr. Ian Paisley is Chairman of the Agriculture Committee. When he stands up to speak for his committee, which includes not only unionists and nationalists, but also members of Sinn Fein, he represents that whole committee and he speaks about the EU Common Agricultural Policy, subsidies for farmers, and the dangers of brucellosis, TB and Foot and Mouth Disease. He works with the Agriculture Minister, Ms. Brid Rodgers, a Gaelic speaking, Catholic nationalist woman, and not infrequently compliments her on the quality of her work. Sinn Fein, although it is the fourth largest party in the Assembly, now controls more than half of the government's expenditure. Its two Ministers, Mr. Martin McGuinness and Ms. Bairbre de Brun, run Education and Health, Social Services and Public Safety—all the schools (Catholic, state, integrated and Irish language), all the hospitals, the Fire Service and so on. They too must find ways of working with unionist politicians and people—and they do.

This is currently working remarkably well but will it continue to work? Who knows? This is truly an experiment. It is a completely different system from anywhere else. The first election is not the most important. The real value of democratic elections is not who is elected the first time, but the fact that they are the only mechanism we know for the transfer of power peacefully from one administration to another. It remains to be seen whether this can be achieved in Northern Ireland, but there is one final element which gives me some hope.

I mentioned at the start of this paper how and why humiliation was a driving factor in the bitterness and violence of my patient. I also drew attention to the same factor at a community level. I have never met anyone who did not want to be treated with respect, and my experience of politicians is that we have an almost insatiable desire to be respected. Conversely disrespect and humiliation is rarely either forgotten or forgiven. Of course it is not reasonable to expect Dr. Paisley and Mr. Adams to feel respect for each other but it is important to ask them to behave in a respectful way in the Assembly. Without this there is no prospect of even a working arrangement. With respectful behavior much can be achieved. One of the reasons why conflicts in countries such as mine run so deep and create such violence is because each side treats the most essential features of the other with disrespect. This is true of nationhood. The disregard of my nation's language—even if I myself cannot speak it—is felt as a disrespect of me. The same is true of religion. Religious beliefs fulfil a fundamental need to create order out of the uncertain experiences of life. When our belief structure, religious or otherwise, is attacked it is perceived as a threat to that which protects us from chaos. We defend against it for fear of a breakdown of our way of making sense of life, and dealing with the disappointments of the past, the vagaries of the present and our fears for the future. Such an attack may be overt as in the Crusades and all their more recent counterparts, or it may be the less obviously brutal but none the less threatening march of modernity. Modernity has rarely been sensitive to conservatism; indeed its advocates often proclaim their successes with some arrogance less in what they say than in how they behave. No surprise then that with a combination of fear and envy almost all the religious families are now developing fundamentalist wings which in their different ways, and sometimes with violence, fight against the very culture that the West sees as offering the best hope for the future. Of course there are issues about world development, inequality, ignorance, disease and poverty, but I hope that I have shown that these are not the only threats to world order.

In Northern Ireland we have found that patient reflection on the motivations of those who have acted with extreme violence and positive engagement with their representatives has taken us as a community towards a hopeful place which is beyond the merely economic, and in the process stretched our capacity to contain our own feelings and responses. We have tried to develop ways in which both sides, and those who do not wish to be described as from either side, are able to behave with respect in order to be treated with respect. In time we may come to know whether this effort is as productive of peace as we hope, but in Ireland we have already tried the alternative and it brought us some hundreds of years of misery.

The Altered Psychoanalytic Space

SHMUEL ERLICH

I Introduction

DURING THE GULF WAR IN ISRAEL WE WERE FACED with an unknown and dangerous
threat of Iraqi missiles carrying chemical or biological warheads. Unknown since
nobody knew for sure whether such warheads existed, nor whether Iraq had the
capacity to deliver them. Dealing with an unknown threat made things much worse
and fueled fears and fantasies. We were ordered to carry gasmasks with us wherev-
er we went and to set up and take refuge in "sealed-rooms." Sealed-rooms would be
safe from lethal gases leaking in unlike the usual mandatory air-raid shelters.

An indication of the extent of tremendously intensified fearfulness and panic
mobilized by the threat was the fact that about a dozen people, small children and
adults, died of suffocation because they failed to open the air valves of their gasmasks. When the air-raid sirens would go off, we would grab our gasmasks and hurry
to the shelter of the "sealed room."

For several tense and anxious weeks most people complied with these public
safety instructions, which eventually turned out to have been wrong. Most psychoanalysts and psychotherapists in Israel practice at home and continued to practice
during this difficult period. A new and hitherto unfamiliar dilemma emerged: The
"sealed-room" at home served the entire family, often augmented with relatives and
friends who came to take refuge.

The "sealed-rooms"—sometimes closets—were typically very small and
extremely crowded; people might be emotionally upset and not fully dressed, small
children often cried and balked, and the stay in them could last for hours on end. You
can imagine that it was not the kind of situation one would want to be thrust into with
one's patient, nor could it be considered particularly comfortable for the patient,
although in some cases it might also have gratified some deep curiosity and the need
to peep into the analyst's personal and "private" space.

At this point I had an experience from which I learned a great deal. Faced with
this dilemma, and given my overall analytic understanding of the frame, it appeared
to me at first unthinkable to introduce my patients into my family's small sealed
room. Instead I bought a "sealed suit" which I would offer to my patient in case of
an attack.

Fortunately I had to offer the "sealed-suit" only to one patient, a woman. Her
reaction was one of shock and disbelief. It wasn't because I would not let her into
my "private space" with my family, or because what I offered to her might be infe-
rior to a sealed-room but because it meant that if anything happened I would rush off
to be with my family and leave her alone in my consulting room. This was some-

thing for which she severely—and rightly—chastised me. Reflecting on her reaction I agreed with her.

My patient's reaction helped to highlight and focus on a clinical dilemma. Should psychoanalysts remain with their patients or be with their family at a moment of potential trauma and disaster? For me the situation became a moment of poignant clarity, as if suddenly the depths were illuminated by what Bion referred to as a "a beam of intense darkness" (Grotstein, 1981, p. 10). What stood out in stark realness were the dilemmas of professional and personal responsibility, of loyalty and dedication. It illuminated the fragility and tenuousness of the psychoanalytic frame and the psychoanalytic situation and the need for reconsidering what I understood by psychoanalytic space.

Before I attempt to consider psychoanalytic space, however, it is important to describe the current crisis in Israel. Most Israelis have known adverse circumstances, including numerous wars and terror attacks. Our fifty-four years of statehood are marked by struggle and survival. It would be equally true, however, to say that these adversities span the entire one hundred years of Jewish Zionist settlement in the land. There is also no doubting the heavy shadow cast over all of this by the Holocaust, as well as the current reverberations of remote echoes of Jewish history. Today in Israel we are faced not only with the terrible ordeal of daily death and carnage, but also with the more searching questions about our present and future life, our fundamental right to exist, and the grim prospects of an endless period of living with terror. Since the breakdown of the Camp David talks and the outbreak of the current Intifada, Israeli society has suffered an acute crisis of deepening divisiveness, dearth of credible leadership and increasing hopelessness.

The impact of this acute crisis can be charted as several concentric circles: the direct victims of terror attacks, who suffered personally or through the death or injury of someone close; those who became victims by personally witnessing acts of terror; those who are traumatized through helping and working with the victims; and the rest of society, which for the most part (excepting those who are even more vociferously calling for action) seem to be affected by a curious mixture of "active passivity," anxiously curtailing their freedom of movement, worrying about themselves, their children, relatives and friends, and frequently unable to work and concentrate.

This paper delves into my own and others' experience in daily psychoanalytic and psychotherapeutic practice with people of the last group mentioned, those affected by "active passivity," therefore not directly traumatized. These patients come to their sessions immediately after or while the bombs are going off, while sirens are heard blasting, and attention is riveted on the next radio announcement of where disaster has struck, or while trying to conjure the map of the whereabouts of family members and friends.

My practice is located in Jerusalem near the Mount Scopus Hadassah hospital and national police headquarters, overlooking a major transportation artery. Sessions are frequently punctured by sirens of ambulances and police cars rushing to or from a terror event. By now, my patients and I realize that more than three separate, successively heard sirens signify that such an event has taken place. External reality has impinged upon the psychoanalytic space.

II On the Nature of the Psychoanalytic Space

So much has been written and said about the psychoanalytic situation as to make it virtually impossible to review. "The psychoanalytic situation," writes Arlow (1987), "is perhaps the greatest and most original of Freud's contributions to the study of human psychology" (p. 382). With its historical origins in hypnosis, what may be unique to the psychoanalytic situation is its capacity to lend itself for use as a "potential space" (Winnicott, 1971), an intermediate area of experience in which people may allow themselves altered states while being "held" by the analytic setting and the presence of the analyst, a transitional area of experience that is felt as both self and not-self (Bromberg, 1996; Aron and Bushra, 1998). Yet even this sensitive description is too coarse and not finely tuned enough to the complexities that make up the psychoanalytic situation.

There is a difference between the psychoanalytic 'situation' and psychoanalytic 'space.' A situation is physically and objectively definable, describable, and manageable. So indeed is 'space' when referring to physical space. But the psychoanalytic 'space' is a creation, brought about by its two participants. It makes use of the interplay of forces and meaning introduced, mainly by the analyst, to fashion a context of meaning and understanding that can potentially serve both partners of the psychoanalytic dyad. In this sense the psychoanalytic 'space' is nowhere to be seen, being a psychic operational reality.

We need to attend to the transformation of the psychoanalytic situation into a psychoanalytic space (Viderman, 1979). We may also wonder about the extent to which this transformation has actually occurred in a given analytic process and study its vicissitudes. The differentiation between 'situations' and 'space' notwithstanding, it is striking that both concepts derive from the physical world. It suggests that psychic reality is not divorced from and antagonistic to physical or external reality.

Just as the ego is first and foremost a body ego, psychic reality is at its base our perception and construction of physical reality. What is at stake is not a choice between Cartesian dualism and the transcendental, fused oneness of opposites. More modestly put and practiced, it is a transformational mode that we as analysts are in charge of applying and developing. We become "experts" at transforming physical, concrete facts into meaningful and psychically poignant experience. A cigar is indeed a cigar, so long as it has not been transformed into and experienced as something else.

We find ourselves at the conceptual junction of subjectivity and objectivity. My own view, which I cannot elaborate in this paper, considers all internal processes as experientially mediated, therefore subjective. In previous work I have drawn attention to the important distinction between two fundamental modalities that process, fashion and organize inner experience (e.g., Erlich & Blatt, 1985; Erlich, 2002a). The crucial difference stems from the experienced unity of subject and object in one mode, as against their experienced separateness and distinctiveness in the other.

We tend to refer to as 'subjective' those experiences in which subject and object are experienced as merged and indistinguishably fused; and we typically regard as 'objective' experiences marked by clearly defined, separate and distinguishable subject and object. In turn, such 'objective' and 'subjective' modes influence and determine our stance on the objectivity or subjectivity of our own and others' experience.

I suggest that we regard psychoanalytic space as an experiential construction shaped and created by both these experiential modes. Attending to our own and our patient's experience is not contingent on how objective and subjective it is, but on the experiential mode, within which we 'take up,' absorb and process this experience.

III External Reality: Its Role in Psychoanalytic Treatment

The issue of the place and impact of external reality is woven deeply into the fabric of psychoanalytic treatment, and influences its entire development. It is marked by decisive turns and stances, such as Freud's giving preference to internal fantasy over external trauma, or Melanie Klein's all-inclusive view of transference (1952), as well as others, too many to enumerate. The issue is very much alive: it finds expression in the writings of Ferenczi, Winnicott and Kohut, recent emphases on attachment theory or inter-subjectivity, and the ensuing internal controversies within psychoanalysis.

Considering the impact on psychoanalytic space of the kind of traumatic horrors such as September 11 and our daily terror-ridden existence in Israel is essentially different from assessing the place of a specific personal trauma within a patient's life or treatment. The obvious difference lies in the fact that, quite unlike individually sustained traumata, in mass traumas we are dealing with traumatized communities and societies to which both patient and analyst belong.

Both the traumatic impact and its understanding must therefore partake of the dynamics of group and social processes. Several pertinent consequences to this level and extent of traumatization may be noted. Being both members of the traumatized group or society, the trauma affects both analyst and patient. The common traumatic experience sets and re-defines what is considered to be external reality. Indeed, it provides a new, jointly held, mutually reality-tested basis of experience. This is in contradistinction to an individually sustained, isolated traumatic experience of either patient or analyst, shared or not shared by one, empathically or non-empathically received by the other.

Beyond defining external and internal reality, new trauma-linked group identifications and social affiliations are established by the shared experience. The commonly sustained trauma forges membership in a social group that encompasses and confirms both patient and analyst as its members. These new affiliations are derived from and based on the commonly experienced trauma, and beyond it on shared survival guilt, depression, reparation, and possibly hope.

The newly drawn social group affiliation and boundaries may be potentially problematic for the analyst as well as the patient. One facet of the problem that is suddenly and "extraneously" thrust on them is whether to acknowledge this "camaraderie," or to resist and deny it. Another facet may present itself when analyst and patient are on opposite sides of the political fence, blaming and holding the other "responsible" for the crisis. An Israeli instance of this is when the analyst is identified with the political left and the peace movement, and the patient is a right wing settler living in the occupied territories. Such issues are always present within psychoanalytic space, but are usually confined to the background. A common trauma would thrust them onto the foreground.

These observations may explain, to a certain extent, the peculiar fact observed by me as well as by many of my colleagues. By and large, our patients (particularly analytic patients) do not speak much, or at all, about the events we all live through. This is not easy to understand, and seems rather puzzling. It is reminiscent of Winnicott's wartime experience, when he "hardly noticed the blitz, being all the time engaged in analysis of psychotic patients who are notoriously oblivious of bombs, earthquakes, and floods" (1945, p. 145). The patients I am talking about, however, are not psychotic. One may consider that in Israel the external reality is psychotic, and the psychoanalytic space becomes a welcome haven of sanity and personal integration. Clearly there are also remarkable differences among analysts and patients in this regard, some apparently being more 'inviting' to talking about external reality than others.

Often during session I have tried, mostly in vain, to decipher clues to the external events that followed horrendous attacks. Patients may refer briefly at the beginning of a session to the attack, and then launch into what "really" bothers them. Sometimes doing so is accompanied by guilt for attending to their petty private concerns and pains. In some sessions I think I can detect an unconscious link with the events, but I am left wondering whether it would serve a useful purpose to bring this level up.

Clinical Vignettes

These cases are not meant to represent three definite varieties or prescribed methods for dealing with a terrible external reality. They merely underscore the endlessly rich and baffling variety in which external reality finds its way into and can be worked with in the psychoanalytic space. It is significant that this 'space' is not a single, overarching, monolithic entity offered to all three patients. In each case, this space is the singular one created by the specific pair involved. In each case, external reality is treated and appreciated very differently within the context of the unique and prevailing psychoanalytic space.

Vignette 1

A woman in her fifties came to her session minutes after a car bomb exploded on a Jerusalem street killing two passers by. Her young daughter had just moved into an apartment around the corner from the blast, and all her glass windows were shattered. She started the session shakily informing me of this, with a mixture of concern and relief. Usually she is very anxious about this daughter—her need for autonomy, her relationship with her and with men, etc. The real external danger, acknowledged and then gratefully put aside by her, seemed "unreal" in comparison to her internal concerns.

Vignette 2

A highly narcissistic young man in a long treatment came in following a weekend of violence and terror attacks. Through the session he did not allude to them at all. He did speak of his neglectfulness and messiness, and the chaos in his life and private spaces—in his car, home, and study. He would really like to dedicate himself to philosophy, which encompasses everything. He lacks his father's capacity for total dedication. He feels a need to attach himself to outstanding men, like Nietzsche and

Schopenhauer. He feels that everything in his life is a compromise, a matter of ful-filling obligations. He searches for an idea he can link with. He wonders whether I can understand all of this? He mentions Yona Wallach and wonders—would I have been able to treat her? He thinks that actually I could have. She went all the way, reaching places no one else has. But it is so hard to live this way. Perhaps it is best to give up on life? Yet to live the way he does is to give up on life. I pointed to his tremendous need "to go all the way," to find and cling to something "pure" and larg-er than himself amidst the chaos and the mess, while also acknowledging his seri-ous, life long dilemma of "living and not living." He agreed and left with a smile.

Vignette 3

A highly intelligent obsessive man, who usually feels guilt ridden, depressed and severely compromised in his competence, came to treatment looking rather pleased and happy during an unusually sad and difficult week with an unprecedented num-ber of dead, both Israelis and Palestinians. He remarked gleefully that his wife had said that he seemed to be the only happy person in Israel at the moment. His pro-fessional work brings him in actual close contact with people from both feuding par-ties. A seasoned veteran of a number of previous psychotherapies, he readily inter-preted his good mood as "unrealistic" and crazy, and attributed it to his neurotic needs. The horrible external circumstances serve to relieve his inner guilt. When things are really bad externally, he can feel less guilt ridden and sad inside.

As the session unfolded it turned out that he had been involved with people and talks of both sides and had actually marveled at their sanity. I suggested that, far from merely serving neurotic needs, he was carrying within himself a tiny bit of sanity and hopefulness, derived from his actual experience that week, and not available to most others in the society. Nonetheless, this bit of sanity and hope was as "real" as any-thing else going on. He could see that if more people had shared his particular expe-rience they might well have shared his optimism and good mood too.

These three vignettes are clearly totally different from one another, though they all take place against the common background of the same external horrors and ter-ror. All three deal with external reality, though very differently. The first patient does it by acknowledging it briefly and proceeding full force to her internal world. The second one deals with external reality by consciously or manifestly failing to refer to it. Yet, I believe that in the second case external reality is symbolically and uncon-sciously present in the patient's longstanding yearning for a larger-than-self, "pure" state, with which he may fuse, and without which life is not fully experienced. I see this quest as inherent to terrorist acts (Erlich, 2002b), and it may well be stirred up in those who, because of their personal makeup and pathology, resonate with it. The third patient brings in the external reality at its face value, but interprets it in terms of his neurotic conflict and in line with his intellectual defenses. My interpretation acknowledged and expanded this reality further, in a way that might allow him to feel less isolated and more a part of the social group, and, at the same time, to get in touch with his individual voice.

IV The Analyst's Responsibility for the Patient's Welfare

The psychoanalytic situation and space are quintessential expressions of the analyst's technical and professional skill. They therefore also constitute the sphere of the analyst's professional responsibility. Clearly this means doing the best one can to help the patient work out the vicissitudes of external impingements and internal motives and fantasies. This work, as always, will best be furthered by the creation and maintenance of the psychoanalytic space. But additional questions present themselves, such as: the necessity and responsibility for continuing psychoanalytic work in the face of external conditions; the relative share of responsibility held by analyst and patient for what may happen; and the technical questions that come up as a result of these.

Let me consider the following example of shared responsibility. If traveling to and from one's session endangers the patient, should the analyst draw his attention to it? Is it solely the patient's decision whether to continue to come? What if this becomes self-destructive? Do we charge the patient for sessions missed under dangerous circumstances? When do we actually collude and collaborate with the patient's aggressive fantasies, or his fantasies of his or our own indestructibility? How far does our own responsibility extend in "allowing" or "forbidding" his coming to see us? Do we invariably regard coming to analysis or therapy as the most sane and psychologically constructive course of action?

The above mentioned example taken from the Gulf War experience pointed out to me what I have come to appreciate as an ethical and professional stance: As long as I do practice, and invite patients to come and see me, I am responsible for their welfare while they are with me. My conflict between being with my family or with my patient, though understandable, is nonetheless misplaced. My primary commitment while practicing is to the patient, not to my family. In many ways, this is the essence of my professional stance and responsibility. If I wish to alter this commitment and feel that I must be with my family, whether to protect or to seek protection, I have to take at least temporary leave from my practice. I certainly should not saddle my patient with this conflict. The dilemma I face is whether, under these pulls and tensions, it is possible to carry on serving as a therapeutic container and to preserve the psychoanalytic space. Obviously this dilemma does not permit a standardized answer and resolution.

V Fraternity in Face of Danger and External Threat

The analyst must exert his or her freedom to make responsible ethical choices, and the freedom to claim the "equality" regarding the equally experienced external trauma. It is natural that "fraternity" should come next. I refer to the feeling of camaraderie and brotherhood aroused in both analyst and patient, directly or indirectly, by the commonly experienced external threat. Fraternity is linked to narcissistic identifications and rewards, as in Shakespeare's "We few, we happy few, we band of brothers" (*Henry V*). Beyond survivors' guilt there is a special bond formed by having lived through the same horrendous events together, of being "brothers in arms."

In analysis, unlike most relationships, this fraternity may involve a flight from transference and, paradoxically, the undermining of the "psychoanalytic space." At the same time, the analyst has to be ready to acknowledge the deeply disconcerting events both he/she and the patient have lived through. This is a fine line that needs to be walked with warmth, understanding and sympathy, but without the loss of overall analytic purpose and task.

This is certainly not only the patient's problem. The analyst may well feel the need to "share" his experience and to find comfort in the patient's fraternal representation of the community. We do not often speak about the essential loneliness of the analyst (Erlich, 1998). Undoubtedly, to maintain the analytic stance and posture, to create, offer and maintain the analytic space, requires an effort that frequently leaves the analyst feeling alone and isolated. Our patients may then become our links for communicating with the world at large. They supply us with information, evidence, and a feeling of being in touch with people and social reality. This need intensifies during periods of external threat and disaster, rendering us more prone than ever to needing and utilizing our patients as links and messengers, through whom we wish to join the social network, when our loneliness becomes acute and unbearable.

VI The Impact of Political-Religious Views

Reality impingements demand realistic responses. The kind and scope of response are determined by the understanding of the sources and meaning of the precipitating events. Such understanding involves interpretation that is colored by one's political views. This subject deserves a full discussion in itself, but there are several points that can be briefly addressed, relying again on my Israeli experience.

Analysts and psychotherapists typically belong to the socio-political spectrum that may be loosely characterized as liberal or left wing. Our patients are less clearly definable. For the most part, they seem to have similar political orientation. In Israel, right wing, ultra-religious, and until recently, nationalistic religious people are seldom candidates for exploratory treatment. Nor are Arab patients usually interested in it. There are however, some right wing, religious and even Arab patients, who raise specific and unique issues. One of these is a very different, politically inspired and identifiable view of external reality.

Political differences may easily become the cause for therapeutic impasse unless very sensitively and skillfully handled. Ideologically most psychoanalysts reject and condemn violence. They believe in the efficacy of discussion and the power of dialogue, especially under the beneficent influence of personal relatedness. These beliefs are based on our experience in a one-to-one prolonged situation, where psychoanalytic space has ideal developmental conditions. This stance does not take into account the tremendous forces inherent in groups and supra-group processes that represent very different dynamic levels that reach beyond the intra-psychic.

Stemming from Bion's (1961) work with groups and its integration with open systems theory in the Tavistock Institute, a more powerful understanding of the issues involved in dealing with enemies and adversaries (Erlich, 1997) has been attained. Although this understanding derives fully from psychoanalytic insights and tools, psychoanalysts tend to be suspicious of it, and to regard it as the alloy of applied psychoanalysis, as compared to the pure gold of psychoanalytic treatment.

Certain theoretical constraints inherent in psychoanalytic theory, especially in the area of early development and narcissism, bias us toward regarding fervent ideological adherence as immature, regressive and pathological. This stance not only considerably limits our understanding of adolescence, but more to the point, it stands in the way of a fuller understanding of the role of religious, political and ideological commitment in adult life. It particularly makes it nearly impossible to understand a suicidal self-sacrifice, which under certain religious and social circumstances actually becomes normative (Erlich, 2002/b). Our view is clouded by Western value systems that lean heavily toward exulting individual, autonomous, circumscribed existence as the paramount achievement and condition for happiness and fulfillment. This view has heavily influenced psychoanalysis and infiltrated its theoretical infrastructure. When faced with different orientations and values, we tend to characterize them as pathological and regressive, instead of adapting our theories and understanding to dealing with them. This juncture is well worth exploration since it is the point at which our theories become transformed in our politics and religion.

VII Conclusion

As analysts we are keenly attuned to a slice of reality or actuality that to most people seems impractical and non-pragmatic, the stuff dreams are made of. This paper strives to consider the impact of harsh and unusually cruel realities on us and our patients, and the space within which we meet and work.

Do we need to alter or amplify our analytic space and technique? Or have these been altered in ways that need to be acknowledged and explored? My own view is that it is not the psychoanalytic space that needs to be revised. In the face of such horrendous external events, it must be maintained and continue to be offered. We need to be alert, however, to the complexities and dangers I pointed to, as well as the social and political horizons within which we operate.

REFERENCES

Arlow, J. (1987). The dynamics of interpretation. In *Psychoanalysis: Clinical Theory and Practice* (pp. 381-396). Madison CT: International Universities Press.

Aron, L. and Bushra, A. (1998). Mutual regression: Altered states in the psychoanalytic situation. *J. Amer. Psychoanal. Assn. 46,* 389-412.

Bion, W. R. (1961). *Experiences in Groups.* London: Tavistock Publications.

Bromberg, P.M. (1996). Standing in the spaces: The multiplicity of self and the psychoanalytic relationship. *Contemp. Psychoanal., 32,* 509-535.

Erlich, H. S. (1997). On discourse with an enemy. In Edward R Shapiro (Ed.) *The Inner World in the Outer World: Psychoanalytic Perspectives* (pp. 123-42). New Haven: Yale University Press.

Erlich, H.S. (1998). On loneliness, narcissism, and intimacy. *Amer. J. of Psychoanalysis, 58,* 135-162.

Erlich, H. S. (2002a). Experience—what is it? (Unpublished manuscript).

Erlich, R.S. (2002b). Reflections on the terrorist mind. *IPA Newsletter* June 2002.

Erlich, H. S. and Blatt, S. J. (1985). Narcissism and object love: The metapsychology of experience. *Psychoanal. Study Child, 4,* 57-79.

Grotstein. I. S. (1981). *Do I Dare Disturb the Universe?* London: Karnac.

Klein, M. (1952). The origins of transference. *Int. J. Psycho-Anal., 33,* 433-438.

Viderman, S. (1979). The analytic space: meaning and problems. *Psychoanal Q., 48,* 257-291.

Winnicott, D. (1945). Primitive emotional experience. In *Through Paediatrics to Psycho-Analysis* (pp. 145-156). New York: Basic Books, 1975.

Winnicott, D. (1971). *Playing and Reality.* Harmondsworth: Penguin Books.

Social Catastrophe and Mental Space

MARCELO N. VINAR

I WANT TO EXPRESS MY DEEPEST APPRECIATION TO the organizers of this event. You have offered psychoanalysts from around the world a unique opportunity. Psychoanalysts are called to reflect on the aftermath of disruptive violence that alters individuals' normal interaction. We are here to share our experiences and points of view, and to exchange our thoughts on a subject that till today has remained at the margins of psychoanalytical conferences and meetings.

Despite the overall neglect from part of our field, current circumstances force us to think about the relation between social space and mind in ordinary, day-to-day political and cultural life. The experience of horror unleashed by violence or social catastrophe, brings to the fore the hidden relation between internal and external spaces, that is to say, between the mind and the socio-cultural environment. Violent events—like September 11—evoke horror, and this horror tends to uncover a normal and permanent feature of mental function that for the most part is kept silent, mute.

A comprehensive conceptualization of the relationship between the social matrix and intra-psychic processes is, in my opinion, necessary. Various psychoanalytical formulations and/or theories have attempted to define the boundaries between the two utilizing Freudian paradigms with limited success. I think that we must continue to explore and delve into those relationships rather than apply ready-made pre-established explanatory models.

Early in its development psychoanalysis, reacting perhaps to Victorian morality, emphasized the significance of infantile sexuality. The hidden dimensions of private lives and conflict connected to intimacy provided sufficient material and enough challenges to psychoanalysis. However, the world has changed since Freud discovered psychoanalysis, and it continues to change. Consequently our minds have changed as well. The narratives of contemporary patients pose new questions that may or may not be answered by a reductionistic application of Freudian principles.

How should we analysts respond to our analysands' tales of terror and political violence? Which position should we assume in front of these narratives?

Oedipus was not just a perpetrator of incest and parricide. As King he could not avoid being involved with political realities. Regarding political realities, I have more questions than answers. However I am convinced that the mind of an analyst must be as widely opened to external, political reality, as it must be to the analysand's sexuality. But one cannot be reduced to the other, even when we are prone to consider the disruptive amount of excitation that violent trauma introduces in the clinical setting. This excitation, which is sexual excitation, overwhelms the ego precluding the possibility of the work of representation, and with it the transformation of the excess of energy into discrete units of language.

Freud's structural theory of the mind is one possible model. Its basic assumptions are that the social domain acts (*agieren*) during infancy through the parental objects. The influence of father and mother is exerted with a stable, unidirectional cause-effect law. Things are clear and evident. Another Freudian reference, which I prefer for the subject under discussion, is proposed in "Totem and Taboo" (1911) and in "Group Psychology and the Analysis of the Ego" (1921).

The premise in these two papers is that the logical antecedent to individuals' suffering following social catastrophes lies in a disorganization of the social link. In other words, group psychology and culture precedes individual psychic organization. I would like to propose that disruptive violence attacks the virtual and symbolic place where individuals engage with one another, and in this attack the oath that engages individuals and the social body is damaged.

These two different Freudian pathways are not easy to reconcile. Ideals and sacrifices, stated in "The Ego and the Id," lead to an individual profile, and to the specificity of a single, isolated subject. Accordingly, the individual will react to social events based on personal style, defining what is normal and what is pathological.

"Totem and Taboo" and "Group Psychology and the Analysis of the Ego" convey a not so clear and simple solution as "The Ego and the Id" seems to. Although in the former two works social reality comes first and is the trigger for subjective reactions, the two papers raise more questions than answers, invoking problems that pertain to the border of psychoanalysis with other social sciences.

The main thesis of "Group Pychology" is that the social link is always there, before the acquisition of conscience. The social link is silent and mute until a violent disruption breaks the equilibrium and fuels panic. Panic illustrates that a solid link, which was always there silent, mute, becomes evident during its dissolution.

Jose Bleger elaborated this concept in his paper "The Psychoanalytical Frame." Bleger's position is that the implicit or explicit social codes, usually silent and mute, are not only specific to each community, but they are also a condition of mental functioning. Bleger referred to this condition as the Meta-Ego. If the social code is broken, as in cases of disruptive or unexpected violence, chaos and panic in individuals' mental space will follow. This chaos and panic reveals in action the strength of the social link.

It is the group, and not the individual, that defines the event. Certainly there is no single objective account of the reality of extreme violence. On the contrary a multiplicity of stories will attempt to make sense of what has happened. In my view, psychoanalysts have to "hold" the extreme dramatic situation and handle the transference. They must allow and respect the singular timing for working through. In this process psychoanalysts must be able to recognize the power of their patients' testimony and the intensity of their negation and denial. We must also learn to deal with a double and contradictory requirement, namely the work of memory and oblivion.

The movement from silence to explosion, from virtual to actual expression seems to me an important Freudian discovery. It stresses movement instead of fixed essences, and illustrates the link between individual and group psychology.

Terrorism and the Psychoanalytic Space

A main concern of mine is to understand how psychoanalysts can maintain alive a situation such as the one generated by an excess of excitation. This is a crucial issue since an excess of excitation normally tends to its own extinction, gravitating towards a return to silence or mutism. Indeed, the Death instinct works by emptying and erasing the representational chain. This is a radical and opposite action from that of Eros where the drives push towards an increment of emotionality linked to representations.

How to listen to silence without violently imposing on our patient our own conceptions, beliefs, or ideals? How can we preserve the analytical frame without contaminating it with a dogmatic and ideological imposture? Octave Mannoni stated that the power of the psychoanalyst is so enormous that perhaps the only legitimate way to exercise it is to abdicate it.

After the planes crashed into the Towers, normality was reinstated. Some individuals appeared to be non-affected, symptom free; others seemed to suffer from traumatic neurosis. Which are the criteria one may refer to in defining "normality?" Psychiatry and psychoanalysis do not concur in this respect. Psychiatry aims at reestablishing health while silencing the symptoms. Psychoanalysis delves beyond the individuals' suffering, searching for the quality of psychic inscriptions that eventually may facilitate an internal, meaningful reorganization of the traumatic experience. The un-symbolized, non-representational terror stemming from violence may be regarded as a central theoretical and ethical dilemma in psychoanalytical practice.

The agent in political terrorism is quite different from the one identified in accidental or natural traumatic events such as earthquakes or tornados. Political terrorism is the product of human action deliberately designed to hurt other human beings. The psychic collapse resulting from this kind of action mobilizes psychotic mechanisms with the concomitant confusion between the internal and external world.

The nature of the disruptive event encloses an unbelievable dimension that must be explored for a long time. A creative inscription of trauma and the building of internal links are possible when the reality of human diversity is re-established.

Freud held a not too very angelic view of the eternal human tension between egotism and altruism, or between object and narcissistic libido. The creator of psychoanalysis alluded to the need that humans seem to have to celebrate the fact that the dead person is somebody else, and not oneself. The need to celebrate occurs regardless whether the dead person is a beloved one or an enemy. The prevalence of egotism above altruism doesn't seem to limit itself to the dying, but to all catastrophic experiences. One of these catastrophic experiences is the attack on the Twin Towers.

A splitting takes place then between the most affected and the least affected, between the victims and the unharmed, between those who were wounded or mutilated, between those who lost one or more beloved persons, or those who suffered the impact of the collapse closely or from a distance, or those whose body was not damaged, but their psyche severely wounded. The excess of emotionality perturbs the normal cognitive operations of thinking, exploring and discovering. The obvious character of these descriptions may be regarded as defense mechanisms, or better yet active mechanisms at the service of not-knowing.

The analytical space is not exempt from splitting, and in it the excess of emotionality disturbs the capacity for thinking, exploring, and discovering. Perhaps the disturbance is exacerbated due to the involvement of the actors in the catastrophic experience. The latter places the therapist in the role of the unharmed, protective mother, while the patient assumes the role of the victim. Could it be that stressing the victimization of the patient may not be the best approach in working through trauma?

The hallucinatory insistence of the traumatic experience is a powerful and recurrent point of attraction during a session. Many of us may be prone to fall into the old trap that tends to rationalize the efficacy of the cathartic method. Undoubtedly one must accept and tolerate the repeated horror tale, but also it is essential to acknowledge this position as a preliminary one to elaboration and working through.

The eruption of terror that follows war, terrorists' attacks, or bombings, threatens to disorganize and disarticulate the ordinary ways of psychic functioning, and those that sustain the social links. Individuals, families and communities who are acutely or chronically affected by those eruptions will require a long period of time to begin to integrate them and eventually begin to re-signify them in the fabric of their memories.

Terror horrifies and fascinates; it both paralyses the psyche and leads to active mechanisms that foster ignorance. A specific part of the therapeutic work consists in localizing and making explicit in analyst and analysand these pockets of ignorance.

We usually conceive the psychoanalytic space as a bubble that exists in isolation from social and political life. Thus, a space of intimacy is built where the meanderings of the psychic life, the excesses of love, hate and sexuality converge. Analyst and analysand reside in this essentially ambiguous space where everything happens and nothing happens.

The essential ambiguity of the analytic space is shaken under the invasion of terror. In the analytic space the facts of daily life collude and resonate with the most archaic and regressive aspects of mental functioning. The analytic work seems to go then almost in the opposite direction to its original intent. While attempting to understand neurotic pathology, the psychoanalyst's interventions aim at linking or relating shifting levels and moments of psychic life. However, when the analyst is submerged himself or herself in the disorienting experience of terror, the need to discriminate and re-establish different moments and levels of psychic life, to differentiate present and past, consensual from "phantasmatic" reality, becomes a central aspect of the therapeutic work.

The affected person expresses grief. The analyst can neither reject nor accept her or his analysand's complaint and accompanying affective expression. The sufferer persistently introduces herself or himself licking hers or his wounds, wounds that seem refractory to healing. The timing of the interventions should neither encourage nor tolerate regressive complacency. Our interventions must be directed to prevent mourning from becoming melancholia, or the residual symptom from transforming itself by assuming the pleasurable nature of secondary gains.

REFERENCES

Bleger, J. (1967). Psychoanalysis of the psychoanalytic frame. *Int. J. Psycho-anal.,* *48*, 511-519.

Freud, S. (1911). *Totem and Taboo.* Standard Edition. 13, 1-162.

Freud, S. (1921). Group psychology and the analysis of the ego. Standard Edition. 18, 167-143.

Freud, S. (1923). The ego and the id. Standard Edition. 19, 13-66.

Mannoni, O. (1967). L'Analyse originalle. *Temps Moderne,* 22, 2136-2151.

PART II

Developmental Effects on Children
and Adolescents: Developmental and
Educational Aspects of the
Experience of Terrorism

*Trauma born failure to symbolize and
mourn, and its impact
on identity formation*

Introduction

MARIBETH ROURKE

THIS SYMPOSIUM, MADE UP OF TWO PANELS OF speakers, provided the audience with a unique opportunity to consider the effects of terrorism on the development of children and adolescents. The first panel presented research findings and theory related to how terrorism and trauma can interfere with and influence development. The second panel was more clinically focused and presented clinical material from interviews with and treatments of children and adolescents, following a traumatic event. The speakers addressed the difficult task of helping child and adolescent patients get back on track developmentally.

The first panel began with a presentation by Dr. Paulina Kernberg. She began the morning by reminding us of the powerful influence that adults have over children, particularly as educators and transmitters of culture. Her comments were focused on the Arab culture. This influence can have both positive and negative outcomes. Unfortunately, her paper will not be included here.

Dr. Kernberg's presentation was followed by Dr. Shmuel Erlich's paper, "Trauma, Terror and Identity Formation." Dr. Erlich proposed that the adolescent faces a unique set of dangers vis à vis terrorism. He believes that because of the developmental task at hand, that of integrating the experiential modes of being and doing, and consolidating an identity, the adolescent is particularly susceptible to the appeal of "the paradise" of merger, and terrorism.

Dr. Myrna Gannagé's paper, "Children and War: Consequences and Treatment," was read by Yasmine Saad, a candidate at IPTAR, as Dr. Gannagé was unable to attend the conference for political reasons. Dr. Gannagé presented her study of the effects on its children of the war in Lebanon, from 1975 to 1991, by comparing the development of Parisian children, children raised in Lebanon and Lebanese children in Paris. She found that there were important differences in reactions among the Lebanese children, even those exposed to similar traumatic situations. Gannagé linked these differences to the quality of maternal care received in early childhood. She posited that the availability of the parental preconscious to act as a protective filter for the child determined the degree to which the child was traumatized. These three presentations were then discussed by Dr. Irving Steingart.

The second part of the morning began with a presentation by Dr. Martha Bragin, who shared her experiences with children living with war in Afghanistan. Her interviews with these children led her to the conclusion that exposure to literal enactments of violent phantasy causes regression to a state prior to symbol formation. This experience is particularly psychologically destructive for children who have not fully consolidated the capacity to symbolize.

Karen Proner next presented a vivid example of the working through process in the case of an eight year old girl. Ms. Proner showed how the current catastrophe of the Twin Towers allowed patient and therapist to gain access to and begin working through an earlier trauma.

The last clinical example, presented by Laura Kleinerman, was that of Anna. Her development and thinking had been impacted by a series of traumas, and Ms. Kleinerman shared how the process of treatment enabled Anna to reestablish the capacity for symbolic functioning.

Children live in a kingdom of metaphor and play. Freud (1908, p.144) said, "the opposite of play is not what is serious, but what is real. In spite of all the emotion with which he cathects his world of play, the child distinguishes it quite well from reality." But in the case of terrorism or war, what is play and what is real become indistinguishable. Symbolization and meaning are lost, as Ms. Proner and Ms. Kleinerman both experienced with their patients, feeling themselves "dunced" and "stunned." Dr. Gannagé and Dr. Erlich tell us that the impact of such a trauma is largely determined by the current developmental task faced by the child or adolescent, and their early care-taking experiences. Often, the capacity for memory and historicizing are interfered with.

Our strength as analysts, Dr. Bragin believes, lies in our ability to help patients re-symbolize by reaching for the unconscious meaning of external events. As Dr. Steingart points out, it is through this therapeutic work that a sense of self in time can be reestablished. Ms. Kleinerman's work with Anna, Ms. Proner's work with Christina, and Dr. Gannagé's work with Lara and Fadia, all poignantly demonstrate both the vulnerability and resilience of children, and the power of symbols. This moving collection of papers marks the beginning of what must be an ongoing effort to help ourselves and our patients find words and symbols for the unimaginable.

REFERENCES

Freud, S. (1908). Creative writers and day-dreaming. Standard Edition. 9, 142-153.

Children and War: Consequences and Treatment

MYRNA GANNAGÉ

THE WAR SITUATION IS CHARACTERIZED BY ITS SUDDENNESS, its brutality, and the unexpected confrontation with mortal danger or death. It brings about various disorders, physical of course, but also psychological, sometimes labeled as wounds. To think about this situation is to attempt to reflect on the effects of traumatic events on the individual. This brings us to a debate, which though quite ancient, remains essential for an in-depth study of our subject, namely the status of causality in psychopathology, and the role of trauma in the etiology of psychological disorders.

The war in Lebanon started in 1975 and stopped in 1991 in all of the country, except the South. During those sixteen years, residential neighborhoods, schools, hospitals and other institutions were often systematically shelled. Lulls in the fighting, when life could be almost normal, were interrupted, often without prior notice, by explosions of terrorism or acts of war: car bombs, shelling and gunfights. Active life could neither stop, nor follow a normal course. The unforeseen, on a practically daily basis, made projection into the future difficult. Danger was a part of daily life.

In order to understand how children can live through war, I will present the results of research that we carried out in Lebanon (Gannagé 1997).

Results of the Research

Within the framework of a survey published as a thesis in clinical psychology (Gannagé 1999), I attempted to study the effects of the war in Lebanon on its children. I collected my material during the 1991-1992 school year, one year after peace had been re-established in Lebanon. In this research, I compared three groups of children aged between six and ten: thirty children born and living in Lebanon (LL), fourteen children living in Paris and born of emigrant Lebanese parents (LP), fourteen French children living in Paris (PP); the children were sampled according to their socio-cultural environment, age and sex. The purpose of the study of Lebanese children born in France was to ascertain whether they were affected by the traumatic events that their parents had experienced. I also interviewed French children to find out how they react when exposed to trying events. The study of each child included a clinical examination, a psychological examination comprising a series of tests (P.M. 47, the WISC-R vocabulary test, the Rorschach, the T.A.T., the "figure of Rey") and a conversation with the parents. I also asked their teachers to evaluate the children's schoolwork and to answer the Rutter questionnaire.

The comparison of the three groups of children shows that the pathogenic power of the event doesn't lie solely in its characteristics. The main effect is the way it severs the parental support; in this way the event disturbs the child. Traumatic events affect certain parents in a particular way, which prevents them from carrying out the normal functions of support they are supposed to ensure.

Within the group of children born and living in Lebanon, there are important differences. Some are affected with an anaclitic organization (9); others suffer from depressive disorders (12), whereas others are healthy and have no problem whatsoever (9). These differences are not caused only by varying levels of exposure to stress, but are also linked mainly to the quality of maternal care received during early childhood. It is interesting to note that real events that took place during early childhood—such as a change in the living environment, the mother's or father's nervous breakdown—are more important and more difficult to bear for the children presenting an anaclitic organization than for the other children. However, external conditions alone do not explain the specificity of the anaclitic depression. What is established during the child's development through interrelations with his/her family environment affects his/her mental health. Depressed children and those who present an anaclitic organization either had during their early childhood an over-present, overprotective mother or, on the contrary, an overly absent mother who could not have a healthy relation with her child. These overprotective or absent mothers couldn't control their anxiety in the face of stress. Without satisfactory interaction, the ideal situation leading to proper development didn't take place.

In Lebanese children born and living in Paris and in French children, I made a distinction between those who were in good health and those who were vulnerable, presenting either an inhibition (children of emigrant parents), or behavioral disorders (French children). However, the vulnerable children belonging to these two groups coped much better than vulnerable children born and living in Lebanon.

Of course, one cannot compare the traumatic events suffered by the children born and living in Lebanon or the parents who immigrated to France with the childhood traumas that certain native French children were subjected to. Contrary to the children living in Beirut, the children living in Paris grew up in an environment that made them feel secure and gave them a "continuity of being."

The concept of "psychic cover" in its pathological aspects, resulting from the breakdown of the exterior and interior world and the loss of "container," allows a better understanding of the psyche of the disturbed children from group LL. In the children of this group with an anaclitic organization and important learning disorders, we note a breakage of the psychological envelope and consequently a deficit in the function of "containing" of thought. Anzieu considers that the function of "containing" is metaphorized by a network of contact barriers (Anzieu et al., 1993). Contact barriers control the circulation of thoughts and passage to consciousness. Thinking is to encompass, to surround a domain, an epistemic territory. Thinking also sets limits and struggles against the illusion of a certain life, of unlimited knowledge. The establishment of the psychological "container" is, according to Anzieu, the result of a double process:

—The interiorization of the "narrative envelope" (Stern, 1993) provided by the environment;

—The attraction exercised on the psyche by a virtual "container" form, which should be acknowledged as a phylogenetically transmitted imago, striving to carry out the experiences leading to its realization.

Grinberg (1972, quoted by Anzieu et al., 1993) gives a detailed description of the effects of the loss of "container" that we recognize in the children of the LL group described as presenting an anaclitic organization: fragmentation of the psychological "contents," search for artificial "containers," confusion between inner and outer space, use of "adhesive identification" instead of projective identification; and, "sticking" to the object.

I spoke of "holes" in memory's envelope to account for attacks on memory. From the interviews carried out with many of the children's parents, it seems that certain events leave no trace in their experience, except as a non-event, a kind of blank. It must be noted that in societies that emerge from war, certain persons try to repress traumatic events, whereas others keep their pain and horror alive. For them it is impossible to repress them. The process of rememoration and oblivion, the process of "historicizing," are hindered both for internal reasons, and for reasons pertaining to a faulty imprint of the events in the collective memory.

In twenty-one families of the LL group (the families of children suffering from depression or presenting an anaclitical organization), parents cannot speak of what they experienced during the war. In the LP group as well, the parents of ten of the children (those suffering from an inhibition) fight rememoration. The interviews I carried out with them show that they fight by denial. The order "not to remember" is not given to suppress horror, but to cancel out history and experience. This cancellation, in fact, maintains and prolongs the effect of the horror they experienced and the annihilation of their thought process.

Exploring the question of trauma is no simple matter. The diversity of traumas that I mention in this study tends to prove the elasticity of the concept.

I noted that the effect of the event depends mainly on the state of the defense mechanisms of the individual who experiences it. From a clinical point of view, the disorder in the child corresponds to a dysfunction of the Ego. So the notion of psychological trauma is not conceivable without its reference to the Ego that sustains it and to this Ego's "energetic economy." The traumatic event triggers a conflict in the Ego. The Ego's strength is linked to its capacity to activate defensive measures, of which repression is the paradigm. Conflict triggered in the Ego becomes negotiable through the preconscious. Linkage belongs to the preconscious; it is an operation, which is essential to unify and channel the flow of stimuli, and to maintain stability. The outcome of a balanced treatment of the stimuli which occur depends on how the preconscious functions, and on its capacity to transform these stimuli into representations. I demonstrated that the parents' preconscious acts as a protective filter, which constitutes the child's protection system against stimuli.

From this angle, trauma can be assimilated to a brutal lack of representative binding overrun by an excess of stimuli, as if a hole appeared in the activity of the preconscious. In this case, the "psychic apparatus" cannot transform what is unbearable into representations, much less into thoughts. Thus, the memory generating processes, and any possibility of "historicizing," cannot be set into motion.

The Therapeutic Treatment of the Children of the War

This research has allowed me to better understand the difficulties of the disturbed children I encountered and treated in the medical and psychological centers that specialize in the care of children of the war. After the shelling by the Israelis of Cana in South Lebanon—which took place in April 1996 and killed 104 civilians, among whom were 39 children and 24 women, psychological and medical consultation centers were set up for the children and their families who had suffered from the war in Beirut and South-Lebanon (Tyre, Nabatieh). They were designed on the model of similar centers in France.

The children are treated through outpatient consultations with psychotherapeutic support. A team of specialists comprising psychiatrists, psychologists and social workers treat the children who come for consultation. The therapeutic follow-up that I undertook with these children brought me to the brink of the "unthinkable" and the "unrepresentable" on a daily basis. "The unthinkable" according to R. Kaës "is something like a void, a waste, a hole, a wound." He refers to certain perceptions that can awaken intolerable affects and cannot be put into words. J. Puget mentions "the unthinkable linked to possible but intolerable knowledge, when thinking is associated with frightful strangeness causing limitless anguish" (p. 37). These are situations where reality is so terrifying that it goes far beyond imagination. Two clinical vignettes, the cases of Lara and Fadia, will illustrate what I mean.

Lara was eight and a half years old when I met her in Tyre for the first time. She was the youngest of a family of twelve children. Like many children of the South, Lara experienced a tragedy: the Cana massacre. She lost her father and a sister that she was very fond of. Her brothers and sisters were all wounded in the massacre. She herself suffered a head wound and her brain was seriously affected. She was admitted to a hospital in Saida in a comatose state and paralyzed on the right side. She was operated on under extremely difficult circumstances. However, the doctor managed to take out part of the shrapnel that was embedded in the left temporal lobe of her brain. She made some progress following the operation, but was still suffering from aphasia.

Lara was hospitalized on her own for one month in Saida. During this period, her brothers and sisters were hospitalized in Tyre. Two months after the tragedy, a charity decided to send her to London for treatment, without her family. According to the family, Lara wouldn't be able to bear the separation, so she was told that she would be taking a plane and going away for twenty-four hours. In reality she stayed six months in London without any family member by her side, but often spoke on the telephone to her mother and brothers and sisters.

When she came back from London, she brought a bag full of dolls for her beloved sister, who she thought was still alive. As the family didn't want to tell her about the death of her father and sister, she was told that they were being treated in Beirut. But Lara saw their pictures hanging on the wall and asked why they were there. The family could no longer conceal the truth.

Lara was sent to us by an NGO with which we were working to evaluate her intellectual capacities. She had never been to school. I saw her for the first time in June 1998, two years after the Cana massacre. The team's psychiatrist and the school psychologist had examined her. But something attracted me to her. I will tell you what struck me during the eight sessions of therapy that we had together.

Lara was a pretty little girl who seemed to come from another world. It was difficult for her to make contact with others. During the first session, she played with a doll. The doll opened and closed its eyes several times. Lara mothered the doll, hugged it, and squeezed it tightly against her. Then she dressed it and undressed it, changing its clothes. She talked to it: "Do you see how nice this is? All of this is for you. These are your clothes. Tomorrow I'll bring you something else…" During this time, I had to sit two or three meters away. As soon as I tried to come closer, to understand what was happening, she would get angry and say: "You are going to offer me the doll today." Then there was a sequence in the game when the doll was going to die. I was not allowed to ask Lara how or why. Any question asked on the subject was met with resistance from the child. Then, in a third stage, the doll changed into a ghost, a ghost with no hands or feet. The ghost lived in an abandoned house.

During the following sessions, the same scenario was repeated with a few modifications: Lara looked at the doll for a few minutes, held it close, then further away. When she was spoken to, she was there, but there was always a sort of screen between her and the therapist. Any acceleration in the rhythm of communication, any intrusive attitude reinforced this screen, which was however made bearable by a constant smile. But then, ghosts intervened much more quickly in the story; as in the other story, they lived in abandoned houses. These handless and footless things were going to die and resurrect. It was only after she had played with ghosts during several sessions that Lara was able to arrange, during the eighth session, a play-space that was much closer to the reality that she had experienced. Lara lined up soldiers. The soldiers played with rifles. Next to the soldiers, she placed animals: a dog, a goat, some geese … and a little further away, a doll holding a knife in her hand. In the game, the doll struck me with the knife, but I didn't die. It also struck a man-doll that lost a foot. The play-space comprised two different, non-communicating spaces: one for the dolls, another for the soldiers and the animals.

During these different sessions, the game allowed her to create an area, which attenuated the separation. In this intermediate play area, between internal and external reality, between the reality of life and that of death, was the ghost. The ghost was a central character in Lara's productions. It was a dead person but a peculiar dead person. It tried to inhabit a space, a place: an abandoned house, a privileged place for encounters between life and death. The ghost thus contributed to the creation of a space that went beyond the categories of real and unreal, of true and false. Each time I was clumsy enough to ask Lara whether the ghost really existed, I felt that my question embarrassed the child and didn't allow her to find an answer.

The place occupied by the ghost in Lara's sessions brings us to adopt Pierre Ferrari's hypothesis, that "the ghost is a sort of transitional, mortal object used by the child in its relationship to death." By giving it this label, Ferrari considers that one might paraphrase Winnicott and say that the ghost precedes the experience of the reality of death whose work is never finished, as accepting the reality of death is a never ending task; no living being can free himself completely from the tension created by comparing the reality of the living and that of the dead. However, this tension can be alleviated by the intermediate play area. In Lara's case, thanks to the detour of childish phantasms, the play area induces an alleviation of horror into tragedy, of reality into the imaginary. It allowed the process of history to come about, and for reality to be given a name.

But all children cannot, during an individual therapy, function as Lara did in this land of ghosts, which constitutes an intermediate area of experience. Fadia's case illustrates the necessity of a different treatment.

Fadia (11 years old) lost her mother, two older sisters (Hiam, twenty two years old, and Fatmé, fourteen) and two younger brothers (Fahd, seven years old and Ahmad, five) during the Cana massacre. She herself suffered serious burns on her arms and legs. When I saw her alone, during an interview two months after the tragedy, Fadia couldn't talk about what she had gone through. When she tried to express herself, it was hard to understand what she was trying to say. She often repeated the same drawing: a large house with lots of flowers. Fadia's inhibition during the interviews brought me to believe that she might benefit from group activities. It was only one year after the massacre that the team and I decided to create several groups within the school framework for those children who had lost family members during the massacre. As for practical and material reasons we couldn't create these groups at the Center, we hesitated for a long time before we decided to do it in school. These children, when they speak of themselves, describe themselves as the "children of the Cana massacre."

Within the group, we recommended a rather free method: the children expressed themselves freely. They imagined games or improvised sketches, using the material at their disposal. No interpretation was given to the subjects. In this framework, Fadia and her friends chose to draw. In a first stage, as during her interviews, Fadia often drew a house with trees and flowers. We were in autumn. It was cloudy and raining. Afterwards, she drew a wedding. For the first time there were people, whom she hadn't represented previously. Then, four months after the beginning of these sessions, Fadia drew what she had seen during the massacre: "The planes are bombing Cana. A boy got his head cut off, another lost an arm. He is yelling. These are people inside the house. Outside the house, a woman is breast-feeding her son. The child is dead. She has no head." After she commented on the drawing, Fadia told her story, in front of the other children: she had lost her mother, two younger brothers and two older sisters. After this session, Fadia and her friends decided to stop drawing and played with Lego blocks.

The following sessions were very difficult to manage. In a very excited atmosphere, the children built castles with very high surrounding walls. The group's progress brought up a theme of aggression, war, casualties and wounds. The children's game changed into something very frightening. It became the equivalent of an acting out. The children dug graves next to the houses, and each child buried the other and destroyed his/her house. For these children, to tell things was the same as to do them: certain words that emerged during the course of talking weighed as much as actions. The acting out seemed to me to be more of a prelude to thought than a means of repeating or reliving the trauma. Later, it would allow the children to elaborate on their experience of the trauma. Many of them, including Fadia, asked to have meetings with their therapist for individual sessions. It was within the therapy that the narrative would reintroduce the time factor in the representation, transforming the traces into thought, the reviviscence into rememoration.

Lara and Fadia both lived through a traumatic situation. This trauma couldn't become meaningful to them. It left traces, which appeared, on the psychological level, as a withdrawal in Lara, and as great instability in Fadia. I must stress here that if we tended to consider these traces in a first stage as destabilizing symptoms which made them more vulnerable, we quickly realized that they are adaptive and regulatory manifestations that the children came to develop following the traumatic situation they experienced. In my view, they constitute a protective device, before therapeutic treatment is initiated.

The treatment of these children has restored the symbolizing potential through games and drawing. Games allowed them to resort to significant predispositions, when the traumatized subject lacks representation. In Fadia's case, the game took place within the group. The group was able to ensure "the conditions of a continuous feeling of existence, of the elaboration of their persecution anxiety, of a capacity to trust a sufficiently good 'container'" (Kaës et al. 1979, p. 35).

To restore the communication potential is to allow the traumatized individual to transform what he has experienced into representations, and to resort to the process of history. According to René Kaës, the process of history consists in working on "the break or rupture in the course of events, on what is missing" (Kaës 1989, p. 190). It is a work of construction and reconstitution, which brings about verbalization, order and meaning both for oneself and for the other.

I would like to stress with Louis Crocq that restoring the process of history doesn't allow one to "recover the experience that was lived and which accompanied each of life's events. This experience was opened on an infinite number of possible futures that the following events of life confirm or cancel or modify constantly. On the contrary, the future doesn't stop remodeling this event and its meaning, reviving it, relating it, denying it, disguising it" (Crocq 1985, pp. 117-18).

But it is not enough to put images, affects or representations into words for things to get better. The process of history must not let us forget something essential: when the process is efficient, it is because a therapeutic framework has been established and the therapist's speech took place in a "container." There was a break, a rupture in these patients, a before and an after in their lives. So it is necessary to establish a "container," i.e. the equivalent of a bandage, so that the continuities can go on being restored. It is important that there be a sort of "protective cover." Moreover, time and continuity are essential to come to terms with the rupture experienced during the war. In a first stage, "the best way to listen to pain is to allow memory to be a place of silence" (Tardy 1993, p. 35). The therapist's urge to talk often made it difficult to listen to stories of tragic situations.

To conclude, I would like to emphasize the fact that war definitely constitutes a risk for the child. But the support provided by the family environment and by society at large could help him overcome difficult situations. Moreover, professionals have an important role to play in the emergence of resilience. The intervention strategies that they resort to must allow the children to give a meaning to an unthinkable experience. Under those difficult circumstances, the psychologist must establish a bond, a therapeutic alliance with the child. He must always have in mind the representation of a future for the child. By that I mean that he must be convinced that, in the child he is treating, there will be a living movement towards development that one stage will follow another, that each stage carries within it the preparation of what is to come. The child depends on the therapeutic follow-up from the very beginning, because the therapist might have a more or less clear anticipation, a vague idea, of the fact that the child will one day be different, that between today and the future there can be an improvement.

I was fully convinced of this when I met Lara for the first time in the waiting room. This conviction was associated with the strong wish to be able to repair something in this little girl's history. But the way in which she quickly communicated through play from the onset humbled me, and made me wonder about my therapeutic project for her. It is true that the efforts exerted during those few sessions allowed me to revive this child's interior world, but they also brought me to realize that she had tremendous psychological resources.

REFERENCES

Anzieu, D., Haag, G., Tisseron, S., Lavallée, G., Boublil, M. & Lassègue, J. (1993). *Les contenants de pensée* (Thought "containers"), Paris: Dunod.

Crocq, L. (1985). Evénement et personnalité dans les névroses traumatiques de guerre (Events and personality in traumatic war neuroses). In *Evénement et psychopathologie* (pp.111-120). Villeurbane: Simep.

Ferrari, P. (1979). L'enfant et la mort (The Child Facing Death). *Neuropsychiatrie de l'Enfance et de l'Adolescence, 27,* 4-5, 177-186.

Gannagé, M. (1997). L'enfant et la guerre: quelle protection? (The child and the war: What protection?). *Psychologie Française 42-3,* 237-42.

Gannagé, M. (1999). *L'enfant, les parents et la guerre, une étude clinique au Liban (The child, parents and war—A clinical study in Lebanon).* Paris: ESF.

Gannagé, M. (2001). La résilience chez l'enfants de la guerre (Resilience in children of the war). In La résilience: résister et se construire (Resilience: To resist and to build). *Cahiers Médico-Sociaux,* Médicine et Hygiène, 107-11.

Kaës, R., Missenard, A., Anzieu, D., Bleger, J., Guillaumin J. (1979). *Crise, rupture et dépassement. Analyse transitionnelle en psychanalyse individuelle et groupale (Crisis, rupture and overcoming. A transitional analysis in individual and group psychoanalysis).* Paris: Dunod.

Kaës, R., Puget, J., et al. (1989). *Violence d'Etat et psychanalyse (State violence and psychoanalysis).* Paris; Dunod.

Stern, D. (1993). *Journal d'un bébé (Diary of a Baby).* Paris: Press Pocket.

Tardy, L. (1993). *Les difficultés de l'alliance, etude basée sur la rencontre entre les Roumains et les Occidentaux (The difficulties of alliance—A study based on the encounter between Rumania and the West).* Foreword by Francis Maqueda.

Terror, Trauma and Identity Formation

SHMUEL ERLICH

CAN WE DELINEATE WHAT MAKES A PERSON CAPABLE of committing the kind of heinous acts that took place on September 11? The question harbors a poignant anxiety: Unless we can sharply draw the lines, how can we be sure that the person next to us in the office or supermarket, riding the bus or subway with us, or living next door, is not a terrorist? Moreover, without well-based knowledge of the development of the terrorist mind, how can we contribute to ameliorative and preventive action that might diminish the probability of a young person becoming a terrorist? Yet this anxiety is not only about identifying the terrorist in the other. It has as much to do with uncertainty and fear about our own terrorist parts. In this sense, it not only represents the fear of the power of our unconscious, but is an issue of personal identity: How can we be certain that in some essential way we can never be that person? It is very reminiscent of the anxiety I have encountered among adolescents in the wake of a classmate's suicide. The lurking question in such circumstances, often expressed out loud, is: "Could I possibly be next? How do I know it won't suddenly happen to me?" In attempting to give psychoanalytic consideration and answers to these anxieties we must devote special space to adolescent development. Not only because adolescents are among those seriously affected by terror and violence, and not only because adolescents are among the perpetrators of current terror and suicide bombing. We must deal with adolescents because, to my mind, the developmental transformations at this particular stage are crucial to the understanding of terrorism.

It is instructive that the term "terrorism" was introduced into psychoanalysis in Ferenczi's[1] (1949) phrase, "the terrorism of suffering." Ferenczi described a relationship in which the adult (parent) is unavailable to, yet controls, the child by adopting a narcissistic, self-indulging, masochistic, complaining and suffering stance. One possible outcome is the child's precocious assumption of an adult caretaker's role, spawned by identification with the aggressor. "Terrorism" here refers to the obliteration of and disregard for the real needs and existence of the other. The traumatized childhood of such a sadomasochistic adult is implied by Ferenczi as the root cause for terrorizing the child, suggesting an endless chain of "exogenous" environmental mistreatment. Winnicott similarly linked delinquency with early deprivation. Rizzuto observed that "Present-day violence and systematic terrorism from nations and individual groups make Winnicott's observations about the connection between emotional deprivation and delinquency an important source of reflection for those who may be interested in working preventively with children who are at risk" (1990,

---

[1]Presented as a paper to the International Psychoanalytic Congress in 1932 and first published in 1933.

p. 811). A widely held psychoanalytic stance is clearly expressed in these formulations: Mistreatment, delinquency and disregard for others stem from faulty or traumatogenic early object relations. While this formulation definitely applies to some individual terrorists, it is neither sufficient nor even relevant to all. It is especially lacking in its disregard of adolescent development and dynamics and their interrelatedness with cultural and ideological factors, which together play a major role in the phenomenon of terrorism as we currently face it.

The anarchism of the students' revolt of the late 1960s and the spate of terrorist activities that followed in the 1970s (notably in Germany and the Middle East) gave rise to new psychoanalytic understanding. In addition to an object-relations perspective, the need for an experience of paradisical bliss and perfection was recognized. Greenacre (1970) saw this as a youthful wish for a Utopian state, "a *death and rebirth fantasy*, which is externalized and put upon society. But back of it is the eternal Utopian dream of a perfect world" (p. 357, my emphasis). Her thoughts are echoed by Ostow (1986), who described the powerful social tendency for an apocalyptic experience, marked by an initial phase of savage destruction followed by a phase of messianic rebirth. This dimension is exceedingly important, but suffers from the procrustean constraint of casting such tendencies exclusively in a regressive and possibly psychotic mold for an etiological explanation.

The attempt to depict "The Terrorist" as a deranged, emotionally deprived, impoverished, and mentally ill person is misleading and basically wrong. Many of the suicide bombers are youths, ranging in age from mid teens to early twenties. Several early adolescents were also used. Recently a fourteen year-old boy changed his mind at the last moment, while his friend proceeded to blow himself up. Four boys aged fourteen were recently killed while trying to infiltrate an Israeli settlement. Young girls are doing their best not to be left behind in this "race." There is real concern among Palestinians about the increasing number of adolescents who, whether sent or on their own accord, go on suicidal missions. One sometimes gets a glimpse of the families as they mourn their deaths. Difficult and superficial as it is to judge, the impression is not of depriving or unloving families, or of deprived, unloved children. Real grief and sorrow are usually evident, often mixed with pride. A significant corollary is the social as well as the considerable financial support these families receive. They establish the traditional "mourners' hut" to which visitors, family and friends, come to pay their respects and support and share in their bereavement. Their son's heroic death is regarded a noble sacrifice and the achievement of martyrdom, and it has the open support and endorsement of the community.

To understand these youths we need to take into account several factors. Some are cultural, others are specific to adolescent development. Adolescents and young adults need to integrate drives, object relations, and intersubjective experience. I have formulated my understanding of what this integration consists in and requires within a theoretical model of the *processing of experience* mediated by *two distinct modalities*. Let me present the principal underpinnings of this model in order to examine its implications for relatedness and identity formation.

Experiential Modalities

In the conceptual framework I developed, the dimensions of *"fusion"* and *"separateness"* form parallel and complementary internal tracks, or modalities, through which experience is constantly processed and organized (Erlich & Blatt, 1985; Erlich, 1988, 1990, 1991, 1993, 1995, 1996, 1998). What is processed by *both* modalities is the *experienced relatedness of subject and object*, which comprises the range of object relations. These modalities, or dimensions, are inborn, yet to a considerable extent socially shaped and influenced. They digest, assimilate, and structure subjective experience continuously and unendingly, mostly outside consciousness and volitional control. The quality of subject-object relatedness, as processed by these two modalities, is reflected in very different experiences, which I will briefly describe.

In the first modality, subject and Other are experienced as separate and distinct. They are therefore functionally and instrumentally related: the relationship between them is instrumental, dominated by purpose and intentionality, by causality, directionality, and chronology. It is also the modality in which instinctual drives and conflicts are experienced. The central question here might be phrased as, "Who is doing what to whom?" which is why I named this the *Doing* modality. Time, the temporal dimension in which this mode of relatedness takes place, is experienced as linear, chronological and realistic, as are all other components that make for good reality testing. Thinking is adaptively geared, and emphasizes objective, logico-scientific aims and methods. The overall tendency is goal-directed and aims for efficiency of function, task, and accomplishment. Boundaries are vitally important in this modality: the separateness, distinctiveness, and relatedness of subject and object all find expression in the clarity, definition, strength and flexibility of the boundaries that set them apart.

In the second modality, the fundamental experience is of merger, identity, and fusion of subject and object. Boundaries here exist only insofar as they encompass and contain *both* subject and object, suspended in relative fusion and unity, allowing and safeguarding the ongoing continuity of experience. Time, space, and other dimensions of physical and factual reality are experienced in drastically altered ways (e.g., as varieties of non-linear time or multi-dimensional, unbounded space). Thinking is *not* geared towards reality testing, precision, and objectivity. On the contrary, the guiding tendency in this modality is towards *subjectivity:* allowing the subject to experience himself fully as ongoing, with ontological continuity and security, and existing in interconnectedness and union with the Other. The central experience is one of *"Being"* (hence its name) in fusion, togetherness and *"inter-being."* In Western thought "being" is typically conceived as an attribute within a singular subject. As I see it, however, the experience of *Being* is never singular—it always encompasses subject *and* object, hence involving "inter-being." This experiential modality does not give rise to or support conflict or drive urges and wishes. It harbors only experiences of "being" vs. "non-being," with needs, wishes, wants and anxieties along these lines (Erlich & Blatt, 1985; Erlich, 1990).[2]

---

[2]Both experiential modes are related in no small measure to cognitive dimensions. This raises and supports their association with primary and secondary thought processes. It is

The terminology of Being and Doing has its origins and parallels in Winnicott's work (see especially 1971, pp. 76-100), yet there are significant and fundamental differences between his conception and mine. These differences can be summarized in several major points: (1) Winnicott regarded *Being* as the prerequisite developmental antecedent to *Doing;* I do not. (2) In Winnicott's (and most psychoanalytic writers') view, *Doing*/separateness are not present at birth, and develop out of *Being.* I regard *Being/Doing* as parallel and complementary modalities, present and interactive from the start. With few exceptions, only one of these two modes gains ascendancy and dominance at any given time. On the other hand, in the course of development, the permutations of their complementary, overlapping and intermixing become increasingly more subtle and available for symbolization. (3) Although we both see in these modalities different aspects of relatedness, I regard *Being/Doing* as much more general, encompassing, and inherent psychological modes, affecting (ego) functioning and adaptation. (4) Winnicott gender-linked *Being* with femaleness and *Doing* with maleness (Guntrip further extended this distinction and linked it to maternal/paternal [1969, p. 258]). I do not see *Being/Doing* as intrinsically gender-linked, but as operating across gender lines, and subject to selective cultural reinforcement.

One further point must be added to this brief account. Developmentally speaking, I see *both* these modalities as present and operative from the onset of life. There is increasing evidence that the newborn infant is equipped and functions from the start with *both* an acute, sharply differentiated capacity for reality assessment, based on the infant's inherent separateness from his mother; but also with a capacity for fusion and merger with her:

> Infants . . . are predesigned to be aware of self-organizing processes. They never experience a period of total self/other undifferentiation. There is no confusion between self and other in the beginning or at any point during infancy. They are also predesigned to be selectively responsive to external social events and never experience an autistic-like phase . . . Union experiences are thus viewed as the successful result of actively organizing the experience of self-being-with-another, rather than the passive failure of the ability to differentiate self from other (Stern, 1985, p. 10).

Mothers equally function in *both* modalities. What is crucial in maternal attunement is not the mother's readiness to enter into symbiotic fusion with the infant (Mahler, 1975), or to engage in pure "Being" relatedness with him (Winnicott, 1971). It rather lies in her capacity to *shift* gears and adapt herself flexibly to whichever modality the infant experiences and requires at the moment, which is either that of *Being* and union or of separateness and *Doing.* Mother and infant gradually share increasingly fine gradations and combinations of *Being/Doing.* What really counts is the *experiential "goodness of fit"* between them. This mutual attune-

---

notable, however, that though a valid correspondence, I see thinking as derived and determined by the experiential modes, and not vice versa, so that primary and secondary processes are created through them. This seems to have considerable heuristic advantage: primary process, for instance, is defined by two attributes: 'rawness' or 'primitiveness,' as well as formal criteria, such as looseness, lack of boundaries, etc. It may thus partake of both modalities, and in turn, they refine the concept.

ment possesses demonstrable characteristics of rhythmicity and synchronicity along a temporal dimension (Feldman, 1993; Feldman et al, 1997). In a similar vein, patient and analyst are constantly faced with the problem of finding and establishing, or failing to do so, the "best experiential fit" between them (Erlich, 1990, 1991, 1995). The analyst/therapist functions simultaneously and paradoxically in *both* experiential modes. In the separateness-*Doing* mode he experiences himself and the patient functionally and "does" to (i.e., treats) the patient, who is directly affected by his doings. The prime example of this *Doing*-dominated mode in the analytic situation is interpretation. When in this modality, the patient is similarly engaged in a *Doing*-mode: he resists, defends, struggles, opposes, internalizes, and so on. On the other hand, the analyst (and the patient as well) is also "present" in a non-functional, *Being*-mode. This latter is typically referred to as "holding," "containing," etc. It is, perhaps, best exemplified by the *psychoanalytic situation,* which is set up, offered, and painstakingly maintained by the analyst as a physical, psychological, and pseudo-normative situation. Typically underrated and viewed as the mere "setting" for the "real work" and effectiveness of interpretation, the psychoanalytic situation is a vehicle and expression of the *Being*-mode and contributes enormously, though in causally unspecifiable terms, to the potential and actual curative effects of psychoanalysis and psychotherapy (Erlich, 1995).

Experiential Dimensions and Identity

Let us now integrate these notions with adolescence and identity formation. For the first time in the course of development, adolescence demands the successful blending and integration of the two experiential modalities (Erlich, 1990, 1993). Identity formation takes place only when one experiences oneself as both "being" *and* "doing" a specific role (e.g., one "*is*" a teacher and that is also what one "*does*") within a particular society and culture. The adolescent experience must combine being fused with some entity or Other, and at the same time be capable of feeling distinct and separate, so as to have instrumental goals and libidinal and aggressive wishes. A complete answer to the question, "Who am I?" requires much more than just the modality of well-established separation of self and object, of drive and conflict, and the subtleties of intellectual differentiation. Equally so, it cannot come solely from merger and union with an object or psychic state, and the safety, security, and substance such union provides for the self as an entity capable of continuous existence. Both modalities must be present, contributory, and sufficiently well integrated in order to appropriately resolve one's identity.

Successful integration of separateness and fusion enables the adolescent to experience himself as fully merged with a particular role provided by society, while at the same time to be fully engaged in the acquisition and mastery of the functional, technical, factual or mechanical skills it calls for. Where such an integration of the two modalities cannot be accomplished, we meet various forms and expressions of imbalance, such as arid technical or intellectual absorption, or an overriding quest for spiritual communion and otherworldliness. The crucial element is always the failure to integrate the two modalities and stressing one at the expense of the other.

In severe cases, the inability to "be" in the role, to join and merge with it, may become so overwhelming as to bring about a defensive withdrawal. The adolescent refuses to "do" the role, even as an external measure, because that might reveal the extent of his "not-being," his inner emptiness and deadness, which he cannot afford to risk. The adolescent who suffers from this kind and extent of *Being* disturbance will usually show various other signs of difficulty in joining socially. These may take a variety of forms and shapes, ranging from an inability to identify with the values and norms of his culture to openly anti-social behavior, or to social withdrawal and isolation, as in schizoid personalities and schizophrenic disturbances. These are some of the ways in which identity, relatedness, and the experiential dimensions are interconnected.

Going beyond Hamlet's dilemma, we may see the adolescent's passage into adulthood as contingent on the simultaneous acceptance and internalization of two contradictory possibilities: "to be or not to be," as well as "to do or not to do." The only solution to this paradox is through the experience that "to be is to do, and to do is to be." This paradox, once internalized, enriches both self and identity, and consolidates more mature and integrative forms of *Being/Doing*. Its rejection, on the other hand, creates tremendous narcissistic sensitivity around the limitations and terminability of the self, culminating in death and suicide (Erlich, 1978, 1990).

So far I have outlined why the integration of the two experiential modalities within a social role is mandatory for successful identity formation. A social role is one specific component of belonging to a society. It is further balanced, couched, buttressed and fueled by the equally important contribution of values and ideologies. Values and ideologies are indispensable not only from the societal point of view. They are the "life stuff" through which the individual experiences himself as belonging—merged with a community that holds, contains and roots him to a social soil and its nourishment, without which he will be disconnected, isolated, alienated, vulnerable and non-existent. Ideology and values, faith and beliefs are the glue that connects the individual psyche with a larger entity or Being, just as imperative for one's existence as are interpersonal love and intimacy. As Freud put it: "To the ego... living means the same as being loved—being loved by the superego" (1923, p. 58). Without the experience of oneness with the internal representations of values and ideologies—with "the ideologies of the super-ego" (Freud, 1933, p. 67), living, or being, is impossible.

For the adolescent and young adult this need to be submerged in something greater than one's self is crucial. In early adolescence it is often an adored personality that is invested and merged with. Later it becomes more abstract, and may be a cause, an ideology, a religion, or any idea that holds the promise of an idealized state. Unlike the Western conception, in which the well circumscribed and autonomous "subject" chooses and adopts an externally presented idea, the mind of youths in general, and of suicide bombers in particular, works differently. An idea (an ideology, religious belief, philanthropic cause, etc.) is not something external that needs to be adopted. It is the inner mode of actualization of the self—of doing what one is and of being what one does. Selfhood, life, and existence are meaningless if not suffused with this life-giving force. An endless array of possibilities, supplied by the dominant culture or counter-culture, beckons to be taken up in this way. It is where these ideological aims fail, usually because of individual and familial psychopathology, that there will be recourse to other means to achieve this end, ranging from drugs to sex, from suicide to self-mutilation. The force behind these manifestations is always the same: the need to submerge oneself in order to regain oneself in a "new" form, in which one is united with a larger-than-self entity. This is not, however, regressive. It is a progressive, developmental adolescent need, whose residues and impact linger on.

The form this need takes varies enormously, not so much along individual psychopathological lines (though these play a role) as along culturally preexisting molds. There is a crucial dovetailing here of intrapsychic development with actual reality, represented through cultural aims and expectations, transmitted and made available as values and ideals. These "ideologies" are the "glue" that bonds and connects—to one's family, social group and history; but also with one's self, body and identity. Without them one is doomed to shrivel, to feel empty and adrift.

It is important to study and articulate the ideologies that actually underline terrorism. Clearly religion plays a major role, and especially religious fundamentalism (Bohleber, 2002). Every religion offers the prospect of "joining" by merging with a greater-than-self entity, group or Supreme Being, and this is its attractiveness. Yet the ways such merger can be achieved or enacted differ from one religion to another, as well as within a given religion, subject to interpretation. Of the several factors affecting this merger, probably the most crucial is the attitude to death. It includes and shapes the view taken of the Afterlife, and this deeply affects the perception of reality shared by the co-religionists. In Islam, for example, the Afterlife of the *Shahid* (martyr) is an eternal pleasure-filled existence in paradise, where seventy virgins attend every "*Shahid*." It is not simply the promise of easy eternal bliss that is so attractive; it is the *idea* of merging with eternal bliss, the perfect Utopian state referred to by Greenacre. But it is not a psychotic regression that enables the youth to throw his life away. It is the immense power and blissful peace that comes from merging oneself with the larger cause—this *is* paradise. It is a state of mind that no longer needs to make calculations or instrumental choices. It is characterized by calmness and serenity, as if one has been transposed to another realm of existence. It is the state in which one's self is taken over, swallowed up and engulfed by something greater—internally venerated by one's ego-ideal and externally by one's family and community. This does not necessarily mean that the families of these young men actively encourage their undertaking a suicidal mission. The same bonds of love and fears of loss and bereavement operate in them as in all human beings. The support usually comes afterwards, but the youth "knows" it will come, and along with the pain there will be acceptance, approval and pride. Contrary to the commonly held Western view, these deaths are not considered "suicides" (forbidden by Islam as by other religions). They are martyrdoms, through which one's personal existence is forever fused and welded with a timeless community—the greater Islamic Ummah.

A widely prevalent form of surrender to ideology is the notion of *purity*. I believe that in all of us an inner "*purity-of-self*" must be maintained and protected from contamination. This "purity" is also an emanation of the *Being* dimension (Erlich, 1998). It *cannot* be understood or approached in rational, functional or instrumental terms. It does not partake of power struggles or territorial greed, and all attempts to study it along such lines are doomed. Ideologies are the breeding grounds for ideas of purity as well as impurity. Religions are expressly concerned with purity—of soul, body, and living—and are thus major contributors to the formation of prejudice. Adolescents are immensely concerned with and anxious about the purity of their mind, soul and body, in which so much is happening. Their craving for purity is linked to the quest for an idealized state, projected and supported through ideological, pseudo-religious visions. Such quests are highly significant expressions of the modality of *being* and fusion, as they hold out the promise of merging with a greater, better, and ennobled state. They belong to a realm that has nothing to do with the logic and rationality of the modality of *doing*-separateness, and are immune to such an approach or understanding. Equally so, they are not the derivatives of drive and conflict.

In closing, I suggest that terrorist acts are not only expressions of hatred, destructiveness and deprivation, though these may play a role. Especially where adolescents are involved in terror activities, we encounter a need to obliterate one's boundaries and merge with something greater. This wish and need does not primarily stem from the pressures of sexuality and aggression, but from another sphere: the experiential need to unite with something larger and more pure, something that promises eternal being. This quest is made possible through merger with an idea or ideology, and is driven by the wish to preserve the "purity" of the self from contaminating impurity. As a developmental stage, it enjoys the implicit support and endorsement of the community, which the adolescent and young adult wishes to join and be a part of. Where and when the religious, political or cultural ideology holds out the promise of attaining purity and eternity, the adolescent's actual death is experienced as a gateway to everlasting union and being.

REFERENCES

Bion, W. R. (1967). *Second Thoughts*. London: Karnac.
Bohleber, W. (2002). Kollektive Phantasmen, Destruktivität, und Terrorismus. EPF Conference in Prague, April 2002, EPF Internet Website: http://www.epf-eu.org/pub/bulletinv04/bulltin_articles_liste_en.html
Erlich, H. S. (1978). Adolescent suicide: Maternal longing and cognitive development. *Psychoanal. Study Child, 33*, 261-277.
Erlich, H. S. (1988). The terminability of adolescence and psychoanalysis. *Psychoanal. Study Child, 43*, 199-211.
Erlich, H. S. (1990). Boundaries, limitations, and the wish for fusion in the treatment of adolescents. *Psychoanal. Study Child, 45*, 195-213.
Erlich, H. S. (1991). Die Erlebnisdimensionen "Being" und "Doing" in Psychoanalyse und Psychotherapie. *Zeitschrift (J. Psychoanal. Theory & Practice), 4*, 317-334.
Erlich, H. S. (1993). Reality, fantasy and adolescence. *Psychoanal. Study Child, 48*, 209-223.
Erlich, H. S. (1995). Two kinds of change facilitating factors. *Israel J. Psychiatry, 32*, 194-204.
Erlich, H. S. (1996). Ego and self in the group. *Group Analysis, 29*, 229-243.

Erlich, H. S. (1998). On loneliness, narcissism, and intimacy. *Amer. J. Psychoanal.,* *58*, 135-162.

Erlich, H. S. and Blatt, S. J. (1985). Narcissism and object love: The metapsychology of experience. *Psychoanal. Study Child, 40*, 57-79.

Feldman, R. (1993). *Rhythmicity and synchronicity between mother and infant in the first year of life.* Unpublished doctoral dissertation, The Hebrew University of Jerusalem.

Feldman, R., Greenbaum, C. W., Mayes, L. C., Erlich, H. S. (1997). Change in mother-infant interactive behavior; relations to change in the mother, the infant, and the social context. *Infant Behavior and Development, 20*, 151-163.

Ferenczi, S. (1949). Confusion of the tongues between the adults and the child (The language of tenderness and of passion). *Int. J. Psycho-Anal., 30*, 225-230.

Freud, S. (1985). Project for a scientific psychology. Standard Edition, 1, 295-387.

Freud, S. (1915). Instincts and their vicissitudes. Standard Edition, 14, 117-140.

Freud, S. (1923). The ego and the id. Standard Edition, 19, 12-59.

Freud, S. (1933). New introductory lectures, Lecture XXXI . Standard Edition, 22 57-80.

Greenacre, P. (1970). Youth, growth, and violence. *Psychoanal. Study Child, 25*, 340-359.

Guntrip, H. (1969). *Schizoid Phenomena, Object Relations, and the Self.* New York: Int. Univers. Press.

Mahler, M., Pine, F., & Bergman, A. (1975). *The Psychological Birth of the Human Infant.* New York: Basic.

Ostow, M. (1986). The psychodynamics of apocalyptic: Discussion of papers on identification and the Nazi phenomenon. *Int. J. Psycho-Anal., 67*, 277-285.

Rizzuto, A. (1990). Deprivation and delinquency. *J. Amer. Psychoanal. Assn., 38*, 811-815.

Stern, D. N. (1985). *The interpersonal world of the infant.* New York: Basic Books.

Winnicott, D. W. (1971). *Playing and Reality.* Harmondsworth: Penguin Books.

Discussion: Developmental Effects of Terror and Trauma

IRVING STEINGART

FIRST, I WILL MAKE A COMMENT ABOUT EACH OF THESE PAPERS, then consider certain common, thematic material, and finally, I will elaborate upon these papers in a way which I trust will provoke useful discussion.

A major finding of Dr. Gannagé's study supports certain of our foundational psychoanalytic constructs having to do with psychic reality and early, maternal object relations. Those Lebanese children who lived through the trauma of a type of completely unpredictable warfare, and who showed depression or anaclitic disturbance, also were characterized either by "overprotective" or "overly absent" mothers, contrasted to a "healthy" group. One is immediately reminded of the report made by Anna Freud and Dorothy Burlingham (1943) involving children living in London during the Nazis' continuous bombing of the city in World War II. The clinical observation involved children and their mothers suffering the bombing in underground air raid shelters and how the children appeared clinically. Those children who remained calm, and played with toys with imaginative but conventional content, were only those children who had the good fortune to have mothers who were calmly connected. Of course, we can understand this, but I, at least, could not have said this was to be expected considering the unrelenting horror and carnage to which these London children were exposed. In any event, such a clinical observation made during a trauma does nicely complement Dr. Gannagé's work, which is retrospective.

Further, and this does not surprise us, the Freud/Burlingham material reports that the younger the child, the more pronounced and clear is the association between the mothering agent's composure and the child's clinical state. I just said "mothering" agent because, according to Freud/Burlingham, a child could remain in such a calm state even if it was a familiar adult figure who was providing the caretaking.

I want to cite a final observation about these London children: "It is a widely different matter when . . . children are separated from or even lose their parents" (p.21). Again, we would expect this, but, taken together, these findings suggest a connection to certain of Erlich's ideas which I will get to shortly.

I realize Dr. Gannagé's sample size is small, but it is impossible not to think further, differentiating questions. I will raise just one such question because it directly bears upon Dr. Gannagé's thesis, that trauma disturbs and disrupts "historicizing" and "continuity of being." All the children in this study were living out their entire lives during the war. But the oldest children studied, the ten year olds, had spent almost twice as much time with such trauma as compared to the six year olds. One might simply—but I think naively—conclude that it must be worse for the oldest child who lived longer with such trauma. But we would expect that the younger a child, the more that child would be influenced by qualities of maternal care. That is, of course, influenced for better or worse, so things cannot be so simple.

In this regard, Dr. Gannagé describes to us how peer "group activity" seemed to be a more effective, expressive therapeutic vehicle for an older, eleven year old Lebanese girl named Fadia. Fadia, some two months before an effort to initiate a therapeutic intervention, had lost her mother and four siblings to war. Evidently, it became clinically apparent that for an initial period Fadia had a better chance to become expressive within a therapeutic, peer group rather than the transference of an individual therapy. Can we think that, for this girl, her peer group was felt to be the most reliable object relationship in her life? Indeed, we are told that Fadia and her peers at school had given themselves a group identity—"children of the Cana massacre." We find another example of such a war trauma instigated peer bonding (for better or for worse) in Rossellini's powerful film "Open City."

On the other hand, Gannagé writes of Lara. Some two years before she accepted the initiation of individual treatment, this girl had suffered enormous physical and emotional trauma inflicted by the war upon her body and mind. She was a somewhat younger, eight and a half year old child. Lara also had lost her father as well as a sister in the war, but not her mother. Lara had to endure a six month separation for extensive medical treatment, but we are told that Lara "often spoke" on the telephone with her mother and remaining siblings. Also, one realizes, and it is a horrible twist of fate, that this child, described as a "pretty little girl," likely had obtained considerable nurturance from medical personnel during her extended medical care. The point is that Lara readily accepted individual treatment from the beginning, unlike Fadia, and somewhere obtained or retained sufficient, stable nurturance experience in connection with adults.

My comments about Dr. Erlich's paper have to do with these ideas of "merger" and "fusion," with consequent renewal of oneself, and especially how this bears upon adolescence and young adulthood. First, I want to ask Dr. Erlich to consider certain additional factors I believe to be pertinent to the difficulty of adolescent identity renewal. Then, later, I will take up this matter of "merging."

Especially due to Erickson (1950), we understand how such identity recreation is an urgent, developmental task. If it is not resolved, with the achievement of a personal/social as well as work identity felt to be both subjectively fulfilling and societally affirmed, then that individual's Self is in jeopardy. So is that individual's society. That society has an individual who, while a member, has no sufficient sense of membership in that society as it is currently constituted by his/her parental generation. I say sufficient because there is a kind of healthy alienation from society which is both the lot and potential of adolescence, together with young adults, and which can be a productive resource for a society. We understand that all adolescent and young adults in any modern, post-tribal, post-ritual society must go through such subjective crises, must work through into some satisfactory integration of change and continuity for themselves and their society (Steingart,1969). Whether or not a society makes available to its adolescents and young adults viable, felt-to-be meaningful, future oriented work identities is of course critical. But things are not so simple for these age groups.

I believe there is an awful irony here for such adolescents or young adults in a modern, or even worse, modernizing society, wherein ritualized, traditional practices now only carry power for the parental generation. With prior developmental tasks of achievement, for a growing child exposed to modernity, there are nevertheless concrete, palpable markers through which, and around which, that child can experience him/herself to be growing up toward adulthood in significant ways. First, there is vivid growth in one's body and new physical skills. Second, there is, in its own way, equally vivid mental growth and new intellectual-emotional capabilities. The terrible irony is this: With the accomplishment of the physical and sexual intellectual capabilities obtained in adolescence and young adulthood, it is dangerously easy to lapse into a dark conclusion that there is nothing more for one to envision for one's future development, and that the outcome of all such growth only has been to become a copy of one's parents. This can be experienced in the extreme as annihilating to one's Self. In this condition one's body and mind cannot offer a substantive aspiration, and hence solution, as in the past (notwithstanding teenage pregnancy).

With these comments, I believe I touch upon certain of Dr. Kernberg's thoughts. After all, she is considering whether the growing child is free to develop and this also must mean develop throughout with a clinically healthy sense of productive choice. We don't have to get all hung up on this notion of freedom. A close examination of our traditional construct of identification always has implicated a sense of freedom which is psychoanalytically viable whatever its murkiness philosophically.

I subscribe to Dr. Kernberg's values with respect to the rights of children to grow with such freedom. But it does raise devilishly difficult questions for the child psychoanalyst who wants to perform such a critique. In the first place, we have to accept that what we propose derives from modernity and thus really does threaten the existence of any ritual and tradition bound, tribally structured society. Second, we then will apply this critique across the board. The deeply religious, orthodox, Israeli young adult who killed Rabin, we would assume, also did not have this growing child's entitlement to freedom. What if we were considering Pennsylvania Amish society? Would we really be so concerned?

But a still more serious question arises. The evidence is that a significant number of terrorists, including suicide bombers, were not so immersed, we would say indoctrinated, into such a prison of uniformity. The leader of the group who used two planes to destroy the World Trade Center Towers was an Egyptian, middle class young adult who seemingly was raised and schooled in the context of modernity. He certainly felt alienated from his family and society. But he was someone who turned to violent extremism as a solution for his identity crises. He was not alone in this regard. From what we learn in the newspapers, there were and are others like him. In this respect, I believe I emphasize along with Dr. Erlich the attractiveness of such extremism for certain alienated youth rather than their helpless exposure to indoctrination.

Finally, this brings me back to this notion of "merging," or "fusion." Also, I will want to add to it some comments about one's experience of time. Taken together, I hope to draw out some lines of conceptual tension which will further discussion.

There always have been two quite different images of "merging," or "fusion," which can be such a tinder box for adolescents and young adults. The first image is that of a sort of inchoate mix or mush with no discernible structuralization of any sort. The second image is like a very well made seam on a garment. The seam stitches together what are factually two separate pieces of cloth. But the seam is so well made that it is not at all noticeable; one has to adopt a certain, critical eye to see it at all, and so one easily and naturally has the experience that one sees a single, unitary piece of cloth. This is merging as "good enough" fit (Winnicott, e.g., 1971). It is what Mahler (with Pine and Bergman, 1975) meant by their term "dual unity." This can occur as part of one's ordinary, immediate and unreflective, subjective experience at any point in our lives. But this does not mean that such experience does not undergo its own kind of development. Of course it does: for example, the acquisition of new sorts of subjective, emotional experience such as guilt.

Dr. Erlich cites Stern to the effect that "Infants . . . are predesigned to be aware of self-organizing process" (p.10). I think this is a confusing way of saying something about psychic structure in this subjective mode. That infants are designed is the structural point and they are aware of the effects of such design upon their experience. But infants are most certainly not aware of these self-organizing processes in themselves which would involve a level of self-reflection about their subjectivity which is beyond them.

I believe the "seam image" is the kind of merging idea that Dr. Gannagé uses. For Dr. Gannagé, damage to the "psychic apparatus" makes impossible the influence of a maternal "container form" which enables "continuity of being." But the very idea of such a "container" implicates, I believe, a structure of "dual unity" (Mahler, Pine, and Bergman, 1975). I think, but I am not sure, that Dr. Erlich works with the other image of merging, or fusion, when he speaks about a "non-linear" time operating in the subjective mode. If "non-linear" means only non-metric, that is one thing. But if it means a not uniform and powerful directional sense of time that is another thing, and I think, not correct.

Simply put, such horrendous trauma (but not only such trauma) destroys a vibrant sense of a powerful, forward, directional sense of time for these children, and this includes their subjective experience. Normally, naturally, one's experience of time can be cognitized as such (i.e. objectified) or be simply subjectively felt. We would all agree that when we speak about a Self construct we include both subjective and objective perspectives. It is evident that without such a conjoined, substantive sense of time there can be no good enough experience of development (continuity) for one's Self. If a Self construct is anything, it surely at least has gestalt property, and it surely must possess such good enough temporal, gestalt quality. We have in our language the expression "Time heals all wounds." I would think there is a similar statement in other languages. I believe all three panelists would agree that such horribly traumatized children have lost their sense of an evolving Self over time, and thus development. It is not even correct to say they live only in the present because this implies a Self time perspective. Therapeutic intervention must rekindle for them the passage of time and thus what Gannagé refers to as their capacity for "*historicizing*" (italics mine).

REFERENCES

Erikson, E. H. (1950). *Childhood and society*. New York: Norton.

Freud, A. & Burlingham, D. T. (1943). *War and children*. New York: I. U. P.

Mahler, M., Pine, F. & Bergman, A. (1975). *The psychological birth of the human infant: Symbiosis and individuation*. New York: Basic Books.

Steingart, I. (1969). On self, character, and the development of a psychic apparatus. *Psychoanal Study Child 24,* 271-300.

Winnicott, D. W. (1971). Creativity and its origins. In *Playing and reality*. New York: Basic Books.

The Effect of Terror on the Capacity for Symbol Formation: Case Studies from Afghanistan to New York

MARTHA BRAGIN

It may be true that the uncanny [unheimlich] IS something which is secretly famil-
iar [heimlich-heimisch], which has undergone repression and then returned from
it, and that everything that is uncanny fulfills this condition. —Sigmund Freud,
"The 'Uncanny'" (1919/1974 p. 245)

THE PLANE CRASHES INTO THE TOWERS. First one building is knocked to the ground, then another, then all of those around. A family rushes to the roof calling for help, the rescue trucks arrive, accompanied by sirens. There is a loud noise and then everything in the vicinity falls with a thud when the teacher announces cleanup time in the block corner of the four year olds' room at the Child Care Collective one morning in the spring of 1985. One of the most terrible things about acts of extreme violence is the way that they take scenarios that belong to the realm of dream and fantasy and make them literal. Thus these events become enactments of our worst nightmares, or force us to be actors in the nightmares of others.

Children, as has been pointed out by Kate Fincke just recently in her *JCAP* paper of 2001 live in the world of metaphor. Living the literal experience of that which has only been imagined causes regression because it removes metaphor—it de-symbolizes, leaving us in the stark world of Kant's *ding-an-sich* or Hegel and Lacan's Real (Lacan 1948). (In his 1948 paper "On Aggressivity" Lacan reminds us of both Hieronymous Bosch and children's play in nursery school.) Real life acts of terrible violence leave us in a world of things stark and without any meaning that can be attached to them. These observations were made before, by Laub and Auerhahn (1993) and Marion Oliner (1996, 1998), writing about the experience of being in Auschwitz.

Fonagy and Target (1999) state that violent acting out in patients is often the result of a failure to symbolize or to be able to think about thinking, forcing the patient to act instead. We must now move to an inverse—from the effect of the fail-ure of symbol formation back to its cause—from the perpetrator of violent acts to their witness.

Marion Oliner points out, "Many individuals suffer from too much reality and the concomitant rage engendered by their own victimization. They cannot use the outside world, and the task of analysis is not to restore the external reality to them but to probe the conflicts standing in the way of its use."

Those of us who work with torture survivors have been struck by a difficult truth: that survivors often experience themselves as locked in a guilty secret with the tor-turer. The torturer and the tortured alike know the hideous, sadistic world that they have inhabited together. The rest of us can blissfully repress all of that. But they know that there is no nightmare too terrible to be enacted. And soon neither knows whose nightmare it is anyway.

Melanie Klein's work on "Criminal tendencies in normal children" (1927) and *On Criminality* (1934) are reminiscent here—she quotes children talking about cutting people up and eating them, and sausages made of people's insides, and notes that children's fantasies often presage the work of criminals. She remind us of Jack the Ripper and contemporary criminals stalking London in her day, acting in real life the play of her little patients—not because the patients had heard of adults talking about the crimes—her patients' play predated the criminal actions—but because the crimes were enactments of what children phantasized.

I found strong resonance with Klein's infant only after having treated some survivors of explicit tortures and a variety of wars. A world in which outside cannot be distinguished from inside, in which one's own devouring wishes cannot be distinguished from the devouring pains of hunger or discomfort of wet. Over time and through maternal care, the outside world acquires meaning; words are formed—"clock," "pot," and so forth. Klein points out that symbol formation is the way in which the internal world is made useful to the external one. It begins through children's play.

In every consultation I was asked to do following the attack on the World Trade Center in New York City on September 11, the question arose as to the management of the intense anxiety, in both patient and therapist, created by witnessing and awareness of thousands of living human beings burning to death, as buildings toppled around them. Over and over the one new thing that I could add to the prodigious knowledge of the therapists in question was encouragement to evoke the unconscious meaning of external events, not to the perpetrators (those people are dead after all), but to the survivors. In a quest to be helpful in my own home town (*heimat* in Freud's 1919 vocabulary), I called on work I know well from Sub-Saharan Africa, South East Asia, Central America and the published work of psychoanalysts in Latin America such as the Vinars, who are among us here. In these far off places, colleagues had been working over the years to help their patients and themselves contain the anxieties evoked by the appearance of piles of bodies in the streets, the smell of burning flesh, the experience of massive destruction, of torture, of death that knows no reason and no end. And in that work I discovered resonances in the actions of terrorists, a terrible resonance to our own fantasies, remembered child's play and to our dreams.

But how can one evoke unconscious meaning if the events have been desymbolized—are simply what Oliner (1996) calls "representations" of universal parts of the unconscious?

What I propose is that exposure to literal enactments of violent phantasy causes regression to a state prior to symbol formation, because this regression is a necessary protection from knowledge of the violent infantile propensities that lay within—the very propensities that have been repressed over time through the care of loved and loving objects whose good enough constancy has allowed us to use the world over time. (In other words, while the capacity to mentalize may protect against the worst symptomatic responses to exposure to extreme violence, exposure to extreme violence may inhibit the ability to mentalize in order to protect against the knowledge of internal destructive capacity too painful to bear.) In order to mitigate these effects, then, one must work in the treatment process to build the capacity for acceptance of the violence within, in order to assist in the re-symbolization of the violence that has in fact been committed without. I will discuss here two issues raised by the de-symbolization of phantasy:

—The disorganizing effect that the literal evocation of phantasy material has on the developing child who is struggling to complete a process of repression and integration.

—The disorganizing effect that the literal evocation of phantasy material has on the therapist and society at large, where a tendency to regress to paranoid schizoid modes of thought are sometimes utilized to protect the self from disintegration, after the integration has been completed.

> *Now the metaphor has become literal: children are children and the*
> *terrors are terrible and there you have the difference.*
> —Boris Pasternak, *Dr. Zhivago*, p. 431

> *Suppose the lions all get up and go,*
> *And all the brooks and soldiers run away;*
> *Will time say nothing but I told you so?*
> *If I could tell you I would let you know*
> —W. H. Auden, (1939) "If I Could Tell You."

How do you survive a war that has gone on for ten years before your birth, and already exhausted your parents? You hear that there were cities once, but without books or media, there is little to tell you what a city might be—or a cinema—school is an exciting new event—every moment on the floor of the unheated classroom to be cherished.

By way of illustration, I present a story told to me in Northern Afghanistan by a group of boys aged 14–17 who had been soldiers prior to the fall of the Taliban. (The area that they lived in was part of what was called the "frontline" because it had been the scene of fighting throughout the twenty-three years of war. This particular city only fell to the Taliban in 2000, followed by expulsion of the population and continued fighting in the east.) First, the Soviet tanks came from the North (these children lived very close to that border), then, when the Soviets were defeated (they were very young), came the almost random destructiveness by the various mujahadeen factions as they fought for power, then the united front against the Taliban, with the front often breaking into fragments, then the American bombing, which left several hundred dead and some children paralyzed. Unexploded ordinance and landmine removal was underway, but children were still frequently at risk for blowing up or losing a leg. Schools had just re-opened after being closed following the fall of the pro-Soviet government in 1992.

These particular boys had been fighting with various factions during the last few years. They would be taken by one side, and if the town that they were holding fell, start home only to be captured by another. They fought for individual war lords, the

Taliban and the Northern Alliance. Because they were under age, these boys were rarely asked to participate in direct fighting. Instead, they would dig trenches, carry ammunition, gather fuel for cooking, and bury the dead. A particularly gruesome task was to collect body parts of the dead on the battlefield and prepare them for burial.

I asked them to name something that they really liked.

> "Peace we like peace."
> "What do you like about peace?"
> "School and kite flying."
> "Is there anything that you don't like?" "Fighting." (When I asked about the fighting I learned about their wartime occupations.)
> "Now that the fighting is over is there anything that you don't like?"
> "We don't like dogs—especially mad dogs—and bits of house that could fall on you."

The boys talk among themselves—

> "When I go to get fuel the mad dogs are there." "Where *I* go there are dogs but I am not scared of them, no, it is the *wolves* that scare me." "Oh no stupid, we can manage the wolves—we just shoot them—but—what's really scary is the *lion.*"
> "What lion ? There's no lion."
> "For sure there is a lion. I've SEEN the lion!"
> "Oh that's true there is a lion, I've seen him too! And a lion can definitely eat a person, gun or no gun."

We then got into long discussion about the lion, with a group of younger boys describing him quite carefully, length of mane, paws, tail, etc. The boys also discussed whether the lion was Muslim, since if he were a Muslim he should not eat people, since eating people was unclean according to Holy Koran. It emerged at the end of the discussion that this lion was ignorant and simply ate people up all the same. "That is why we like to go to school. If someone is illiterate he might not know *what is actually written* in Holy Koran correctly and then he could do any terrible thing. Like the lion."

I asked the boys about the afterlife, and none felt sure that his entrance into heaven was assured. They said that they were probably bad boys because they had lived through drought and terrible sorts of things. And they see bad things in their minds—not just when they are dreaming but sometimes when awake. Some have been taken to the traditional healer if things have gotten very serious. Most have not because of the expense of this treatment.

I would like to unpeel this conversation in layers. Clearly, there is much more that could be explored here, with time and care and the opportunity to work more closely over time with these boys. To what extent is this fantasy adaptive? Are there aspects that are in fact maladaptive and if so what are they? Are they actually able to learn at school or is symbol formation a pervasive problem for them?

Since the boys are not here, and there is not more time, one must avoid the temptation to speculate endlessly about the possible implications of fragmentation fears and fantasies in a fragmented country, behind broken walls in a culture where families are accustomed to live behind walls—what is important for us to remember here is that just as terrorism reduces the phantasy world to the literal, the critical contribution of psychoanalysis to help lies in our ability and interest to re-symbolize through reading symbols.

At first glance we see a clear metaphor for the political situation in Afghanistan and a clever one at that. The pre-Taliban warlords, who professed to Orthodox religious principles, were known to abuse children and conquered populations under their command in spite of the clear injunctions against such behavior in Koranic law. Many of the warlords were said to be illiterate, and it was to their illiteracy and that of the population that many of these excesses were attributed. Had they been unable to read Holy Koran, it was often said, they would have understood its interdictions and mitigated their cruelty. Plenty of symbol formation here.

Then we think about the fact that these boys lived dangerous lives. Unexploded ordinance and landmines littered the earth under their feet; unstable houses sometimes fell in, and roads were strewn with rubble causing accidents. Dismemberment from all of these things was literal, not metaphorical. Yet the boys did not speak about them, they spoke about a lion, prowling the northern desert, eating up hapless young men out in search of fuel.

Was this their (again metaphorical) way of talking to me about their lives and the fear of the uncontrollable forces that had a variety of meanings? Was this their adolescent way of being brave while informing me that they were terrified? Things fall apart and so could they. One thinks again of Klein and Lacan and the experience of most day care teachers, who see children dismembering, devouring and being dismembered in early play. Their most violent childhood phantasies had literally been enacted on the battlefield throughout the vast terrain of their known world.

However, it also reminds one of Oedipus. Jocasta tells him that all men sleep with their mothers in dreams. Oedipus has gone blind and the city has been beset by plague *not* because he dreamed it—but because he has really done it. The punishment and the illness then is not for the idea—but for making a common fantasy literal. The boy soldiers that I interviewed in Kunduz and other northern cities had seen normal childhood phantasies, such as castration and bodily disintegration, turn real in the fighting and its aftermath. The imaginary had become literal—they are *not* guilty of the destruction—someone else is—but they may well be guilty of having phantasized it. Their fantasies have been enacted, they have not been punished and now they are on guard against the terrible punishment that must arrive. It may be that for that reason these teenagers were thinking and dreaming about devouring lions in ways more usual among much younger children.

But the boys did not talk about the lion as though it were a story. Most were consciously afraid of an actual lion. At the same time, these boys were not psychotic. They went to school, helped with chores, and worked at carpet weaving or odd jobs every day. And yet it became clear to me that the lion was *not* a symbol—the lion was a real creature in their minds. The literal and the imagined were conflated beyond recognition. Regression then to an earlier state—the lion more bearable to fear than the horrors that they had frequently witnessed, and the dangerous world to which they had returned. This regression brings with it an infantile omnipotence in which the survivors tend to see themselves as the cause of the violence around them and not its victim. Thus the well-known concept "survivor guilt" has been seen as a result of a defense—regression to a state so early that they are then the creator of the world around them (see Winnicott's infant for more of this in "The use of an object"). This early infantile omnipotence defends against the terrifying helplessness at the hands of a murderous enemy which has been these children's real life.

However, when the actual rather than imagined terror was over these youngsters were left with a complex problem. There had been symbol formation throughout the years and it had worked well. However, the repeated enactment of primitive material that ought to be in the unconscious disturbed the ability to both symbolize and to repair, and left an enormous struggle to do and to be good (to repair), on the one hand, and the intrusive thoughts that plagued them on the other.

This dilemma perpetuates the dangers to us all, as the need to be good and be pure and to purify, unsymbolized, and unintegrated—split off from the rest—can lead to action, and the action, if not mediated by assistance, can lead to behavior that is harmful to both the self and to others. (The Taliban, after all, were former boy soldiers turned religious scholars to whom no help in the mediation of symbols was given.)

Back to the towers—

The recognition of violence enacted in the world as something that lives within as well as without is an unbearable psychic pain. The knowledge that one's own extraordinarily destructive wishes could be carried out—are not just phantasies—is obviously intolerable in the depressive position, and therefore tends to cause splitting, or rather regression to a paranoid schizoid mode of thinking in order to distance oneself from the possibility of destruction within.

My colleague called for consultation with a disturbing case. The young man in question—I will call him Paul—a precociously bright (barely 14 year old) freshman at a competitive public high school, had been referred because of the kind of "defiant attitude" that could get him in trouble in a school in which he was in the minority as an African American.

Trauma in his family had come down through the generations with his own mother having been witness to the attempted lynching of her father by an angry mob. Her untreated psychological difficulties, and real life economic stress, left her unable to be empathic to her son, and often with an unconscious need to be avenged by him. (Maurice Apprey has discussed what he calls "transgenerational haunting" in families such as this, in which enactments of the original horror repeat over time.)

According to the therapist, Paul was responding rather well to treatment until the events of 9/11. Then he began to decompensate in frightening ways, spending all of his time on the internet, writing about his very specific and perfect view of the appropriate response to the events ("how dare you say tragedy—this was evil—this was war"), and a rage at anyone, including his mother, who responded in any way that he considered incorrect. He no longer ate or slept well, awake pacing and writing all night, and refused medication. What was particularly interesting is that he had not seen the events.

He had been at school in a different borough at the time. When he returned home, he repeated to his mother that the smell was of burning bodies, and that the ash was of the dead. That they were breathing the bodies of their neighbors. He began to have difficulty eating and sleeping, and was overwhelmed by the sense of the evil that had been done—the worst anywhere in the world he would announce—worse than Hiroshima and Nagasaki, because it was not committed during an act of war. He began to develop a complex scheme of who was guilty, who was more guilty, and what was appropriate as an expression of grief. His mother, a devout Christian, was cursed for her lack of respect for the dead when she talked of her compassion for the mothers of the boys who died committing the act, a compassion important to her own psychic survival. Every waking moment of Paul's life revolved around the careful construction of behavior and ideas that were such that they could have no connection to the terrorists. Sleep eluded him but for a few hours.

There is a great deal more to say, in a long and complicated story. However, we will focus here on the uncanny. This young man had got stuck on his own fantasies of violent retribution being enacted by bright young men, older and wealthier but perhaps *not* so different from him (Osama bin Laden went to Disneyland as a child). They were smart, educated, and aggrieved. They acted upon their worst phantasies of retribution. Fearful of his rage, most especially at his loving, somewhat seductive mother (who had suffered so very much, but who was so unable to reach out and empathize with him: a strict mother who held him close but made difficult rules), he felt in this enormous crime a frightening breakthrough of his most violent phantasies. He needed to remind himself and everyone else that *he* was no terrorist.

When we became collectively aware of all those people burning to death, we did not want to know, to understand, to symbolize and integrate that awareness. Like Paul, we wanted to keep it utterly apart and horrible and *other*. But remember Jocasta—in dreams we are all perpetrators of the most heinous crimes. In our dreams, *we are all terrorists*.

To be a terrorist is to live in a paranoid-schizoid world, with the self as good and the other as the recipient and embodiment of projected evil.

When we are unable to see beyond the evil of the terrorist act and project all of our rage upon the terrorist, then we oddly enough are most like him. On the other hand, and perhaps ironically, when we are able to understand the common humanity that we share, even with the terrorist, including the capacity to fantasize evil, it is at that very moment that we enter the depressive position and are least like him.

Our contribution as psychoanalysts, then, is to face the darkest fantasies within and without and to help others come to grips with them as well. The phantasies of the perpetrators, who died in their attack, can not be known and understood. However, the survivors, all of us, need our assistance to integrate, symbolize and own the buried parts of ourselves that have been woken up by these acts of cosmic violence. That is our calling. Otherwise we run the risk of joining the same terrorists from whom we wish to differentiate ourselves in a divided world in which we see self as pure and other as evil.

REFERENCES

Apprey, M. (1993). Dreams of urgent/voluntary errands and transgenerational haunting in transsexualism. In M. Apprey & H. Stein, eds. *Intersubjectivity, projective identification and otherness* (pp. 102-31). Pittsburgh: Duquesne U P.

Auden, W. H. (1989). "If I Could Tell You." In E. Mendelson, ed. *W. H. Auden: Selected poems* (p. 110). NY: Vintage.

Becker, D. (1995). The deficiency of the concept of posttraumatic stress disorder when dealing with victims of human rights violations. In R. Kleber, C. Figley, & B. Gersons, eds., *Beyond trauma: Societal and cultural dynamics* (pp. 99-114). NY: Plenum.

Fincke, K. (2002). A love of things irrepressible: The narration of metaphor. *Journal of Infant Child and Adolescent Psychotherapy 2*, 1, 107-23.

Fonagy, P., Target, M. (1999). Towards understanding violence: The use of the body and the role of the father. In R. Perelberg, ed. *Psychoanalytic understandings of violence and suicide.* London and NY: Routledge.

Freud, S. (1919). The 'uncanny.' Standard Edition 17, 273-53. London: Hogarth Press.

Freud, S. (1918). Lecture XIX: Resistance and repression. Standard Edition 15, 286-303. London: Hogarth Press.

Kant, I. (1781). *The critique of pure reason.* Amherst: Prometheus Books, 1990.

Klein, M. (1927). Criminal tendencies in normal children. In M. Klein, *The writings of Melanie Klein.* Vol. 1: *Love, guilt and reparation and other works, 1921-1945* (pp. 170-86). NY: Free Press, 1975.

Klein, M. (1928). Early stages of the Oedipus conflict. In M. Klein, *The writings of Melanie Klein.* Vol. 1: *Love, guilt and reparation and other works, 1921-1945* (pp. 186-99). NY: Free Press, 1975.

Klein, M. (1930). The importance of symbol formation in the development of the ego. In M. Klein, *The writings of Melanie Klein.* Vol. 1: *Love, guilt and reparation and other works, 1921-1945* (pp. 219-33). NY: Free Press, 1975.

Klein, M. (1934) On criminality. In M. Klein, *The writings of Melanie Klein.* Vol. 1: *Love, guilt and reparation and other works, 1921-1945* (pp. 258-62). NY: Free Press, 1975.

Klein, M. (1937). Love, guilt and reparation. In M. Klein, *The writings of Melanie Klein.* Vol. 1: *Love, guilt and reparation and other works, 1921-1945* (pp. 306-44). NY: Free Press, 1975.

Klein, M. (1975). *The writings of Melanie Klein.* Vol. 1: *Love, guilt and reparation and other works, 1921-1945.* NY: Free Press.

Klein, M. (1975). *The writings of Melanie Klein.* Vol. 3: *Envy and gratitude and other works, 1946-1963.* NY: The Free Press.

Lacan, J. (1948). Aggressivity in psychoanalysis. In *Ecrits: A Selection* (pp. 8-29). NY: W. W. Norton, 1977.

Lattimore, R., Ed. (1992). *Sophocles 1:* Oedipus, Oedipus at Colonus, Antigone. Chicago: U of Chicago P.

Laub, D. & Auerhahn, N. (1993). Knowing and not knowing in massive psychic trauma: forms of traumatic memory. *International Journal of Psychoanalysis, 74*, 287-302.

Oliner, M. (1996). External reality: The elusive dimension of psychoanalysis. *Psychoanalytic Quarterly 65*, 267-300.

Oliner, M. (1998). Analysts confront the holocaust. The unsolved puzzle of trauma: The impact of the Holocaust on Sexuality. Paper delivered to the New York Freudian Society, October 4, 1998.

Mitchell, J., Ed. (1986). *The selected Melanie Klein.* NY: Free Press.

Pasternak, B. (1958). *Dr. Zhivago* (M. Hayward & M. Harari, trans.). NY: Pantheon.

Vinar, M. (1989). Pedro or the demolition: A psychoanalytic look at torture. *British Journal of Psychotherapy 5*, 353-62.

Winnicott, D. W. (1971). *Playing and reality.* London: Routledge/Tavistock.

Winnicott, D. W. (1969). The use of an object and relating through identifications. In *Playing and reality* (pp. 86-95). London: Routledge/Tavistock, 1971.

Terror, Persecution and Dread Revisited

KAREN KOMISAR PRONER

Introduction

CATASTROPHIC CHANGE IS A TERM CHOSEN BY Wilfred Bion to describe a disruption to the constant conjunction of facts that can be found in diverse fields: among them the mind, the group, the psychoanalytic session and society itself. These facts can be observed when a new idea appears in any of these areas. New ideas contain a potentially destructive force which violates to a greater or lesser degree the structure of the field in which it appears. Thus the new discovery violates the structure of the pre-existing theory and it can revolutionize the structure of society and the structure of the personality.

Violence, invariance, and subversion are words that Bion uses to describe the elements inherent in the change.[1] He maintains that the development of personality proceeds by a series of leaps forward under the thrust of a new idea which generates anxiety by virtue of its requirements that all previous experience must be reviewed and reorganized in the new light or at least from a different perspective. Later, he used these words to describe an internal process that he found useful in work with borderline and psychotic patients.

In a workshop that I led for IPTAR members, not long after September 11, I asked the question: Are these concepts relevant to a situation that we and our patients have experienced in the last months? I believe now as I believed then that these are useful concepts in understanding how the psyche deals with variance of enormous proportion. We focused on the mourning and healing process and how it can be prevented, or facilitated.

Clinical Material of an Eight-year-old Child

To illustrate these ideas, I would like to offer some material of an eight year old girl who had started in psychotherapy with me just before Christmas; that is just three months after the September 11 event. I want to make it clear that this child has no direct link to this disaster nor does anyone she knows, except that she lived in the city of New York where it happened. However, the disaster had a great effect in

---

[1] It is interesting that Bion first used these ideas when working with soldiers with war neurosis in a military psychiatric hospital after the Second World War. He plots the vicissitudes of a new idea in groups, describing the evasive tactics of the basic assumption group. He describes how the primordial anxieties that are stirred by catastrophic change are dealt with. I found his concept useful last year in thinking about how affected we and our patients were by the disasters of September 11. But I seem to have moved on from thinking about trauma and its immediate effects, to thinking about what one might call a working through of that which was generated by this event.

bringing about a process that began the working through of an earlier trauma that had been repressed for years.

We know that trauma can influence children's thinking, symbolization, play and learning capacities. However, in the preliminary consultations with Christina, her ability to articulate her history and to express her worries and to draw and play was quite remarkable, one might say precocious. Choosing the couch, to perch, which is next to my chair, she proceeded to outline her history, with a pseudo-mature air. I wondered if she had been primed by her mother's thinking. She talked of her worries about separations from her mother when her mother traveled on flights for her work. She spoke about her fear of her father's anger. She also spoke about friendships, which let her down or left her out. But she talked with insight and with clarity. She talked to me easily about her parents' separation and her complicated life of moving between two houses and two needy, anxious adults. She spoke of her mother's anxieties. I spoke to her about how close she felt to her mother and how confused she sometimes became between her worries and her mother's worries. She seemed relieved when I commented on how exhausting it was for her to have to look after her parents, and it left very little space for her to be looked after. She talked about how she worried about her father when she was with her mother. She also worried about her mother when she wasn't with her. She sat and talked easily in these initial sessions. My overall sense was that time seemed irrelevant as in the unconscious. She seemed to know when her father moved from the home, which was when she was four years old. However, she presented it as though it had just happened. I was left with the sense that the loss was not worked through at the time.

The next session she drew a picture of me. I was depicted as a gigantic head with piercing blue eyes and a large red mouth that dominated the face. A strange cone-like hat, fringed by fur like Santa Claus' that was shaped like a dunce-hat perched on my head. The point of the hat was cut off at the top of the picture. She accompanied this figure with a picture of herself, smiling. I interpreted that I looked quite frightening, with my eyes and my mouth. I wondered with her that perhaps I stood for a process here of looking at herself and thinking about herself and the things in her life that she is frightened of. I commented on the cut off bit of the hat and posited that some part of her was cut off and not able to think about things that have been difficult for her, as opposed to the part of her that smiles and pretends that everything is fine. I wondered with her whether the girl was laughing at the clown-like figure, to which she did not respond.

I felt that I had made contact with her and she seemed very happy to return the next time. We began therapy after Christmas. She seemed to like the drawing materials that were offered. She sat pondering over the paper. She scribbled circles that expressed an inner confusion. She began by making rather sterile conventional pictures: flowers, sun, and clouds. She drew three flowers all placed very far apart. The smallest flower was drawn in the middle. I commented how apart they were and seemed to grow in separate gardens. She stared at it and circled it with her pen. She then moved to making folded shapes that she attempted to fly. These forms began as strange amorphous shapes, folded and stapled and then thrown into the air across the room, away from both of us. She remained silent. All efforts were directed to folding and shaping these bits of paper.

The following session, she made more shapes in a silent repetition. She would begin with a scribbling mass and then she would move to folding and shaping these flying shapes. It was only after several sessions, that she began to name them "planes" and struggled with the aerodynamics. A dull repetitive silence prevailed in the session as plane after plane was made and tried and retried. My mind wandered trying to maintain thought: thinking about gender and boy's games; and "dunced" Santa Claus daddies, but after attempting some comments, I succumbed to dullness. I found myself in a space that was only defined by the beginning and the end of the session. I found myself thinking of Frances Tustin's black hole images of autistic children, and the autistic and psychotic children with whom I have worked.

A terrible sameness descended on each subsequent session and the only hope I maintained was that I had seen my patient in a different state of mind. Some part of her seemed determined to rejoin to an experience, perhaps to a memory. I struggled to talk only of the atmosphere in the room, trying to find words to describe the despair that nothing would change, and the shapes seemed shapeless. Then one session after she had placed many flying shapes in her box (ten sessions), she constructed another one and wrote " twin tower" on both sides of the plane. I realized the link to the World Trade Center disaster. I spoke then of the Twin Towers as Mummy and Daddy, whom she felt were demolished as a couple by her attacks and her wish to have mummy all to herself. This feeling that she was so close to Mummy makes her feel that she "dunced" Daddy. She responded, "Did you see the people jumping out of the windows?" She added, "they must have been mush on the sidewalk." I said that I thought she was worried that her wish to separate Mummy and Daddy had really "dunced" Daddy's penis so that he could no longer make babies for Mummy. Mummy's babies were all thrown out of the window, and made to mush. Further that she believed that this was the reason that she was Mummy and Daddy's only child. This was something she could not tell anyone about when she was little, but seeing these things really happen at the World Trade Center made her think of this earlier disaster in her life. I wondered with her that through her 'shape' attacks she felt that I too was "dunced" and not able to think and no longer able to make "thought babies" as we began to do in the beginning. I linked it with the frightening eyes she had drawn in the beginning. Perhaps she worried that I would see what she felt she had done to Mummy and her potential babies and Daddy.

I would like to stop and think about this process. It seems that there was an earlier trauma, perhaps even earlier than the separation between father and mother. The timeless quality to her emotional life was a clue to me that Christina's problems were more to do with an earlier loss of mother. Mother had said she was depressed after a miscarriage; things began to go badly between mother and father. This is recollected when she was a toddler but no doubt had its antecedents in attachment and separation in her infancy. The disaster of the World Trade Center triggered the earlier traumas as her mother reported her to be very anxious in school since September; clinging, regressed, and easily persecuted by other children and expressing a dread of her mother leaving her. The sense of a "black hole" in the room, session after session, seemed to be a breach in container-contained functioning (Bion), perhaps as she experienced it in the original trauma. I also was reminded of the "sameness" quality that is so often the psyche's response to the immediate impact of trauma. Would this be an area of breakdown? What Hannah Segal would call the "isolated pocket of schizophrenia," or Wilfred Bion would call "the psychotic part of the personality"? Caroline Garland writes, "Isolated pockets of disturbance, of madness, of raw untransformed primitive experience, inhabit us all. We can be skilful, or we can be just lucky, and they may never emerge fully into the light of day; but whatever the nature of the degree of failure in the original relationship with the primary object, the experience of external disaster will seek it out and give it fresh life and fresh significance." Was Christina's experience that she brought to psychotherapy an untransformed primitive experience, perhaps from infancy? Her play had a repetitive, evacuative sensate quality; the quality that you might observe in infancy. It had the look of an infant in a repeated sequence of actions, not yet transformed into phantasy or representation. It had a quality of a protomental level of thinking with its intimate relations with bodily processes.

It was after many sessions that Christina's thinking began to evolve into a thought looking for a thinker: an attempt at projective identification for which I was meant to become the recipient thinker. When I succumbed to and began to reflect on it, it was a turning point in building this container. I was slow to come to it. My own counter-transference to the September events, no doubt, played an important part. What interests me is that the meaning that was latently in those shapes could only be thought about when I was clearly in the affective state of despair struggling with her to find thoughts/ words for the helplessness. When I could deal with my own resistance to the horror of the image ("mushed babies"), I could speak to the level of the communication, which may have been encapsulated since the original experiences perhaps in infancy. The new experiences of the World Trade Center adhered to this early un-processed experience. To speak to the conscious awareness of the disaster would be to deny the import of the communication.

She began to draw again. She drew a series of persecuting pictures of her braces; a picture of a wire drawn between two objects; holding them together; as though her mouth (she connected) held the breast and the nipple together. She drew a line down the middle of the picture and then added a picture of herself with the brace on her mouth. Thus the picture had the brace on one side and a picture of her wearing the brace on the other side. In another picture she pasted a large red heart in the center with an arrow drawn through it with two figures on either side of the heart. They were male and female and were decidedly smaller than the heart. The male figure was in short trousers. The overall sense was these were parental figures but they were reduced in size. However, they were smiling, connected by the arrow of the heart.

Many of her pictures have a dividing line diagonally across it. She drew a picture of a rather large phallic cigarette that was drawn diagonally across a piece of paper with a line drawn diagonally across the cigarette. She told me that she did not want her mother to smoke and felt that she needed to remind her. She began to more freely depict a controlling part of herself. She made "The BAD Girl Book." This book depicted "hot dog girls," "pigs" and "lusers." It also had an interesting abstract configuration on the cover page. She drew two conical shapes, one larger than the other. The larger one on top is in red and rather sketchily drawn, and the smaller of the two is solid dark green, but under the weight of this larger figure it does not seem to have much substance. In yet another picture, she draws a gigantic shoe in the right hand corner of the page in a diagonal action of stepping on a flower growing in the center of the picture. Perhaps the most disturbing depiction is done in pencil of a girl with eyes shut and whose body is depicted as a set of segments of rigid shapes, interlocking shapes that look somewhat like a sarcophagus. It reminded me of the character in the play *Happy Days* by Samuel Beckett, who is so buried up to her neck in the sand of her rigid defenses that it doesn't allow for any new thought or experience to take place with the help of her objects.

Donald Meltzer's Theory

In trying to understand this material, a classic paper by Donald Meltzer came to mind which is called "Terror, Persecution and Dread." I find this paper helpful, because these words are particularly around in our minds at the moment, both consciously and unconsciously. In his paper Meltzer attempts to differentiate between these three states in the unconscious world of phantasy. *Terror* he says is paranoid anxiety whose essential quality, paralysis, leaves no avenue of action. The object of terror is *dead objects* that cannot be fled from. You can only bring life back to your objects through the reparative capacity of your internal objects and their creative coitus. Christina's manic superior attitude to her objects did not allow her to get into a position for her internal or her external objects to help her with this. *Persecution* is of the damaged objects; the collapsed towers, the decapitated penis/nipple, the defective analyst. *Dread* is to do with submission to the tyranny of a part of the personality; the basis of perversion that prevents infantile dependence on its objects; hence a know it all, controlling Christina who keeps the flowers separate, placing herself between her parents; she is the arrow that binds the parents but keeps them diminished sexually as in short pants; who clings to mother or wires the couple as it were (as represented by the braces). She joins the parents together in phantasy and in reality in order to protect herself from the terror of the dead babies. The power of this tyrannical part of the self makes her feel nothing can stop her. This is depicted by the larger red conical shape that dominates the smaller insubstantial green one. It is also represented by the braces, that are both on her mouth and outside her. These seem to represent un-integrated parts of herself, like a bad girl part that feels to blame for all disasters, or the tyrannical part that feels she dominates the parental couple and therefore stops all disasters from happening.

One might ask; what produces this tyrannical structure? Donald Meltzer believes that "the addictive constellation of submission to the tyrant is not produced by depressive anxieties alone, nor is produced in combination with persecution by the damaged object." Where a dread of loss of an addictive relation to a tyrant is found in psychic structure, the problem of terror as the force behind the dread and the submission will be found at its core. Hence the most important thing that Christina wanted to convey to me was the "mushed babies."

Conclusion

I would like to return once more to ideas of catastrophic change. Christina not only felt the new and catastrophic idea with all its catastrophic anxiety on a conscious level; that is, that such disasters can befall her own city, and could even attack her, her schoolmates, her mother, her father. These events also brought her back to a previous trauma in which her unconscious experience had been left unprocessed, unworked through; an unconscious phantasy that parts of herself could attack her parental couple and their babies and collapse them in a devastating way. This would then render her internal objects unable to come to her aid or to protect her from these terrifying unpredictable objects, in this new external devastation. This working through brought new ideas and we are just in the beginning of this struggle to work it through.

Postscript

A few months after September 11 there was a magazine article written by a female Israeli journalist who happens to be a mother as well. The title is "We've All Been Irrevocably Changed and Not for the Better," written by Eetta Prince-Gibson. She writes:

> We all pretend to be normal here. We try to manage normal daily routines. But nothing is normal when daily life has become life threatening. Normalcy is one of the first casualties of terror. We even have a buzzword for it all—*ha-matzav*—"the situation." "How's the situation?" we greet each other inanely. "Lousy," we answer, even more insipidly.
>
> I have always been proud that I am many things to myself and to others: a journalist, an activist, a wife and friend. But now above all I am a frightened mother trying to keep her children safe, and knowing, so fatally, that I really can't.
>
> I push that thought away because it is intolerable to confront the truth--that I am helpless to protect my family from that hateful someone who is right now lurking somewhere, planning, in intricate detail, the death of everyone and everything I love. It is intolerable to think about that man or woman who is, right now, mapping out the best spot to stop, to ambush, to explode, to maim, to murder.
>
> Palestinians say the terrorists are motivated by desperation. I am motivated by dread. (p. 22)

One can only respond to Eetta Prince-Gibson's outcry with serious understanding of the reality of the Israeli situation for those living in this state of terror. One can hear in her description, her choice of words, her choice of images of this state of terror that which I have been exploring in my eight year old patient's internal world. It is not soldiers going to war, on battlefields. It is the commonplace, everyday, unpredictable nature of it. In workplaces, familiar buildings, in pizzerias and bus stops. The words she uses and the images seem to me to link the images of infantile phantasy that already exists in all of us. And perhaps it isn't surprising then that it gathers up all the infantile emotions of terror, persecution, and dread. In a world that is dominated by "nameless dread" in which no maternal figure can protect you, the overwhelming dread is that you can not keep these parts of the world from your loved ones. It is a world which seems to have "changed"; where death instinct seems to rival life instinct and the terror and persecution that it engenders overwhelm one and make one feel that to survive, you have to cut off and call it *ha-matzav*, "the situation."

REFERENCES

Bion, W. R. (1970). *Attention and interpretation*. London: Tavistock. (Repr. London: Karnac Books, 1984).

Bion, W. R. (1961) *Experience in groups and other papers*. London: Tavistock.

Garland, C. (1991). External disaster and the internal world. In J. Holmes, ed. *Textbook of psychotherapy in psychiatric practice*. Chap. 22.

Meltzer, D. (1973). Terror, persecution and dread. In *Sexual states of mind*. Perthshire: Clunie P.

Prince-Gibson, Eetta (2002, May) We've all been irrevocably changed and not for the better. *The Progressive, 66*, 5, 22-23.

A Young Girl's Reaction to 9/11

LAURA KLEINERMAN

ANNA IS A LATENCY AGE GIRL FOR WHOM THE EVENTS of the past six months, in New York, Afghanistan, and in the Middle East have personal connections, in the present and in the past. Anna's internal experience illustrates the effects of trauma, fear and loss on the capacity to symbolize and on the development of thinking. Her efforts to grapple with and to defend against the recent world events this year shows the ways in which current trauma can overwhelm defenses, and reach directly and immediately to past difficulties. Disaster is most difficult for children who have previously experienced a major loss, have suffered earlier trauma, have other challenges such as difficulties at home or at school, or are already living with anxiety and depression. Anna's revelations in her treatment attest to the profound effects on a child's thinking and development that this combination of factors can engender.

Anna was referred to me at the beginning of 2001. She was nine years old; symptoms of anxiety were getting in her way at home and at school. Her parents told me that she could not finish her homework and she was going to bed later and later because she would anxiously keep going back to the beginning of her assignments and starting over, or she would endlessly correct imagined or real mistakes. When I met her, she had huge circles under her eyes. Except for her tiny size, she looked older than her age because of those circles and a serious, even sober countenance. Her smile was minimal, and I never heard her laugh.

With the help of a niece to translate, the parents told me that they had come to New York three years earlier, from an area near Afghanistan that had been affected by the Russian/Afghan war. They were able to leave through the sponsorship of the family of the niece. The wife's parents were able to go to relatives in Israel. The family is Jewish; once in America the practice of Judaism became a central aspect of school and family life.

When Anna was a baby, before she turned one, her mother had become very depressed. Anna was her first and only child; she was twenty when Anna was born. Her parents moved in with the family and took care of Anna. The mother was embarrassed and apologetic; she wanted to be sure that I understood that she had recovered from this depression after some months. Although their history was told in a style that was tense and constricted, I sensed that underneath some nervousness and discomfort, Anna's parents were caring and concerned, and anxious to find help for their daughter.

In New York, both parents found work and Anna and a baby sibling born in America were cared for by the aunt and nieces who had sponsored the family and who lived in the same building. Anna had not met this family before moving to NY, but the sense of family was very strong, and listening to Anna, I heard how she had earnestly invoked this sense to feel safe with these new people. She did miss her grandparents terribly; tears would come to her eyes when she spoke of them. I noted that she tried not to speak of them, therefore.

From the first session, Anna tried to curb and control emotion. She told me what her difficulties were and in the same sentence she told me that perhaps she wasn't doing the homework over so much anymore. During sessions, she would try to focus on something like drawing or making something. She would talk more easily once she was engaged in the activity. As we talked, there would often be a word I said that she wasn't absolutely sure of. She would immediately interrupt, and ask almost aggressively, "what does that mean?" She was constantly worried about words. By the time I met her, she spoke three languages fluently: her native language, English, Hebrew. She criticized herself in all three. In English, she felt that her vocabulary was deficient. She berated herself because classmates from Israel spoke Hebrew more fluently and wrote more easily. She was embarrassed because she could hardly read and write at all in Russian, but those were the words that came first and the language in which she most often had dreams. Anna was insistent on the subject of her deficiencies against the standard of perfection.

Before we parted for three weeks in August, Anna had begun to tentatively ask me, with an affectedly casual attitude, questions about fears, rituals and superstitions which seemed to plague her quite a lot. I worked to help her find a more realistic, less fearful and less harsh view of herself and of the world. It was only after September 11 that I could appreciate quite how adaptive, how necessary her symptoms were for her. In the harshness toward herself, I recognized her desperate attempt to create some containment and safety. She felt that if she could be perfect, if she could have control of something, then she could be safe. Although I felt I understood well the importance of recognizing and understanding what is or was adaptive and useful about symptoms for each patient, working with Anna through this re-traumatizing year has given me a much greater respect for and deeper understanding of this phenomenon.

Anna's uncle, of the family in the same building, worked in the World Trade Center. On September 11, it was difficult for the family to get back home from their various locations, and there was no word from the uncle. Needless to say, everyone was frantic and afraid, but late in the afternoon, he arrived home, having walked about as far as one can and still be in Manhattan. He was covered with the dust, exhausted, devastated. He had seen horrible things, he had tried to help, and he had lost friends and colleagues.

Anna had become gradually more connected and more lively over the months we had worked together, and more expressive. When I saw her two days after the disaster, she was pale, flat, and shaken. She seemed not to be able to allow herself to experience the uncertainty and vulnerability of affect and connection. She told me about the day of September 11 in terse, factual sentences. She fought back tears, literally using fists to her eyes. I was quiet; I thought it would be helpful to just give her a moment in time and some mental space in the context of not being alone and not being intruded upon, perhaps to better tolerate her feelings. She said her few sentences, and sat, upright on a little stool, head hanging down for several minutes. In desultory fashion, she reached for a pencil but did nothing with it. She stood up and started to move some things in the doll house, but then sat down. I waited and then asked her what happened. She said some of the doll house family was not there, where were they? Finally some tears escaped. I commented on how awful it felt to think about people who could just disappear. She was quiet for most of the rest of that session; she went back to her father's experience, and to her own fear that day. She punctuated her sentences by looking up at me; I thought that finding me to look at and being seen by me seemed to steady her, and when she left she managed a little smile and touched my arm and said, "thank you." Then she turned back anxiously at the door and asked, "am I here next week? will everything be the same?" I was too stunned to say anything, so I nodded, and she left. I was left wondering why I had not responded as I usually would, saying to her that of course it was hard for a child (or anyone) in her present situation to imagine, right now, that things could return to what they had been. Instead, I was left feeling shocked and empty. I thought soon after that perhaps in being too stunned to think, I was getting a taste of what Anna's experience was.

Over the next weeks and months, we seemed to be starting from some point before we had met. Anna seemed tired and sad, she had trouble doing anything, and she had trouble concentrating or talking. She made efforts to diminish her obvious feelings and she seemed to feel ashamed that what had happened was affecting her so much. "It was nothing, so much worse happened to people, it is wrong to feel bad about this." She worried that God would punish her for feeling so bad when nothing had happened to her. She also made valiant efforts to feel safe. Her parents worked downtown and she talked about an expression her teacher said, that "lightning never strikes in the same place twice." But then she would worry, over and over, about whether that meant the World Trade Center site would be spared, or that anywhere downtown was now safe. She wanted me to reassure her. I could not do so, and she began to be upset and angry. As soon as she heard herself, she tried to protect me from her frustration saying, "It's ok, because you can't really know, only God knows, and so if you said you were sure it wouldn't be true, and then God would punish you and He would punish me for making you answer. I'm sorry."

The greater freedom of expression that Anna had just begun to develop disappeared and she was preoccupied with superstitions and patterns that she hoped would make her family safe and make her safe. It was painful to see the intensity of this effort and its failure to comfort her, and her resulting depression. Eventually, however, as she told me these thoughts, and as she saw that I accepted them, her anxiety abated somewhat. (Anna sometimes worried that I would laugh at her and she was relieved when I did not.) Although the sober demeanor and worries continued, Anna began to make progress again, slowly, making drawings and plasticene figures and gradually elaborating stories about them, putting her worries in more symbolic form. She started to be more animated and engaged as she talked about school, or her interest in her cousins' boyfriends and adventures. She was less preoccupied with rituals and superstitions. During this period we were able to talk about how it was for her to come to this country, how she missed her grandparents. In tapping into her own past, she began to entertain the idea that feelings have causes that are legitimate in one's own personal context.

Just as Anna was beginning to feel a bit safer internally, the bombings started in Israel, some very near to where her grandparents were living. There was fear and anxious discussion at home. At first she felt anguish for the entire situation. "Why does God let this happen? The children there, are they bad? I don't think so, not even the Arab children are bad, I wish it would stop." She wondered why she had learned conflict resolution in school if grown-ups did not use it. But as the fighting continued, and her anxiety grew for her grandparents and a country that was special to her, she took another point of view. She lectured me, saying intently and seriously, "Israel has to do this, the places they attack only have terrorists, even the children are terrorists. They aren't like other children, they are never afraid and they are brainwashed and dangerous; if Israel doesn't do this it will be really bad."

Anna most recently is worried about danger everywhere. Her drawings again became more simplified and repetitive. Her conversation is often a string of anxious questions and the superstition laden solutions that are her attempt to contain her anxiety. But as we talk about the things that are on her mind, and how we had been understanding the world events that connect to and touch her own internal world, she finds some relief. I was struck by how surprising it was when Anna spontaneously laughed recently. She was talking about fears she had on the subway. When we had looked at the fears from every possible angle more than once, and she was letting herself feel a bit safer, I made a little joke in the next round about going over the same thing yet again. She exaggerated the joke and burst out laughing. It was like the proverbial sun after the storm. She was delighted to see herself and her reactions from a safe distance with me, even if just for a moment.

Our defenses create some safety in the face of everything from real danger to anxiety based in conflict. When extreme defenses are called upon, and safety is still tenuous at best, there are consequences for affects, relationships and for functioning in the world. For a child, there are consequences for development, as well. Anna's treatment has mitigated some of these effects and helps her develop more mature, flexible defenses that help her cope with the pain of her situation and proceed in her development.

PART III

Clinical Challenges

Navigating the altered psychoanalytic space

Introduction

RUTH STEIN

TODAY'S AFTERNOON PANEL IS CLINICALLY ORIENTED, which tallies very fortunately with the workshops this morning, where we have been going into clinical and experiential detail with different facets of our theme. We are going to hear three distinguished speakers who will share with us their experience and their struggles with treating patients who have undergone torture and persecution, or patients amidst situations of terrorist threats (Benyakar), patients who reach the end of their symbolizing capacity after having undergone *actual* injuries of a psychically mortal nature (Garland), and patients whose relationship with their analyst is impacted by the disturbance of the meta-setting, the extra-analytic frame for the therapeutic work (Varvin). We will listen to the individual ways of conceptualizing our authors bring to these difficult materials.

As I sat reading and listening to the creative materials that have been assembled for this conference, I had a sensori-motor feeling of things coming close and getting far away, like a sensory regressive signal, almost a hallucination that indicates: look, we are dealing with life and death issues, the same skulls that sit here and think could be shattered by an explosion, by a shell. How absurd and fragile is life, how precious. And how great our capacity to remove ourselves from the knowledge that destruction can be imminent and how horrible beyond words it is when it happens, beyond the words we are using at this conference. I was thinking about literary critic Kirby Farrell (1998), who wrote: "To recognize representations of trauma in stories is easier than to see how those fictions may express the world that created them" (p. x). He writes exquisitely about a notion that has come to occupy a greater space in our thinking today, which I think should be thought of in psychoanalysis as well. The notion is that *trauma is none other than the unveiling of what lies ahead of and beneath us*, namely, the unspeakable dread of the real, the normal current of insanity that runs through everyday life, and that in times of terror, trauma, persecution and disaster, is exposed. Indeed, trauma is the unveiling of death, finitude and pain that reality holds out for us. At such moments, we have the "opportunity" to feel the power of dissociation. Conversely, as Marcelo Vinar told us last night, we recognize the social ties that hold us, only at the moment of their explosion. That which we take for granted is not granted. We usually shun the realization of how helpless we are, and how invented the human world is.

September 11, the terrorism in different countries, psychically mortal trauma—all these are times when we blunder outside the magic circle of everyday life. In trauma, terror overwhelms not just the self, but the ground of the self, which is to say, our trust in the world. On the other hand, acts of terrorism, suicide or military killings, which are the paradigms addressed by our three panelists today, are themselves the *product* of loss of trust in the very ground of being. And the more aware of and prey we become to these acts, the more we become aware of how absolutely vital culture and its practices are to the keeping of trauma at bay.

Mordechai (Moty) Benyakar participated in wars in Israel, and assisted those injured in terrorist attacks and other disasters in Argentina. These experiences made him a researcher and thinker of "The Traumatic," as he calls it.

Dr. Benyakar deals with the difference between (life confirming, or open) *aggression* and (deadly, unpredictable, sometimes invisible) *violence*. Against an open declaration of war in aggression, and the possibility of fighting back, he positions violence where the harm is hidden or denied, and the *victim cannot locate the threat and cannot develop defenses, but instead is exposed to unprocessed helplessness*. Violence, we learn from him, causes a deformation of reality, and the destruction of judgment and distinction between the dangerous and the harmless (the basis of our feelings of canniness and familiarity).

Benyakar insists that a kind of *analytic setting should be kept*, created and recreated, even under conditions of duress, terror and war, so as to safeguard and enable the working of the analytic space. And he describes two patients, Meir and Dalia, who could be helped analytically after their setting, with its laws and rules, could be maintained.

Caroline Garland is head of the Unit for the Study of Trauma and its Aftermath, and editor of a book, *Understanding Trauma, A Psychoanalytic Approach*. In her paper, "Vengeance and Sacrifice in the Therapeutic Setting," Dr. Garland aims at clarifying man's capacity for *destructiveness*, which is also influenced by social factors, as well as the individual's part in it. Her striving is to deepen our understanding of "destructive forces in the individual that seem so opposed to listening, thinking, and considering other points of view, turning instead to killing and to war" in a mindless immersion in the schizoid-paranoid position.

Following Michael Feldman, Dr. Garland makes the important distinction between *grievance*, which is more within our ordinary (specifically Kleinian) clinical discourse, and *paranoia*—which is a further structure in grievance and which is the issue with the patient she's going to discuss here. *Grievance* is addressed to the object who has gone back on his promise, but who should make up to the entitled person. In paranoia, on the other hand, the split between the bad object who has not fulfilled his promise, and the idealized desired object is deeper. A central point in this paper is that when there is an actual injury (including the gratifications derived from it!), there is an *inability to process that injury through symbolic means alone*. She will illustrate this through a patient for whom there was an apparent reality to his original blissful state, but who at the same time suffered external objective injury that, as she says, "has compounded whatever internal sources of grievance there may already have been." The predicament of this patient is that *as his desire grew, grievance grew with it, until the annihilation of the desired object appears to be the only solution* to the level of pain, frustration, and sense of betrayal. Perhaps this is what is meant by "running out of hope"—the hope of a blissful reunion with mother.

His devotion to his primary object was overwhelmed by his newly discovered hatred for her. The revenge: locating the beloved betraying mother in the analyst and then in his mind depriving her of her most precious possession, her son, as he felt she had deprived him of his most precious possession, the passionate and exclusive relationship with the mother.

Although analytic theory may be able to understand the dynamics of oedipal hatred and resentment, analytic practice may be still unable to undo or modify the passionate intensity of a situation when an *actual betrayal* compounds what is a universal and painful sense of loss that accompanies the recognition of the parents' sexual union. *The thirst for revenge may not be quelled by verbal acknowledgement* alone of the wrong that has been done: "Blood will have blood."

I would like to raise a few comments about Dr. Garland's paper. Let us note, first, that the patient's mother *died* when he was fourteen. She died of *breast* cancer— translated into unconscious phantasy, the very breast that had given him life had died, had been infested, or persecuted, and we can think what all these meanings implied for the patient. I would have also liked to know what were the patient's relations with this lover? Did he abandon her? Did she love him, or hate him? There is a lot by way of death and abandonment. If we agree that the patient's mother's betrayal is also by dying, then we may see his dying as his undoing of his mother's abandonment by identifying with her (as well as merging with her) through dying. In this sense, Dr. Garland uses a model of the suicide bomber as merging with mother. I, for my part, have a model of regression to the father and merging with him in my thinking on this phenomenon (Stein, 2002).

Sverre Varvin, from the Norwegian Psychoanalytic Society, works also at the Psychosocial Center for Refugees, University of Oslo. His paper, "Mental Space and Survival in Times of Terror," is a fascinating study of clinical work in depth with victims of political persecution. Dr. Varvin works on an international scale, and has anticipated in a sense September 11 and its aftermath, which has brought terrorism to the consciousness of larger parts of the Western world.

Varvin's study also contains several examples of another theme of his, which we could call *regressive social dynamics*. He will show us in varied ways how terror and trauma destroy our ability to think. As he says: "terror creates disturbance in the social context and affects the mind and its functioning and it affects how we relate to others and to ourselves." Varvin then investigates as well how such a disturbed social context influences the analytic space and mental functioning both of the patient *and of the analyst*, in the sense also of how what he calls "totalitarian contexts" influence the meaning resounding from the analyst's words as they are transmitted to the patient.

The clinical material concerning a refugee to Norway, who has been tortured in his country by state sponsored terror, is chilling. Hassan's core experience of "being killed" reminded me of the writings of Bollas (1995) and Sue Grand (2000) on evil, perpetrators and serial killers. Here we touch the utmost in human horror and persecution. I feel Dr. Varvin tells us only a tiny bit of what he has seen and gone through with his patient.

REFERENCES

Bollas, C. (1995). The structure of evil. In *Cracking up: The work of unconscious experience*. New York: Hill & Wang.

Farrell, K. (1998). *Post-traumatic culture: injury and interpretation in the nineties*. Baltimore: Johns Hopkins University Press.

Grand, S. (2000). *The reproduction of evil: a clinical and cultural perspective*. Hillsdale, NJ: Analytic Press.

Stein, R. (2002). Evil as love and as liberation: The mind of a religious terrorist. In Moss, D. (Ed.). *Hating in the first person plural: Psychoanalytic perspectives on racism, sexism, homophobia*. New York: Other Press

—(2003). Vertical mystical homoeros: An altered form of desire in fundamentalism. *Studies in Gender & Sexuality, 4*, 38-58.

Vengeance and Sacrifice in the Therapeutic Setting

CAROLINE GARLAND

Introduction

HOMO LUPUS HOMINI—MAN IS A WOLF UNTO MAN. This is how Freud (1929), after the horrors of World War One, described man's capacity for destructiveness, directed both at his fellow man and inward, at himself. We are at the moment very concerned with the *social* factors that we use to account for, to make sense of, that destructiveness: the various political, cultural, religious, and economic philosophies that come into conflict on a global scale, either through diplomacy or through war. Yet there is also the contribution made by the individual. Individuals of both sexes exert their own psychic energies, both consciously and unconsciously, towards whatever goal seems vital for the survival of the self and, by extension, of whatever group that self is attached to—both constructively and destructively. The contributions of individual and group are of course reciprocal. To understand an individual fully one must also know something of his group and of his relations with it. Equally, to understand the group one must know something of the psychic state of those individuals composing it. Neither on its own is sufficient; both are necessary.

As psychoanalysis has developed there has been an increasing recognition of the role of aggression *per se*, not merely aggression in the service of defence. Some of the derivatives in the individual of that "wolfishness" described by Freud may be seen not only in forms of overt aggression, but also in aggression directed inward, and in the compulsion to repeat tragic events arising in part from an accompanying masochistic gratification. This is familiar to us as the negative therapeutic reaction (achievement followed by an attack on that same achievement) or as—very significantly—forms of envy which result in the turning away from, or hatred of, what is most needed and desired *because* it can only be obtained in a relation to another. At this moment in particular, it is hard to account for the existence of certain repetitive and hard-to-shift manifestations of aggression and negativity, as we see it in our patients, without considering some kind of universal human destructive drive.

I am going to talk about one particular manifestation of this destructiveness. Psychoanalysis provides a unique method for studying at close quarters destructiveness, negativity and aggression as expressed in the individual. Potentially at least, if we are careful and thoughtful, we may be able to make some kind of contribution to the understanding of these destructive forces, and perhaps to the knowledge of the early circumstances which foster their development, or which fail to mitigate their expression in the world of adult object relations.

My question is then: what can we learn from the consulting room that might help us understand those impulses and drives that seem so opposed to listening, thinking and considering other points of view, turning instead to killing and to war? How can we help ourselves, our groups and our countries move away from what seems like a paranoid-schizoid mode of functioning and into something that contains a depressive grasp of the realities—that is to say, towards a recognition of the differences between what we value and what others value, and a respect for the need for room, for space, in which those differences can co-exist?

Aggression and Negativity

I address this question through a perspective on the phenomenon of grievance. Clearly it is complex. Internal sources of grievance can be fed and strengthened by external sources, external injuries, leading to a situation in which the structure of grievance becomes entrenched, coming to dominate psychic and hence social functioning. For instance, in certain analyses at certain times we come across an apparent willingness in the patient to forego or sacrifice the analysis, and so his or her own development—in other words the possibility of hope for a better future—in the service of attacking the analyst against whom he is entrenched in a state of grievance. As Feldman (1996) shows, what characterizes a grievance is its persistence and hopelessness—how difficult it is for either analyst or patient to imagine anything that might genuinely lay it to rest. Feldman describes a situation in which an Oedipal configuration underlies the persistence of an unresolvable grievance:

> The object against which the grievance is consciously directed is held responsible for the patient's being deprived of something he was implicitly or explicitly promised, and to which he feels entitled . . . the unconscious structure of this state involves an ideal union with a gratifying and supportive maternal object. The object of the grievance is seen as coming between the patient and this ideal object, in order to possess the object itself, or for more perverse or cruel motives.

Feldman then goes on to contrast grievance with paranoia. In paranoia, the split is more complete. The object of grievance is perceived as more completely bad and hostile, and the object of desire as more completely ideal and desirable, and the patient applies himself in a more single-mindedly delusional fashion to the removal of the obstacles to that blissful union. In the patient I shall present, a man who was psychologically quite ill, I present a further stage in the structure of grievance. In this variation, there was an apparent reality to the original blissful state in which there was exclusive possession of the maternal object. Here there is an important point about the nature of the injury: how the *actuality* of the mother's collusion, and the gratification that derived from it, leads to an apparent inability to process that injury through symbolic means alone—as is eventually possible in certain analyses.

In my patient, what occasioned this destructive impasse was a betrayal felt to be deeply humiliating and painful, of a son by a parent to the advantage of the other parent. The inherent destructiveness I am addressing does not of course exist in isolation, but is expressed within the anchoring framework of the object world. For example, aggression, just as much as love, is part and parcel of the Oedipal template, the triangular structure which determines our basic relations with each other. And of course the management and resolution of this conflict between love and hate is the basis of what we think of as emotional maturity. Yet daily in the consulting room we are forcibly reminded of the sheer risk and intensity of that conflict. In Sophocles' play, the Oedipal triumph carried within it the seeds of its own destruction, the stirring up of passions that led to murder, mutilation, suicide and exile. Perhaps its opposite, an Oedipal betrayal, is equally capable of producing an anguish so intense that at times nothing short of a murder—which can also take the form of suicide— can avenge and redress that sense of betrayal. (And of course added to the pain of the betrayal itself is the sudden exposure of a son to all the guilt and depressive pain that he has been able to avoid while enclosed and secluded with the parent, most usually mother, in their universe of two.)

Clinical Material

The context of the situation I describe is our National Health Service rather than private analytic practice. This patient, Mr. C, during the two weeks' interval between his referral to me for an assessment and the actual appointment, had already been admitted in a state of quite deadly depression to the psychiatric ward of one of the large London teaching hospitals. He was a tall, narrowly built young man of mixed race, with a fluent capacity for expression once he began to talk, though he needed some encouragement before he could do this. During the meeting with me he met my eyes only once. He told me that he had run out of hope. Hope, he said, was a kind of natural resource that existed inside you, the way coal or gas or oil existed in the earth. If the weather was warm and conditions were good, you would not use it up so quickly and it might last you throughout your life. If living was hard and the weather bitter, then it got used up that much more quickly. Now he had none left. There was nothing to do but kill himself. He had grown up in the north of England as the youngest child of a white working-class family, who had apparently adopted him at birth. One by one he had lost his brother, his mother and his father to major illnesses. Only his older sister remained and he had lost touch with her. He had had a very close relationship with his mother. He had memories of lying with his head on her lap, while she stroked his hair and told him how much she loved him, asking him whether he loved her in the same way. He said he remembered as a little boy wishing that the sofa they were on would float out to sea like an island and he and she could be alone together on this island, wanting for nothing since they had each other. His parents seemed to have had a very poor relationship, involving silence and hostility, which made the relationship between the mother and son all the more poignant and meaningful. However, this ended when he was 14, when his mother died of breast cancer. The boy then spent the next dozen years at home caring for his father, who was progressively disabled by a series of strokes. They too had had a vir- tually silent relationship. My patient felt grateful to him for his adoption and regard- ed his caring for his dying father as paying his dues—but he was aware that they did not love each other.

I am now going to jump forward to Mr. C at the age of thirty, when he applied for a job for which he needed certain official documents of identity. He was unable to locate a certificate of adoption, and to cut a long story short, eventually he dis- covered that his adoptive mother had in fact been his birth mother. It is difficult to convey the extent of the deep shock, dismay and emotional turbulence that this pro- duced in him. It let him know that she had kept a deeply important secret from him, and withheld something from him he felt it was his right to have known. Most important, it obliged him to realize—as I took up with him in the consultation—that she had had a lover within the marriage, probably an Afro-Caribbean judging from his own appearance. He did not like my putting this fact about her sexuality into words. He remained silent. After a while he repeated that he wanted to kill himself.

In the transference I recognized I was being required to adopt him myself. I thought that he treated my overt encouragement as an external energy source, designed to ship in fresh supplies of hope. It felt to me impossible to say that we had nothing to offer him, which would have been tantamount to agreeing with his suicide plans. I said that although he was certainly able to go away and kill himself, perhaps there were other possibilities worth exploring. One of them might be to come into treatment with me at the Tavistock, into an analytic group with other people of his age (it was the only vacancy that could have been found for him at that point) and to find out if hope was a renewable commodity. There was a long silence before he finally said he would give it a try. I felt an immense sense of relief as he accepted my offer. In retrospect, I think projected into me was that particular version of the mother with whom he had actually had a very intimate relationship, and by whom he now felt so betrayed. I do not have time to go into the details of the treatment, which was absorbing and gripping in its own right. Certainly he began to recover, once (and only after three months attendance) he decided to speak to his fellow group members, who had handled his presence with great sensitivity. He was revealed to be intelligent, perceptive and witty, and—this should have been a warning sign—I began to feel pleased with his progress and with his return to life. He, I think, knew he was doing well, and knew too that I was pleased. This added to the volatility of the situation, in which the transference took on in his mind a psychotic sense of reality. Now the group was his family, and he was the special child, the one who could bring a sparkle to my eye as he revealed his intelligent and subtle understanding of the difficulties of his fellow group members.

Yet his visible progress brought with it something much bleaker. I think that in this patient's history, he felt it was made plain to him in a variety of ways that he was the favorite, not merely the favorite amongst the children, but in some particular way more special to the mother even than her own partner, the powerful third object who normally stands between the mother and the fulfillment of the most intense of the desires of the Oedipal child. This particular mother was felt to have bypassed the father in conveying the message, "If it weren't for father, you and I would be completely happy together." The child's response was to become good and compliant in relation to the object with whom he shared that secret, and covertly hostile and contemptuous in relation to the parent's real partner. However, that private alliance was then betrayed by none other than its original instigator, the mother. Once my patient had discovered his own real origins, the mother was in phantasy no longer available for the perpetuation of their private alliance. The man for whom he felt contempt and could dismiss was replaced by a powerfully sexual being he could not even know. Morever, and largely because that secret mother-son alliance had existed in the first place, neither was there any effective third party available in the patient's mind to whom he could turn for help or support. The object of desire and the object of grievance were united, and the two had become one.

At this point in this kind of situation a dangerous momentum exists. As the desire grows, the intensity of the grievance grows with it, until the annihilation of the desired object appears to be the only solution to the level of pain, frustration and the sense of betrayal, aggravated by the guilt. Perhaps this was what Mr. C had meant by *"running out of hope"*—he had lost the hope that he could recover the conviction of the blissful union with the mother, in which they were one another's most precious objects. (We might consider the part played by "running out of hope" in contributing to desperate and violent actions in general.)

As my patient recovered from the worst of his severe depression, the rage in him became more apparent and started to feel quite unmanageable. He expressed himself as afraid he would become one of those murderers who shoot up shopping malls, finally turning the gun on themselves. He broke the mirrors and then the windows on the ward and used the pieces of glass to slice his own arm to the bone. He would attend the group stitched and bandaged and listen gravely to the reproaches, which were forceful and coherent, of his fellow group members. I think, although I was not so aware of it at the time, he was watching and gauging carefully the effect this escalating process had on me. At the point that it became clear to me that the current therapeutic regime was inadequate to contain him, and I had more or less had to force the hospital ward to hold a joint meeting with us to discuss the situation, he hung himself, on the ward.

This was a quite devastating experience for both therapist and group members. For some months I was unsure that the group itself could survive it. If one believes that the chosen manner of the suicide contains within it some indication about the psychic meaning of the act, then his choosing to hang himself, a traditional punishment for criminals, perhaps expressed his unbearable guilt over his terrible attacks on his objects and his feeling that they were now irreparable. He left a note, a single word, scrawled on a piece of paper towelling: *Sorry.*

How is this act to be understood? I suggest that the discovery that his exclusive possession of his mother was illusory, that she had had secretly in her mind all along a sexual relationship with a lover, blew open an abscess of murderous hatred in him and a wish for revenge. This revenge was achieved by locating the loved but betraying mother in me, his therapist and then, in his mind, depriving me of my most precious possession, the son, as he felt she had deprived him of his most precious possession, the passionate and exclusive relationship with the mother. Steiner (1996) writes,

> The sense of wrong experienced is made more painful if it follows a period of seduction by the primary object who may have colluded in fostering the belief that Oedipal intimacy is desired by the mother as well as the child. The result is that when this fantasy collapses the child feels that a promise has been broken so that he is not only wronged but betrayed. It is often at this point that the demand for justice turns to the thirst for vengeance.

Steiner suggests that when the resentment and hatred that is stirred up by the enforced recognition of the realities of the parents' relationship can be acknowledged and expressed, albeit in a limited way, then the way is open eventually for understanding and forgiveness. This may well be true within the context of psychoanalysis, where symbolic actions, and symbolic reparations—which are always necessary—are sometimes also adequate for the purposes of redressing psychic betrayals and narcissistic wounds.

However, although analytic theory may be able to understand the dynamics of such an act, analytic practice may still be unable to undo or modify the passionate intensity of a situation when actual, or enacted, betrayals compound that universal and painful loss that accompanies the recognition of the parents' sexual union. At that point the "thirst for vengeance" may not be able to be quelled by the verbal acknowledgement alone of the wrong that has been done, and the symbolic expression alone of the hatred and anger evoked by the act. *"Blood will have blood,"* as Macbeth put it, recognizing that once the king/father has been murdered, there is no way to avoid the bloodbath ahead, the unrestrained expression of an equally murderous violence. Effective intervention in this deathly tit for tat is a long, painful and highly taxing process.

Discussion

Psychoanalysis is perhaps the most intimate connection many individuals have experienced since their own infancy, when survival itself depended upon the benevolent vigilance of the mother, or primary caretaker. In psychoanalytic treatment, the apparent outward quiet of the consulting room disguises the intensity and danger of the primitive forces and passions attaching to that primary relationship, both the most intense love and the most intense hate, which emerge to shake both patient and analyst. My point in this paper has been to look at the origins of a particular source of the intensity and single-mindedness of that state of mind in which death, annihilation of the self, that which Freud described as man's most fundamental anxiety, can be preferred to life in the pursuit of vengeance. The following quotation comes from Isaiah Berlin (1978) and describes vividly the point at which the personal and the political may be seen to come together.

> The oldest and most obsessive of these visions is, perhaps, that of the perfect society on earth, wholly just, wholly happy, entirely rational: a final solution of all human problems within men's grasp, but for one—some one major obstacle—such as . . . class war, or the destructive aspects of materialism, or of Western technology; or, again, the evil consequences of institutions—state or church; or some other false doctrine or wicked practice—one great barrier but for which the ideal is recognised.
>
> It follows that since all that is needed is the removal of this one great obstacle in the path of mankind, no sacrifice can be too great, if only by this means can the goal be attained. No conviction has caused more violence, oppression, suffering. The cry that the real present must be sacrificed to an attainable ideal future—this demand has been used to justify massive cruelties.

We cannot know the complex spectrum of experiences, beliefs and convictions that go to make a suicide bomber, but perhaps we can recognize in that quotation something of the state of mind in which it seems possible to choose death over life in the pursuit of the "perfect society" that was once perhaps experienced by the infant at the breast. I do not think it too fanciful to see "globalization" as having parallels with an unthinking and insensitive intrusion into and over-colonization of the young child's world by an imperious father. Not a helpful Oedipal father who can moderate the intensity of the child's impulses towards his mother, but a wholesale takeover of child's own living-quarters, living space. When there is no room in the father's mind for a recognition of the child's own world view, the child's own beliefs and phantasies and tastes, let alone for time and space with his mother, a murderous hatred can develop for that bombastic way of behaving. Then a vicious cycle is set in motion. The more idealized the longed-for relationship with the mother, the more feared, hated and denigrated becomes the world of the sexual father. In my patient, we saw that in order to attack and punish his once-ideal object, which had become submerged in the hated sexual couple, he was prepared to sacrifice his own life. And as I have suggested, it is often the case that when an injury is *actual*, when an external injury or external betrayal has taken place, the imperative urge is to even the score in an equally actual way.

It is impossible, and certainly inappropriate, to reduce what have been almost daily events in the Middle East, or the major catastrophe in New York of September 11, to an Oedipal drama. There are many crucially important degrees of difference and many stages of differentiation between the psychic world of the ill individual, and the external world; between those social and cultural groupings at odds with each other, and the international political scene. The size of the group involved of course also plays a significant part in how and why thinking and talk become so difficult, since as the group increases in size, the processes involved become more primitive and feel more desperate. Nevertheless, I think it is worth considering how easily these terrible events may be viewed in the light of phantasied events in the internal world. The erosion of or the snatching away of the ideal world once inhabited with the mother can generate a terrible intensity of hatred and destructiveness in the son. We might think about the implications of this for an understanding of the acts lived out in the wish to liberate *the mother country* from what appear to some to be the domineering material seductions, the crass ideology and the lack of spiritual values of the West, even if that means sacrificing oneself in the struggle.

At the very least we can allow ourselves to consider the nature of the internal structures that may incline individuals to align themselves with a cause felt to be "just," in which the splits are very total, the group mentality and group processes reinforce and justify those splits, and the outcome is death in the service of a righteous cause, a righteous search for vengeance. Psychoanalysis is ultimately about freedom of thought. It is of course difficult to think freely about terrifying events while still under threat, but it is imperative we try.

REFERENCES

Berlin, I. (1978). Quoted in Feldman.
Feldman, M. (1996). Grievance. Unpublished manuscript.
Freud, S. (1929). *Civilisation and its discontents.* Standard Edition, 21, 64-145.
    anal., *77*, 433-443.
Steiner, J. (1966). Revenge and resentment in the Oedipus situation. *Int. J. Psychoanal.*, *77*, 433-443.

The Setting and the Psychoanalytic field in Social Disasters, War and Terrorism

MORDECHAI (MOTY) BENYAKAR

IN THE CONFUSION OF WARTIME IN WHICH WE ARE caught up . . . We cannot but feel that no event has ever destroyed so much that is precious in the common possessions of humanity." These contemporary words were those used by Freud to open Chapter One of "Thoughts for the Times on War and Death," referring to the First World War (Freud, S. 1915c). My personal experience as an analyst who has participated actively in five wars in Israel and has assisted those injured by terrorist attacks or other disasters and the recent economic upheaval in Argentina, has prompted me to research and develop different perspectives of "the traumatic."

In this presentation I want to share with you the concept of the "disruptive situation" and its relationship to traumatic experiences. In order to clarify this relationship, I will also describe some differences between aggression and violence, traumatic "experience" and traumatic "experiencing" and the impact of these threats on the transference and counter-transference. Through the application of case material, I will also consider the specificity of the setting and the analytic frame in the deployment of the psychoanalytic field in situations of social disasters, war and terrorism.

The Disruptive Situation

The disruption produced in the psyche by social disasters, war and terrorism emphasizes the interplay between the inner world and external reality, focusing on the way the nonspecific "outside" bursts into the subjective and specific "inside." (Kernberg, O. 1980). A central feature of these *"disruptive situations"* is that the social institutions that normally support human life become flooded or destabilized to great extent and therefore lose their normal protective and holding functions. In my paper "Aggression of life and Violence of death," I propose the distinction between aggression and violence as different kinds of disruptive situations. (Benyakar, M. 2000b).

Violence and Aggression

In situations of *aggression*, the person who causes the harm (the aggressor) presents himself as a threat to the person who will be the injured. Facing clear and direct threats, persons can defend themselves both physically and psychically. Classical examples of situations of aggression are conventional wars, struggles between factions, etc. We could say that aggression tends to evoke signal anxiety through the perception of the threat, generating reactions known today as "stress" (Freud, S. 1926; Winnicott, D. 1979, 1989; Benyakar, M. 1997a, b). Different is the essence of situations of *violence* that lies in the distortion of the external "factual" environment, threatening the stability between internal world and external reality.

Violence tends to obstruct the capacity to discriminate between the dangerous and the harmless in the environment, distorting the familiarity of everyday life. Violence stimulates the development of traumatic experiences (Freud, S. 1919, 1930; Miller, A. 1980; Benyakar, M. 1998c, 2000a).

Examples of violence are rape, a government that claims on one hand to protect its people and on the other annihilates or makes its population disappear, the hug of a father who punishes his son unmercifully while telling him that he is doing it for his own good. All these are examples of the distortion whose extreme expression is terrorism. The goal of terrorism is to distort the everyday environment, to be used as pressure on the population, so that riding a bus or receiving a letter becomes threatening (Reinares, F. 1998).

Traumatic "Experience" and Traumatic "Experiencing"

Unfortunately Freud used the concept of the "traumatic situation," possibly influenced by the popular tendency to characterize situations as pathological (Freud, S. 1917, 1926).

As psychoanalysts we cannot qualify situations a *priori*; for this reason when referring to the traumatic, instead of "traumatic situation," I prefer to use the concept, also proposed by Freud and postulated by Dilthey, of "Erlebnis" (*experience*) or "Erleben" (*experiencing*). As analysts we cannot determine if a situation was traumatic; what we need to detect is whether the subjective experience of the individual confronted with this situation has been traumatic.

I consider "experience" as the articulation between affect and representation. This approach based on Freud of the first and second topic allows us to define the "traumatic experience" as the disarticulation between affect and representation (Benyakar, M. 1996a, 1999a), that is, the failure of the psychic apparatus to articulate or represent affect, what is felt, in the experience of the traumatic. Violent or aggressive acts are situational qualities of these events, whereas stress or "traumatic experience" is their psychic consequence—the subjective experience and psychic reverberation that make these events "traumatic."

Transference and counter-transference

In social disasters, war and terrorism, patient and analyst are threatened in an inclusive, non-differentiating way, which requires specific working through of *transference* and *countertransference*.

The analyst is helped to face this situation through his own analysis, supervisions, or his peer group. The Argentine Psychoanalytic Association (APA) developed special frames of containment in the institution to work through the impact of the economic and social disaster that Argentina faces at this time.

In disruptive situations, the capacity to work through factual events, articulating them with the material that emerges in the *transference* and *counter-transference* material, is not an easy task.

Guilt, compassion, and the demand for concrete answers and immediate help, all confront the analyst with special feelings of impotence that have to be worked through, on the deepest level, to prevent them from being acted out. If the working-through is successful, we can face the implosion or disruption of the external world in the psyche through the material that emerges in the therapeutic relationship, and try to avoid getting caught up by the emotional impact of the factual events, while not denying the threat.

Clinical Vignettes

Meir's Case: An Israeli reserve officer was called to duty during the Lebanese war. He proposed to stop the sessions until his return. I suggested we continue our sessions during his times off duty, with the firm conviction of the importance of preserving this space.

During these sessions the patient spoke about how important it was for him to preserve this frame where he felt he could be himself, stopping doing, and being able to reflect on what he was doing from his subjectivity. In one of the sessions he said: "Here, I stopped doing for my people and my country, here I am simply for myself."

It was impressive to see someone who had been in trenches and shelters able to perceive the psychoanalytic setting as the place where he felt mostly safe because he could count on himself. I have confronted this type of situation over and over in today's Argentina, a country immersed in violence that is a product of an economic distortion, in which some citizens lose their sources of income, for whom it doesn't make sense to continue their analytic work until they can solve their economic situation.

The conviction of the function of the analytic frame, articulated with the reading of factual reality, in a containing and holding attitude, allows us to postulate the analytic frame as a combined paradigm of protection and working through to face disruptive situations.

Dalia's case: During the Gulf war, when all Israeli citizens had to carry their personal gas masks, she came to the session without the box, stating that for her these rules did not make any sense, and that it was all the same for her not to carry her personal mask (Benyakar, M. 2000b).

I had the impression, based on the analytic material, that this was a new expression of her omnipotent and indiscriminate defiance—as if she were flirting with death. It was, possibly, her way of presenting her disavowal (*Verleugnung*) or rejection (*Verwerfung*), or maybe an expression of a negative hallucination (Freud, S. 1915a,b, 1940; Green, A. 1993).

I asked her to go back home (located a few blocks from my office) and to come back with her mask, so that we could start the session. With an expression of distaste, and without any other comment, she went out in search of her box. When she came back, she showed her anger and complained about what I had asked her to do.

Fifteen minutes after her return, the emergency alarm sounded, and at that precise moment we had to put on our masks and share the sealed room, adapted especially for this kind of situation, and thus we stayed there until the missiles stopped falling. This episode was worked through during the treatment as a situation in which she felt truly protected. This protection did not have any behavioral tranquilizing characteristics, but by means of them, Dalia was able to start working through her experiences of helplessness in which childhood experiences emerged. She manifested in the session how she saw herself, acting in an omnipotent manner, rejecting and devaluing the figure of her parents. She characterized them as weak and impotent, lacking the capacity to develop adequate mediating functions, and increasing her feelings of rejection and loneliness that invaded her.

Based on these cases, we can discuss the specificity of the setting, the frame, the process, and the analytic field in these disruptive situations.

The Setting and the Frame

To consider the differences between the *setting* and the *frame*, I will focus on the interplay between laws, rules and norms, three concepts in our therapeutic work that are not always specified.

Laws, as a kind of paradigm, will be those postulates which are not man-made. Each one of the sciences has its own universal laws. Physics has gravity as a basic law, and psychoanalysis postulates the unconscious as a law.

Rules are man-made regulations presumed to be opposed to laws. There would be no need to establish the rule "thou shalt not kill" if there were not a law that drove man to kill.

Norms emerge from the interaction between laws and rules. Norms are open to working through and to being interpreted in the analytic process.

By the interplay of these concepts in our field we can say that in the psychoanalytic setting we formulate *rules* to facilitate the emergence of the unconscious *laws* to be worked through, enabling us to analyze the specificity of the *norms* deployed in every therapeutic relationship.

The setting can be described as the rules in the mind of the analyst before the interaction between patient and analyst. It is the product of the analyst's conception of the way that unconscious laws emerge and could be worked through. The experiences of his or her analysis, supervisions, treatments with other patients, ethical values, his cultural and social environment, and traits of personality, are additional factors that influence the way the analyst stipulates the rules of his setting.

The frame is the setting in action, as it develops from the very first contact between patient and analyst. As this interaction develops, several kinds of phenomena start to appear, part of them conscious and situational, and, part unconscious and irrational, that tend to transform the "setting."

As an analyst, and even more as a supervisor, I have perceived the importance of analyzing the specificity of this process of the transformation of the *frame*. This work can be done only if the establishment of the *setting* that the analyst has stipulated, before the beginning of his therapeutic work, has been kept clear.

When we confront situations of crisis, social attack, wars and especially terrorism, there is a tendency to alter those pre-established rules in the setting and to develop different frames. Faced with these phenomena we must have the necessary elements to evaluate whether these changes are a product of prevailing reality, or simply the product of anxiety and inadequate perception by the analyst, in either case, to maintain or to change the established rules (Benyakar, M. 1982, 1994a,c, 1998a).

In social disasters, war and terrorism, in which the stability of the environment is very fragile, the rules of the setting function as a protection against environmental violence that pretend to distort daily life. These rules enable the frame to preserve the psychic stability of both patient and analyst.

The setting's *rules* are the basic net where psychoanalytic activity can develop, emphasizing the importance of a high frequency of sessions. In my understanding this is not professional capriciousness, but an important factor in the progress of daily clinical activity.

The consistency and solidity of the setting is what will enable the deployment of psychic plasticity, in contrast to those who propose to adapt the extension or frequency of the setting based on what emerges from the patient's psyche. Together with this position and product of the same conception, I recommend being sensitive to the impositions of external reality when it becomes disruptive.

In the two clinical examples we see how the setting has functioned as a transitional space: In Meir's case preserving his subjectivity, in contrast to what is stereotypical in the combat situation; in Dalia's case, preserving the patient's safety, but also, by continuing to work through unconscious content, preventing external events from provoking destructive attitudes.

The Psychoanalytic Field

The "psychoanalytic field" enables us to clarify the special conscious and unconscious net that is knitted between patient and analyst (Baranger, W. 1993).

In social disasters, war and terrorism, the deployment of the capacities of containment and holding become more difficult to handle, because we face the same factual threats as our patients (Benyakar, M. 2001c).

These situations confront the therapeutic frame with the aim to work through "traumatic experiences" and "traumatic experiencing" (Benyakar, M. 1998b). It is beyond the scope of this work to discuss this subject with the specificity required (Benyakar, M. 1989, 1996b, 1999a, 2000a, 2001b).

In clinical practice, we approach the traumatic from the subjective, experiential point of view, meaning that the psyche has remained helpless when facing a disruptive situation. In these situations there is a dangerous tendency to focus on causality of the events. In my understanding, our main function is to face the obstruction of the psychic capacity of processing.

Dalia's example enables us to see the way to be connected with the imposition of the external events that are not the product of the analytic relationship, but belong to it. Facing the implosion from the outside enabled Dalia's elaboration of the unconscious component of the subjective and the idiosyncratic aspects of her experience.

Having been able to sustain the frame in a threatening external situation and offering the conditions of holding (as in the case of the gas masks), enabled Dalia to begin to elaborate the way in which the traumatic developmental experiencing was manifested in her psychic processing. The irruption of this threatening situation was a turning point in the analytic process.

After a few sessions Dalia said: "I have no words to express myself, I know that nobody will ever be able to understand, I'm tired of destroying everything and everybody, of being alone in my world." I thought she was describing a feeling of hardness and lifelessness, so I said that I perceived she felt like a mountain of stone in the desert; she opened her eyes as if she were looking at what she was describing, and answered, "No, not a mountain of stone but an iceberg."

I told her that I understood she was indicating a very important difference, because a mountain of stone is destroyed by force whereas an iceberg melts with warmth.

This way of putting feeling into the relationship through figurative interpretation is the way I consider that the containment and holding of the setting enables us to approach the "traumatic." The use of what I have called "the experiential interpretation" is the articulation of three interpretative dimensions: figurative interpretation, the relational, and the dimension of meaning (Benyakar, M. 2001a).

The Analyst and His Environment in Situations of Social Disasters, War and Terrorism

The goal of terrorism is to produce psychic harm by means of horror and fear. This is why psychoanalysts have a central function in those situations (Benyakar, M. 1999b).

In Israel, for instance, in situations of war generally psychoanalysts are called upon to carry out their functions in mental health. In the Yom Kippur War we had to assist soldiers on the battlefield, and I called this task the passage "*From the Couch to the Rocks*" (Benyakar, M. 1994b).

The therapeutic environment in disruptive situations is not only a frame for dealing with pathology, but also a frame designed to prevent multiplication of pathogenic effects caused by these situations. The analyst has to be able to detect the threatening factors in the environment, and thus facilitates the development of working through of what is internal, while sustaining subjectivity and continuity of being (Lezica, A. 2002).

We can say that the basic functions of the setting in those situations is to protect the person and to enable the processing of his experience. These frames can be developed in different places, depending on the circumstances that are being confronted. The simple act of establishing a specific time and space, anywhere in the desert, where the soldiers could work through their subjective feelings, was a major approach we learned by working in the battlefield. Looking forward to that meeting provided a special bit of hope in these life-threatening situations. In these circumstances, bearing clearly in mind the principal factors in the therapeutic setting has enabled us to highlight the importance of finding a tree, a stone, "a place" that we could use as shelter, to allow us to talk with the soldiers and elaborate what they were experiencing at that time. This tree or rock became the place of reference, different from the rest of the trees or rocks in the desert around us.

I consider it extremely important for psychoanalysts to participate actively in the mental health networks developed in wars, terrorism and social disasters, like those we have created in Israel's wars, and in Argentina in the terrorist attack that destroyed the Jewish community center (AMIA). In this case all the psychoanalytic societies joined forces to fill an important role in assisting the injured (Benyakar, M. 1994c, 1998a,d, 2001a).

The process of working through in those conditions, with the same analytic depth as in our consulting rooms, is not an easy task. We must create frames of containment to deal with these situations, while bearing in mind the essence of our function, which is to preserve mental health and the capacity for psychic processing, both in analyst and in patient.

Our own analysis, supervisions, peer group, the agencies of the institutions we belong to, are examples of paradigms of containment for analysts who are dealing with these situations.

REFERENCES
_____

Agamben, G. (2001). *Childhood and history. Essay on destruction of experience.* Adriana Hidalgo Editora. Argentina

Aulagnier, P. (1977). *The violence of interpretation.* Amorrortu Arg.

Aulagnier, P. (1994*). An interpreter in search of meaning.* Ed. Siglo XXI Méjico. A

Baranger, W., Baranger M. (1993). *Problems of the psychoanalytical field.* Ed. Kargieman. Bs. As. Argentina

Benyakar M., Dasberg, H., Plotkin H. (l982). The influence of various therapeutic milieus on the course of group treatment in two groups of soldiers with combat reaction, stress and anxiety, Vol. 8, Milgram, N. A. Spielgerberg, C. D. Sarason, I. G. NY: McGraw-Hill International Book Company.

Benyakar M., Kutz I., Dasberg H. Stern M. J. (1989). The collapse of a structure: A structural approach to trauma. *Journal of Traumatic Stress 2,* 4.

Benyakar, M., Kretsch, R., Baruch, E. (1994a). Mental health in work with Gulf war evacuees: The use of a transitional therapeutic space. *Israel Journal of Psychiatry, 31,* 2, 78-85.

Benyakar, M. (1994b). Trauma and post-traumatic neurosis: From the experience to a theoretical reflection. *Actualidad Psicológica,* 211: 26-32.

Benyakar, M. (1994c). The program of assistance to persons affected by war, disasters and disaster situations. 1eras. *Jornadas de Salud Mental en Situaciones de Desastre,* Departamento de Salud Mental del Hospital de Clínicas José de San Martín, Facultad de Medicina, U.B.A.

Benyakar, M. (1996a). The traumatic experience: Vicissitudes in clinical psycho-analysis. Conferencia presentada para la categoría de miembro titular de la Asociación Psicoanalítica Argentina.

Benyakar, M. (1996b). Trauma: The mythic construction of the psychoanalytic field. Asociación Psicoanalítica Argentina. IV Simposio Internacional sobre Mitos y sus ámbitos de expresión interpretación psicoanalítica e interdisciplinaria. Buenos Aires, Argentina.

Benyakar, M. (1997a). Trauma and stress, clinical perspectives. Cap. XVI del libro: Conceptos fundamentales de Psicopatología; II Ed. Hector Fischer y colab. C.E.A. Bs. As.

Benyakar, M. (1997b). Definition, diagnosis and stress, clinic and the trauma. Psiquiatría COM [revista electrónica] 1997 Diciembre;1(4): Disponible en: URL: http: //www.psiquiatria.com/psiquiatria/vol1num4/art_5.htm

Benyakar, M. (1998a). Mental health of those evacuated from the Gulf war: The therapeutic spaces of a typical war. Monografías de Psiquiatría. Enero-Febrero de 1998. Año X. Num 1. Pag 14-17. Madrid.

Benyakar, M. (1998b). *Traumatic neurosis or experiencing and traumatic experi-ence.* Reflexiones Teórico-Clínicas. Publicación Psicoanalítca. La Peste de Tebas. Mayo 1998. Bs. As. Argentina

Benyakar, M. (1998c). *Aggression and violence in the millennium: The evil chain.* Revista de Psicoanálisis. Ed. Asociación Psicoanalítica Argentina. Tomo LV, No. 4 Octubre-Diciembre, pp. 875-892.

Benyakar, M., Schejtman C. (1998d). Mental health of children in wars, social attack and natural disasters. Postdata Revista de Psicoanálisis, Ed. Homo Sapiens. Fundación Estudios Clínicos en Psicoanálisis. Año 2 Num. 3, pp.9-20. Bs. As. Argentina of the World Psychiatric Association. Hamburg August 6-11.

Benyakar, M. (1999a). The experience, articulation between affect and representa-tion: A challenge for the theory of technique. Revista de Psicoanálisis. Ed. Asociación Psicoanalítica Argentina. Tomo LVI, No. 3, 591-603. Julio-Septiembre 1999.

Benyakar, M. (1999b). Disasters and disaster: A challenge for the assistance of civil-ians in peace time. XI World Congress of Psychiatry

Benyakar, M. (2000a). The traumatic and the sinister. Theoretical clinical questions about threats. *Journal Dept. Psicosomática de la Asociación Psicoanalítica Argentina.* A.P.A.1.1 pp. 71-77 Mayo del 2000.

Benyakar, M. (2000b). Aggression of life and violence of death. The infant and its environment. Available on URL: http://www.winnicott.net/patron_esp.htm.

Benyakar, M. (2001a). Combat reaction. Facing traumatic and stress experiences. Available on URL: http://www.psychoway.com

Benyakar, M. Lezica, A. (2001b). The traumatic experience in clinical psycho-analysis. *Psychoanalysis in the Clinic and Contemporary Practice.* XXIII Simposio de la Asociación Psicoanalítica de Buenos Aires, (ApdeBA), Tomo I pag. 37. Noviembre 2001.

Benyakar, M. (2001c). About uncertainties in today's world. FEPAL 13 de Noviembre 2001. Montevideo, Uruguay.

Bion, W. (1965). *Transformations.* NY: Basic Books.

Bleger J. (1967). Psychoanalysis of the psychoanalytic setting. *Int. J. Psycho-anal.,* 48: 511-519.

Botella, C., Botella, S. (1992a). Névrose traumatique et cohérence psychique. *Revue Française de Psychosomatique, 2:* 25-36.

Botella, C., Botella, S. (1992b). The metapsychological position of perception and the irrepresentable. *Revista de Psicoanálisis.* Tomo XLIX, N. 3/4 Ed. Asociación Psicoanalítica Argentina.

Botella, C., Botella, S. (1997). *Beyond the Representation.* Ed. Promolibro. Valencia.

Chasseguet-Smirgel, J. (1992). Some thoughts on the psychoanalytic situation. *J. Amer. Psychoanal. Assn., 40:* 3 25.

Crocq, L. (1992). Panorama des séquelles des traumatismes psychiques. Névroses traumatiques, états de stress post-traumatique et autres séquelles. *Psychologie Medicale, 24,* 5: 427-432.

Crocq, L. (1993). Le trauma et ses mythes. *Psychologie Medicale, 25,* 10: 992-999.

Crocq, L. (1996). Critique du concept d'état de stress post-traumatique. *Perspectives Psy. 35,* 5, Décembre 1996.

Etchegoyen, R. H. (1986). *Fundamental Psychoanalytic Technique*, Amorrortu Editores.

Fain, M. (1992). La vie opératoire et les potentialités de névrose traumatique. *Revue Française de Psychosomatiqe, 2*: 5-24.

Ferenczi, S. (1933). On the confusion of tongues between adults and the child. In *Final contributions to the problems and methods of psychoanalysis*, 155-67. NY: Basic Books, 1988.

Freud, S. (1900). *The Interpretation of dreams*. Standard Edition, 4.

Freud, S. (1915a). Instincts and their vicissitudes. Standard Edition, 14.

Freud, S. (1915b) The unconscious. Standard Edition, 14.

Freud, S. (1915c). Thoughts for the times on war and death. Standard Edition, 14.

Freud, S. (1916-17 [1915-1917]). *Introductory lectures on psychoanalysis*. Standard Edition, 15.

Freud, S. (1917 [1916-1917]) *Introductory lectures on psychoanalysis*. Standard Edition, 16.

Freud, S. (1919). The uncanny. Standard Edition, 17.

Freud, S. (1920). *Beyond the pleasure principle*. Standard Edition, 18.

Freud, S. (1926 [1925]). Inhibitions, symptoms and anxiety. Standard Edition, 20.

Freud, S. (1930 [1929]). *Civilization and its discontents*. Standard Edition, 21.

Freud, S. (1937). Constructions in analysis. Standard Edition, 23.

Freud, S. (1940 [1938]). An outline of psychoanalysis. Standard Edition, 23.

Green A. (1975). The analyst, symbolization and absence in the analytic setting. *Int. J. Psychoanal., 56*: 1-22.

Green, A. (1983). *Narcissism of life, narcissism of death*. Amorrortu Editores.

Green, A. (1993). *The work on negative*. Amorrortu Ed., Bs As, Arg.

Kaës, R. (1979). *Crisis, Rupture and Superation: Transitional Analysis in individual and group psychoanalysis*. Ed. Cinco. Bs. As. Argentina.

Kernberg O. (1980). *Internal World and External Reality*. New York: Jason Aronson.

Kijak, M., Pelento, M. L. (1985). Mourning in certain situations of social disaster. *Revista de Psicoanálisis*. XLII, 4: 798-809.

Krakov, H. (2001). Personal communication.

Krystal, H., Krystal, J. H. (1988). *Integration & Self-Healing: Affect, Trauma, Alexithymia.*, New Jersey: The Analytic Press.

Lebigot, F. (1999). The advantages of immediate and post-immediate care following psychic traumas. In *Emergency Psychiatry in a Changing World*. M. De Clercq, Ed.

Lebigot, F. (2000). La clinique de la névrose traumatique dans son rapport à l'événement. (Clinical study of traumatic neurosis in relation to the traumatic event). *Revue Francophone Du Stress Et Du Trauma. 1,* 1: 27-31.

Lezica, A. (2002). Personal communication.

Lifton, R. J. (1979). *The Broken Connection*. NY: Simon & Schuster.

Miller, A. (1980). *For your own good. Roots of child education*. Tusquets Ed.

Ogden, T. (1985). On potential space. *Int. J. Psychoanal., 66*: 129-141.

Puget, J., Wender, L. (1982). Analyst and patient in superimposed worlds. Psicoanálisis. IV, 3:503-536.

Reinares, F. (1998). *Terrorism and antiterrorism*. Ed. Paidós. Barcelona

Winnicott, D. (1972a). Transitional objects and transitional phenomena. In *Reality and Playing*. Ed. Gedisa.

Winnicott, D. (1972b). *Holding and interpretation. Fragment of an analysis.* NY: Grove Press.

Winnicott, D. (1974). Fear of breakdown. *Internat. Rev. Psycho-anal.*, 1: 103-07.

Winnicott, D. (1979 [1947]). Hate in the counter-transference. In *Escritos de Pediatría y Psicoanálisis*. Ed. Laia

Winnicott, D. (1989 [1968]). Roots of aggression. In *Psycho-analytic Explorations.* Cambridge: Harvard University Press.

Mental Space and Survival in Times of Terror

SVERRE VARVIN

Introduction

September 11 brought a new dimension to terrorism. Even though terrorist acts have been commonplace in different areas of the world in the last century and even though the nineties brought an increase in terrorist acts, September 11 with its disastrous effects and immense sufferings, has brought terrorism to consciousness for large parts of the world's population. Mark Juergensmeyer underscores the performative quality of terrorist acts, and describes them as *"dramatic events* intended to impress for their symbolic significance" (Juergensmeyer 2000 p.123). While the aim is to spread fear and terror and to signify some "just" cause, the political strategic value and the political implications of the acts are often not clearly considered. They function like mere acts of violence justified by utopian ideas of a homogenous society or community based on religious, quasi-religious or idealistic political ideas and coupled with hatred of "the others," ideas of purification and a cult of death (Bohleber 2002). A common feature is the dehumanization of the victim, be it children, women or soldiers. The result is widespread fear and often regressive social dynamics including impediment of rational thinking.

In the recent congress of the European Psychoanalytic Federation in Prague, Israeli psychoanalysts called for a meeting to discuss the recent development in the Middle East. The aim, to create a space for thinking and reflecting in times of terror, was met by an almost desperate silence among the many European analysts joining the meeting. An Israeli psychoanalyst from Jerusalem said the obvious: we cannot give the answers, we are in the midst of terror, we are not able to think or reflect.

At the same conference, an Israeli analyst presented a case with a second-generation woman who now feared for her son going into the army and the possibility of being stationed in dangerous places. A detailed analysis of this situation showed that themes from the Shoah were reactivated. The most disturbing fact, however, was that the analyst was in exactly the same situation as the woman. His son was also entering the army at the time and the analyst harbored the same fears as the patient. An honest description of the countertransference problems that arose was most touching and taught us about the struggle to be reflective and to contain difficult emotions under times of stress and war.

A woman in Belgrade said spontaneously, when hearing about the bombing of the Twin Towers, "they deserved it." She believed the planes were empty. Within seconds after hearing that the planes were full, her state of mind changed to compassion and despair for all the lives lost.

During a meeting with psychotherapists discussing the treatment of severely traumatized patients in Diyarbakir in eastern Turkey, the security police suddenly broke into the meeting and started to videotape all the participants. This came as a shock and immediately caused anger and fear. Soon after, several of the participants started to relate stories, some based on personal experience, which involved torture related to anal matters. This lasted for some time until the meeting came to a close in a fearful defensive atmosphere.

I bring these stories to demonstrate how situations of terror disruptively affect the mind, its ability for empathy, for reflection, mentalization and for enduring ambivalence. In all these cases, some stability was re-established. The meeting on the middle-east situation ended with reflection and thoughtfulness. The woman from Belgrade, who had herself endured the recent bombing, regained her empathic capacity after having regressed into a "terrorist state of mind" for some seconds and the analyst, painstakingly, maintained his empathic, listening and reflective capacity during a long process where both patient and analyst suffered. The Turkish/Kurdish colleagues regained some balance by resorting to a defensive attitude of apparent compliance. The fear of terror and persecution was of course not resolved during the seminar.

Terror thus creates a disturbance in the social context, affects the mind and its functioning, and affects how we relate to others and to ourselves.

In this paper I intend to examine some aspects of how such a disturbed social context may influence the analytic space and mental functioning both of the patient and the analyst. My reflections are mostly based on therapeutic work with extremely traumatized patients, but I also have material from supervisions and dialogues with colleagues working under actual conditions of violence and state organized violence in Turkey, Palestine and former Yugoslavia. I will focus on posttraumatic conditions as an extreme example of how external reality, both past and present, may influence the mind, acknowledging that there are both parallels and difference between such conditions and an acute situation of terror or potential terror. As will be evident, posttraumatic conditions after massive social traumas or extreme social violence, include mental states where former terror and fright may make it appear as if the present is as insecure as was the past, and resembles in that way acute states of terror.

The Therapeutic Setting

We are accustomed to consider the setting or the analytic frame as a function of the quality of the relationship between the patient and the analyst, the way they work, the preservation of the analytic rules, preservation of borders and of the privacy of the therapeutic space. This is, as we know, an ideal construction, which is violated every day by the influence of external circumstances. These may represent breaks into the analytic or therapeutic process evident for example in training analyses where the analysand and the analyst share a common world (Bernardi & Nieto 1992). As long as these may be analyzed, the process may again be put on track and they may be seen as accidental circumstances. There may, however, be social contexts where external reality imposes itself on the analytic or therapeutic space in such a way that they appear as "real factors," the meanings of which are for longer or shorter periods of time not possible to analyse. Analysts who have lived under totalitarian regimes or under military dictatorships have reported how the real external reality of persecution may severely influence the analyst's countertransference and also how the external situation may be used in the service of the negative transference (Sebek, personal communication).

Moreover, totalitarian contexts are circumstances where the analyst's words may tend to be listened to with a double perspective, both as addressing the transference and mental space, and as conveying a message about or from external reality. One may say that certain aspects of external reality become very insistent in the analytic process.

There are different levels of representations such as representations at the level of the dyad and the family/group respectively, which make up the habitual frames of reference for psychoanalytic work. De Bianchedi and co-workers refer to the trans-subjective space that contains representations of external reality that refer to the infantile level of relatedness or rather at-one-ness where the subject feels she/he has a basic contract with others and with society at large (de Bianchedi et al. 1991). At this level, the basic need for affirmation of experience is assured, that is, the right to have and express affects and a need for approval of the right to exist (see Killingmo 1995). This concerns a level of basic security that under normal circumstances is taken for granted and which is maintained and supported by a stable social setting. It becomes narcissistically invested and contains a claim for unconditional acceptance. From the point of view of the analytic setting or frame, this refers among others to the basic contract (no time-limit, unconditional listening etc.) that may support an illusion that the analytic process will never end, a safe haven that will be there forever. When this basic narcissistically invested "contract" is questioned, for example in crisis when demands are made upon the person for radical change or when something unexpected and unwanted happens, this may cause a narcissistic injury which may be a starting point either for growth or for stagnation, fixation and regression. Breaks in connection with weekends and holidays may represent minor blows to this illusion and the working through of such events represents possibilities for grief-work, growth and autonomy.

War, totalitarianism, dictatorships, state-organized violence and terror attacks, represent social contexts where this level of "basic contract" is violated. The violent encroachment on the personality represents thus a break in the infantile belief in invulnerability. Many fears are invoked; the fear of one's own death, the fear of the analyst's death or disappearance, the fear of being hurt, damaged, fear for the family etc. From the point of view of the therapy, this may potentially mean the end of it and thus permeates the dialogue with urgency and insecurity.

This social or extra-analytic context supporting this basic contract has been named the metasetting. It is, usually, a silent supporting social context in ordinary analytic work. In times of terror and upheaval, this metasetting may become a major concern (Liberman 1970 cited in Bernardi and Nieto, 1992).

Terror and the Terrorized State of Mind

Juergensmeyer described the symbolic and spectacular aspects of terror acts. This refers mostly to the terrorist acts committed by organized groups such as Al Quaeda even though state organized terrorism certainly has its important symbolic or communicative aspects, the aim of which usually is to put the population or a specific group in fright and terror. The often-used significance of sending the tortured victim back to his local community, serves this purpose.

Terror can also be described as *a state of mind where there is an expectation and readiness for an encounter with an ultimate threat to one's own life*. The mortal danger may appear any time with the accompanying feeling that no measures may be taken to avoid it. The person in a state of terror will try strategies to circumscribe and identify and ultimately avoid the danger, nevertheless knowing it may not be possible. This state of mind may be compared with Bion's concept, "nameless fright" (Bion 1967). The fright has, however, a name and a location somewhere outside the individual; it may be terrorists, Al Quaeda, an airplane with bombs, the torturer or the silent killer waiting at any corner. However, *because it is impossible to locate exactly in time and space it remains indefinable and represents as such a space for projection of internal horrifying fantasies*. In this situation it may be difficult to distinguish internal from external and thus the borders of mental space become blurred.

This state of terror places the person under threat in a readiness to encounter death at any moment. The body will be in a state of high tension, the mind will be focused on the surroundings for signs of danger and one will be alert and ready to take action at any time. Because of the blurring of boundaries, reality testing becomes confused and internal frights and external dangers may be difficult or impossible to distinguish. Schreuder described how the *transitional space* becomes limited in such conditions making it difficult to symbolize and construct different perspectives on reality. He distinguishes two aspects of the transitional space relating to a private and a shared conception of outer reality. The private is what is unique for the person while the latter is more or less shared by others. The latter refers to what we may communicate and agree upon (for example when gathering at a meeting, a football match) while the first refers to what is more or less our private perspective on the outer world (Schreuder 1998). The distinction between these spaces is of course not clear and well defined and may vary according to circumstances.

Under circumstances of terror, suspicion may be life saving and the private perspective may come to dominate at the cost of constructing a shared perspective on outer reality. When incarcerated in a political prison the outer reality may become very limited indeed, often to the point that the limits of the cell coincide with the limits of the outer reality and the transitional space thus become very limited.[1]

During the recent time of stress, the importance of sharing and of opening up the shared and communicative perspective on external reality was well recognized by Salman Akhtar with his "Guidelines for processing the inevitably psychic trauma," produced after the September 11 attack. In a simple but nevertheless profound way, he suggested nine guidelines whose prime function was to preserve the mind's capacities for dealing with such a terrifying event (Akhtar 2001).

The above is a description of terror in its pure forms as can be seen in certain posttraumatic states and also psychosis. In posttraumatic states, there is a time collapse and a sense that what has happened may happen again any time. In some psy-

---

[1] Anecdotal evidence suggests that the capacity to use and expand a transitional space under such circumstances may be lifesaving.

chotic conditions, there is a breakdown in relation to the other with an accompanying breakdown of the ability to represent self and other in any meaningful way and the agent producing the catastrophe is projected and identified outside.

When large populations, nations or ethnic groups are under threat, the basic experience is, I will argue, basically the same. Modifying forces will, however, always be present that may ameliorate the basic fears. The community may offer help, support and comfort, health workers may provide services, and family support may be available and so forth. However, *terror does not only strike the individual, but the group and the community at large. The large-group processes that may be set in motion may be regressive and preclude the ability to take care of oneself and others*. There are therefore three levels or dimensions that must be taken into consideration;

1. *Subject/body-other relation:* The individual's relation to the other on a dyadic level; this is the level of emotional bodily mediated regulation of affective states.

2. *The individual's relation to the group:* this is the level of identity formation, where one finds one identity as both a member of a family, group, community, or nation but also as different and unique.

3. *Subject discourse dimension:* The individual's relation to culture at large, that is, to religion, cultural narratives such as folktales, philosophical texts, moral codes, norms and so forth; this is the level where meaning is established and is the reservoir for finding ways of understanding existential themes, life-crisis, developmental challenges, rites-de-passage etc. (Elaboration of this model is given in Rosenbaum & Varvin 2002a; Rosenbaum & Varvin 1999; Rosenbaum & Varvin 2002b; Rosenbaum & Varvin 2000; Varvin 2001; Varvin 2002).

In each dimension, the subject is pulled between a negative and a positive pole. The subject may be attracted to or repelled by the other or the representations of otherness in each dimension. A child may, for example, be attracted to mother in the dyad seeking proximity and nurturing but be repelled by the fact that the mother also is a part of a family group in a triangular structure (dimension 2), defined by the culture's moral codes and norms (dimension 3). The dynamic interrelations between these three dimensions are thus of significance. Although these dimensions may also be described as developmental stages, they are here viewed as structural levels/dimensions in the subject's relation to others.

In the first dimension, *subject/body-other*, the dialectic concerns the immediate bodily relation on an emotional level to an other. The person may feel attraction (warm feelings) or rejection/detachment (dysphoric emotion) and in normal conditions, these emotions can be reflected upon. In disordered states, the subject may be unable to concretize or symbolize the sensations. Within this dimension, important nonverbal emotional regulatory processes occur between self and others and there is a self-soothing reliance on internalized object relations.

The second dimension concerns the person's *relation to the group*. The salient questions are related to belonging in a group (including the family) and sensing what others want one to be or do, that is, basic identity issues as a person belonging to a family, group, nation etc. One learns from the group and its members and acquires the ability to empathize and take the other's perspective. This does not only mean to understand, persuade or be taken away by the singular other's view, but also, and more important, to be able to view the matter from many possible standard views and establish a consensual validation.[2]

In the distorted or disordered subject-group dimension, the self and the group cannot cognitively act as foreground and background for each other. Empathy is reduced to egocentricity, intimacy perverted to intrusion or exploitation and care is turned to neglect. The community feeling may be abandoned and transformed into psycho-physiological dis-ease. One is no longer a part of a group and may experience a loss of the aspect of personal identity related to the group or the family. Developmentally this relates to the establishment of a sense of *we* in development (Emde 1994). In societies where the family and the group (clan, tribe) is the organizing unit of society, and where belonging to such a group is of fundamental importance both for personal and social identity, disturbances in this dimension may have grave disorganizing effects.

Ideally, the group's intention as a whole is taken into consideration side by side with the subject's own intentions. This inter-intentional dynamic demands a continuing reconstruction of unexpected viewpoints that have their origin in the discourse dimension (e.g. moral and political narratives). In this dimension, the person is allowed then both to be a part of a community and to be a particular individual.

The third, the *subject discourse* dimension, signifies the subject's relationship to discourses represented in myths, philosophies, ideologies, ethics, morals, folklore, poetry, literature, jurisdiction and other social discourses. Discourse is in principle written, temporalized and memorized signs of living in a culture. These signs are not particularly stable over long periods, but stable enough to produce converging and diverging myths, narratives, ideologies and paradigms of beliefs and argumentations.

Cultural discourses may contradict and influence each other. The subject's modes of relating to the differences and divergences, and the expression of social passions based on "higher principles," is part and parcel of the subject-discourse dimension. Included in this dimension are also the subject's fantasies of being grounded in time: linear time, experiential/deictic time (seeing the present in relationship to past and future), and existential time (inchoative, durative, associative, dreaming).

This dimension consequently transforms the group-mind, giving rise to the possibility for the subject to step outside of the group, and still be a part of a cultural movement. It represents in this way a regulatory principle and a dimension that structures meaning in the other dimensions.

This model thus attempts to give a comprehensive picture of the subject's relation to self and the world on a bodily-emotional level, on a group level and on a societal-cultural level. It depicts a system of interrelated dimensions and functions related to each, where each dimension is dependent on the others. It is easy to see how "maladies" in the cultural discourse dimension may, for example, cause disturbances

---

[2] ". . . the process of consensual validation . . . calls in an illusion, an illusory person, in the sense of a critic, more or less like what we think the hearer is. We observe what goes on in him when we make this string of words or say this sentence, and it isn't satisfactory; and so we feel that it is an inadequate statement . . . So we look again at our experience, and we consider him from the standpoint of illusory critics, and so on: How can the thing be made to communicate" (Sullivan 1944 p. 5).

on the person's ability to regulate emotions in a dyadic dimension. The mere fact of persecution of a group, terror or ethnic cleansing, changes the way the group's identity is formed and maintained (i.e., we are now a denigrated group) and has grave effects on personal and intimate relations, e.g. childrearing, caring for the ill etc. This has been observed in several studies (e.g. Lavik et al. 1996).

Terror as well as trauma and posttraumatic states imply disturbances in each dimension, as well as in the relation between them. The uncanny experience produced by extreme trauma affects the individual as well as the group and the culture. Torture is something that happens as a result of perversion in all dimensions, and the consequences for the individual are often enduring disturbances in his/her relations to the other/group/discourse (culture). State organized violence, including torture, is on the other hand also a sign of disturbance in society on the cultural/political level with severe repercussion on individual-group relations, as well as, in specific contexts, the subject-other dimension. Terrorism, especially in the form seen in connection with September 11, may have as effect the destabilization of society in all dimensions including the individual's mental processes and for the practising analyst or therapist, this may have profound repercussions on the therapeutic relationship as well as the internal processes of both analyst and patient.

I will in the following try to illustrate this model using an analysis of a psychotherapy with a severely traumatized refugee from a persecuted minority group in a country with state organized violence (for an extensive analysis, see Varvin 2002). His problems centered on a personally experienced danger of being killed, but related to the effects on a group and cultural level of the organized attacks on his family and his group.

It is important to study what happens in and with the transference when the threat is experienced as coming from without and how is it possible to work in therapy or psychoanalysis under such circumstances. Further, how is it possible to preserve the analytic frame and how is the analyst's ability to contain and mentalize the patient's and his/her own fear affected? What forms of countertransference modes and reactions may be observed?

Clinical Material

When Hassan came to Norway, he had experienced a long journey from his homeland. As an UN-quota refugee, he had been selected for acceptance to Norway from a desert refugee camp in a neighboring country of his own. He had been there almost four years and he aligned this experience with the inhuman experience in the prison in his home country. Before his flight, he had experienced a long time period of persecution, terror (among others, he had been nearly shot dead when walking on the street), imprisonment with the harshest torture including mock executions and killings of close ones. He was exhausted and suffered serious psychic distress as well as physical disabilities and sequels after being maltreated for prolonged periods.

One of Hassan's core problems could be described as *"an experience of being killed,"* the feelings of being unprotected and living in a state of persistent terror and insecurity. This feeling, of possibly not being alive in the next moment, continued to mar him. The way his mind structured these feeling was to live in three partly separated (or dissociated) experiential modes, three "worlds," as he said:

1. *The world of his past.* This was the experiential world before the time of traumas from torture. This world concerned his relation to his father, mother and the rest of the family. It was an idealistic picture with an almost delusional character, especially regarding his relationship to his father.

2. *The imaginary world.* This was the world of persecution, the experiential prison in which he could be killed at any moment and had to take all sorts of precautions.

3. The world "in between," a shadow-like experience of living a normal daily life. This state of mind was not very stable.

This situation improved markedly during therapy, but this is not the topic here. I will illustrate by some excerpts what appeared during therapy, and how his mind was affected in relation to the abovementioned dimensions; that is, what problems he had to deal with as a result of terror and persecution.

Belonging to a population minority, the persecution of him and his family began early in his childhood. He became politically active and the first blow came when his fiancé was arrested, raped and then committed suicide as a consequence of this.

This represented a clash between his relation to culture and his relation to others on a dyadic level. He was unable to protect his fiancée and thereby lost an emotional relation. This had a heavily disorganizing effect.

He was tortured beyond imagination, both physically and mentally. He was shot through his right foot in order to make it impossible for him to practice his sport again (with no medical help afterwards). He was shot through his chest in an attempt at assassination.

Neither his group belonging (dimension 2) nor his culturally designated position (dimension 3) could offer him protection. He was treated as a non-human. This may have reinforced an idealization of the past.

Very early in the therapeutic process, he described a feeling of being alienated. It appeared that he had extreme difficulties in trusting people and lived much of his life alone, having only a few friends. He felt as if he was living in different worlds.

In exile, his relation to his group was dominated by withdrawal. He felt he had failed his assigned task and felt shame. In a large part of the therapy he worked in "splendid isolation," contemplating how to solve the problems in his country. Later he started with practical, goal-directed human rights work and became leader of a human rights organisation, thus reversing his alienation in relation to the group.

One of his "worlds" was, as mentioned, the abundant re-experiencing and dreaming (nightmares) of the traumatization.

This implied a withdrawal to the negative pole of his relation in all dimensions (body-other, group and culture). This withdrawal diminished clearly during therapy, as shown by a decrease in nightmares and re-experiencing.

In between was the "real world" of his daily existence.

He gradually increased this territory. He established lasting intimate relations where he could have emotional support and achieved also a belonging to a new group in exile, a Norwegian family. This implied a step in a gradual reorganization of his relation to discourse and culture in that he established more realistic goals regarding what he was able to achieve as the designated leader of his clan and also gradually achieved a more secure position as an exiled belonging to two cultures.

The third "world" was that of his childhood. As mentioned, this was an idealized version, but nevertheless a retreat to a position of an idealized self with idealized parents.

This represented an imaginary solution bringing the three dimensions "in order." Needless to say, this was a brittle construction. It represented a safe haven, needed when his second, the prison world, threatened to take over.

In long periods his second "world" dominated. In this world, there were persecutors everywhere. When he walked in the street, there were people following him everywhere. When he turned around, the fact that they did not watch him became proof that they had done so, and that they now pretended that they did not notice him. He could therefore not go out except when absolutely necessary and often had to take detours (which made his arrival at sessions quite irregular).

This may be seen as an extreme example of being repelled by the group and isolated. Both his relation to the culture and the emotional relation to others were affected negatively. This aspect improved during therapy and his ideation lost its paranoid quality. He was, however, constantly afraid of deadly attacks. This way of experiencing was of course rooted in the past traumas; once you have experienced the catastrophe, you may never be sure it will not happen again. It had also, however, to do with real present fears, as the dictator's agents were present in the exile milieu.

Hassan had thus been severely affected by a traumatizing environment where his group belonging and his culturally assigned position were of no help. He struggled to survive mentally by dissociating, splitting up and projection. The border between inner and outer reality was, however, blurred both because of his traumatization and because he felt there was a real danger "out there." The transitional space became increasingly privatized and dominated by restricted, concrete representations of persecutors. Not all could be judged as projections, however.

The transference was marked partly by severe suspiciousness and alternatively by idealization. He had for longer periods the habit of walking cautiously into the consulting room, looking carefully behind the door for the possibility of assassins and also, was very careful in relation to the therapist. While this behavior in the beginning had to be treated as fright, it later gained transference significance and could be interpreted to some degree.

I was never really affected by his feeling of persecution in the sense that I imagined a real danger. From his perspective, however, the metasetting was constantly under threat. As this happened in rather peaceful surroundings I did not feel the therapeutic setting threatened. Countertransference was, however, more affected by his wordlessness and lack of symbolization and mentalization of affective states and experiences. The therapeutic work was in great part concentrated on building a common transferential or transitional space where his private world (the world of persecution and of his idealized past) could be transformed into a common transitional area where meanings and perspectives could be negotiated.

Conclusion

I have tried to describe how terror may affect the mind, the ability to relate to and use others, identity and cultural belonging. On all three levels described above, terror tends to tip the balance towards the negative; isolation from others and inability to use others for comfort and emotional regulation, isolation from the group affecting identity and self image, and isolation from culture as a resource for finding meaning and anchoring in a shared reality. It is obvious that individual psychotherapy or psychoanalysis may only be a part of what is needed under such circumstances. Group and family support as well as "the work of culture" (Obeyesekere 1990) is needed in a total effort to help the individuals, groups and societies that are affected. The last may be seen as aspects of the "metasetting" helping to secure the therapeutic space.

REFERENCES

Akhtar, S. (2001). *Guidelines for processing the inevitably psychic trauma.* Philadelphia.

Bernardi, R. & Nieto, M. (1992). What makes the training analysis "Good Enough"? *Int. J. Psycho-Anal, 19,* 137-146.

Bion, W. R. (1967). *Second thoughts. Selected papers on psychoanalysis.* London: Karnac.

Bohleber, W. (2002). Kollektive Phantasmen, Destruktivität und terrorismus. Unpublished.

de Bianchedi, E. T., Bianchedi, M., Braun, J., Pelento, M. L., & Puget, J. (1991). Transgressive social violence., Paper presented at 37th IPA Congress.

Emde, R. N. (1994). Individuality, context, and the search for meaning. *Child Development, 65,* 3, 719-737.

Juergensmeyer, M. (2000). *Terror in the mind of God. Global rise of religious violence.* Berkeley, Los Angeles and London: University of California Press.

Killingmo, B. (1995). Affirmation in psychoanalysis. *Int. J. Psycho-anal., 76* (Pt 3), 503-518.

Lavik, N. J., Christie, H., Solberg, Ø., & Varvin, S. (1996). A refugee protest action in a host country: Possibilities and limitations of an intervention by a mental health unit. *Journal of Refugee Studies, 9,* 1, 73-88.

Liberman, D. (1970). *Lingüística, Interacción Communicativa y Proceso Psicoanalítico Vols. 1-3.* Buenos Aires.: Galerna.

Obeyesekere, G. (1990). *The work of culture* Chicago and London: University of Chicago Press.

Rosenbaum, B. & Varvin, S. (1999). The breaking down of the mind: Trauma in a psychosemiotic perspective. Paper presented at the 30th annual meeting of the Society for Psychotherapy Research. Braga, Portugal, June 1999.

Rosenbaum, B. & Varvin, S. (2000). The enunciation of exiled and traumatized persons: A model and its application., NASS Conference, Copenhagen.

Rosenbaum, B. & Varvin, S. (2002a). The enunciation of exiled and traumatized persons: A model and its application. In *Upheaval: Psychoanalytic perspectives on trauma.* S. Varvin & T. Stajner-Popovic, eds., Belgrade: IAN.

Rosenbaum, B. & Varvin, S. (2002b). The influence of extreme traumatisation on body, mind and social relations. Unpublished.

Schreuder, B. J. N. (1998). How inner and outer realities are separated by persecution and migration. Third Congress of the European Federation for Psychoanalytic Psychotherapy in the Public Sector, Cologne.

Sebek, M. (2001). Personal Communication.

Sullivan, H. S. (1944). The language of schizophrenia. In J. S. Kasanin, ed. *Language and thought in schizophrenia.* NY: Norton, 4-16.

Varvin, S. (2001). Auswirkungen extremer Traumatisierung auf Körper, Seele und soziales Umfeld. edition Diskord. In Press.

Varvin, S. (2002). *Mental survival strategies after extreme traumatization.* Doctoral thesis submitted to the University of Oslo, Medical Faculty, Oslo.

PART IV

Psychoanalysts' Response to Terrorism
and the Expansion of the
Psychoanalytic Space

Working as a Psychoanalyst in the Midst of Terror and Violence

NAAMA KUSHNIR-BARASH

ONE OF THE FUNDAMENTAL COMPONENTS OF THE THERAPEUTIC situation is a sense of safety. One enters treatment in order to deal with internal anxieties, conflicts, psychic pain and various "monsters" that reside in the unconscious, and seek healing. We, as analysts, try to provide an environment that is safe and protected and that will enable the therapeutic regression to unfold—a regression that is so necessary for real and enduring change.

What happens to this "safe haven" when the external conditions are filled with terror and violence? Shall we, as analysts, try to preserve the safety of the setting and stay out of the "troubled waters" outside? Can we avoid it? Shall we encourage exploration of the external events? These are some of the many dilemmas that Israeli analysts have faced in the past eighteen months, since the eruption of the Intifada that brought destruction and terror into our most daily activities.

Joseph Sandler (1960) describes the feeling of safety as a feeling so much a part of us that we take it for granted as a background to our everyday experience. It is a feeling that bears the same relation to anxiety as the positive body states of satiation and contentment bear to instinctual tension. It is a feeling of well-being. The need to maintain a feeling state of safety is of great importance in learning and development. Sandler states that an activity that leads to pleasure may be inhibited if it lowers the level of the feeling safety.

Gampel (1999), using Sandler's concept of the background of safety, postulated an opposite background that she named "background of the uncanny." She uses the term uncanny to describe experiences that cannot be expressed in words and include memories of dread and horror that are aroused by extreme social violence. Experience of such violence can lead to the blurring or destruction of the distinction between that which is possible and that which is imaginary. Such an assault on the boundary between reality and fantasy can become traumatic in itself and may lead one to fear one's own thoughts. Thus the "background of the uncanny" is created. The two backgrounds, according to Gampel, are working at different levels at any given moment. While one is in the foreground, the other is in the background. Both these backgrounds exist in the preconscious, and therefore are not repressed but rather suppressed. People who have experienced extreme traumatic and violent events need to dissociate the two backgrounds in order to continue living without being flooded and overwhelmed by their traumatic past.

What we, as analysts, learn and internalize during our training and experience becomes our own psychoanalytic background of safety. We have our ways of thinking and communicating with patients and colleagues.

During the first few months of the Intifada, many patients and analysts alike tried to preserve the notion that inside the consultation room the world is safe and there is sufficient psychological space to explore the inner reality. When my patients did not mention the latest horror, I did not bring it up. I was trying to hold on to a familiar structure of safety in a world that was growing out of control. As time went on and the violent events continued, there grew a sense of accumulating disaster. As the number of people killed and injured grew, it was becoming impossible to deny or suppress what was going on. As the language of terror filled the news reports, it found its way into the office. For example, a patient would say there was "a bomb" in the room when referring to the mounting tension in the transference or to a "strong" interpretation.

A patient described her mother-in-law as a terrorist, explaining that she appears unexpectedly and destroys the peace in the house. Another patient described herself as exploding with envy. For some patients, the external violence provided a vehicle to reveal their own aggressive fantasies and violent inner world. I am reminded of one patient who would always "reassure" me after some horrible event, that "you ain't seen nothing yet." As a son of holocaust survivors, he would delve into prolonged description of death camps, deportations and cruelty. The external situation helped him to connect to what was before an unspeakable black-hole of his parents' experience in the holocaust. His parents never talked about World War II and for Mr. G. it was the first time he had verbalized something he always felt he knew from his parents' past. However, he did not describe the past. For him it was a prophesy for the future of Israel. As I listened to his predictions I became cold with terror. His analysis was almost convincing and certainly horrifying. I was faced with the question: what shall I address? Should the focus be the past—the internalized parents? Or, perhaps, the external present frightening situation? Or the transference message to me? Or maybe all of the above?

The continuous sense of uncertainty, vulnerability and violence constricts our capacity to think creatively, to be flexible and attentive. Our patients find it difficult to free associate. The buzz of helicopters and the sound of ambulances' sirens, day and night, are a constant reminder of the trouble outside. Bernstein (1987) wrote: "in countries where political and social violence are rife and affect both the analyst and the patient, the analysis, although it may continue, is effectively restricted." Later on he states: "Terror and threats irrupt in a manner incompatible with life" (p. 31).

Ordinarily I do not take part in political discussions with my patients. However, the complicated political situation in Israel (both internal conflicts and vis-à-vis the Palestinians) sometimes enters the consultation room. For example, a patient who comes to treatment from a settlement on the West Bank sees me as spoiled and out of touch with the "real" reality because I live and practice in Tel-Aviv. He drives through dangerous roads, risking his life in order to get to work and to come to my office. I feel that he is endangering himself and his family and complicates the political situation for everybody by choosing to reside in a controversial area. These differences polarize Israel as a nation and have transference-countertransference implications that are present in the material.

A supervisee of mine has been treating a young Arab Israeli graduate student for the past six months. Last week she walked into her weekly session and told her therapist that she is terminating treatment with him. She told him "your people are killing my people. If you are drafted to reserve duty tomorrow you may kill my cousins in Nablus." She continued and said she could not trust him any longer. He was totally surprised and as the session went on he felt increasingly anxious. He tried to pull himself together and told her how painful the war was for both of them. After the session he was flooded with fear that she might hurt him. He became preoccupied with thoughts that she might be a member of a terrorist organization. The patient saw the therapist as dangerous and the therapist saw the patient as potentially dangerous. The aggressive fantasies were fused with the reality of the war and there was no room left for metaphor. When this happened, the safety principle was destroyed and the therapeutic alliance was gone.

Freud (1915) wrote: "It [war] tramples in blind fury on all that comes in its way, as though there were to be no future and no peace among men after it is over. It cuts all the common bonds between the contending peoples, and threatens to leave behind a legacy of embitterment that will make any renewal of those bonds impossible for a long time to come."

The thoughts that run through the minds of many Israelis go like the following:

"Am I driving too close to the bus in front of me which may blow up?" or "Is this man who is struggling to button his coat a terrorist or just a fat guy?" Or, while sitting down for a cup of coffee, wondering: "if a terrorist enters, will he blow himself up near the entrance or closer to the rear?"

At times I find myself drawn to say something about the external events. For some patients, such a comment is important and makes them feel held by the acknowledgment of a shared reality. For others, such a comment can be experienced as desertion and abandonment of my role as the protective shield. They need to believe that as their analyst, I am strong and impervious to danger. One patient recently asked me: "Are you scared?" before I even had a chance to consider my response, he added "I don't want to know." He later elaborated that logically he understands that I must be frightened and worried, but he does not want to hear me say that when he feels so vulnerable.

For certain psychotic and borderline patients, the external violence has a calming effect. When the external terror matches their internal horrors, they calm down. They do not feel so deviant in their suffering and phobic isolation when others are overtly scared and depressed.

There is an interesting dialectic between the "background of safety" and the "background of the uncanny" in relation to dreams. I have observed during the past eighteen months that when the outside is more calm and a sense of some safety is established, even just for a few days, the dreams become more violent and scary. When the external reality is bloody, the dreams are filled with "pink ribbons." Patients who for a long time distanced themselves from the external events and insisted that they don't let any media intrude into their lives, reported dreams that were filled with images of nuclear disasters, fires, weapons and battle fields. Patients who consciously could not escape feeling scared and overwhelmed in their waking hours, dreamt of romantic lovemaking and reconciliation with estranged objects from their past. This is, of course, in harmony with the wish fulfillment function of the dream.

One of the most unpleasant situations for me as an analyst, is to listen to one of my patients describing the Palestinian enemy as the devil, as beasts, as less than human, etc. Under the current fear of suicide bombers, one regresses from the depressive position (characterized by a capacity to recognize one's own aggression and to experience guilt, mourning and compassion) to a paranoid-schizoid position (characterized by denial, massive projection and splitting). This patient, like most of us, finds it impossible to understand the mentality of someone who is willing to annihilate herself or himself and others.

In her article about nuclear terror, Hanna Segal (1987) reminds us of the following, which is relevant today: "In the depth of our unconscious, unintegrated wishes and terrors still exist. We are only partly sane and such circumstances as prevail now mobilize the most primitive parts of ourselves."

We know that helplessness and omnipotence are two sides of the same coin. The helplessness and omnipotence feed on each other in a vicious circle. When one is caught in that mode, it is impossible to find the more middle ground. Perceived helplessness is the basis for trauma. As long as individuals feel they can do something to help themselves, they do not feel so traumatized. There is a sentence you hear everywhere in Israel "We have to go on," even when it is not clear where we are going. As long as one keeps moving, one does not feel victimized and keeps the illusion of safety.

One consequence of all these internal and external pressures is profound fatigue, which makes introspection more difficult and the therapeutic process somewhat less energetic. The work still goes on as we try to listen to the internal world of the patient as well as to the ways in which the outside violence is in the material. We try to consider present and past, inner and outer reality and the ways in which they shape the transference and our own contributions. Yes, the work goes on, heavier at times, with more clumsy humor and less playfulness.

REFERENCES

Bernstein, I. (1987). Analysis terminable and interminable, fifty years on. *Int. J. Psycho-anal., 68*, 21-35.

Freud, S. (1915). Thoughts for the times on war and death. Standard Edition, 14. London: Hogarth Press, 273-302.

Gampel, Y. (1999). Between the background of safety and the background of the uncanny in the context of social violence. In *Psychoanalysis on the move: The work of Joseph Sandler*. London and N.Y.: Routledge.

Sandler, J. (1960). The background of safety. *Int J. Psycho-anal., 41*: 352-365.

Segal, H. (1987). Silence is the real crime. *Internat. Rev. Psycho-anal., 14*: 3-13.

Understanding Terrorism at Close Quarters

LORD JOHN ALDERDICE

as written and reported by Hattie Myers

IN THIS WORKSHOP LORD JOHN ALDERDICE described three patients that he had seen in Northern Ireland, each of whom, because of their own personal and historical circumstances, were touched in different ways by the Troubles there. In each of the vignettes, Alderdice refrained from giving very detailed case histories, but taken together the three sketches highlighted his very explicit message—understanding the psychological impact of terrorism at close quarters involves grasping the fullness of another human being's subjective reality. The full clinical implications of Alderdice's view challenged workshop participants to examine various culturally and professionally determined experiences of subjectivity and objectivity. In particular the discussion touched on the work that therapists need to do in order to contain their own culturally subjective experiences which so profoundly influence their professional clinical (and political) understanding of process. It became clear just how much these personal perspectives intervene (and sometimes interfere) when working in frightening and tragic settings with individuals whose lives have been touched by terror at close quarters. It is to be expected that this will be the case when the therapist or his/her family or friends have experienced profound personal trauma. It is also unsurprising when the therapist is living within such a society and experiencing a sense of general threat and danger from it. What is perhaps less obvious, and therefore more insidious, is how a therapist from outside the situation will also bring their own experiences and perspectives to their work, and how these too can infect their clinical effectiveness if they are not held and explored in the context of a genuinely and rigorously phenomenological approach.

Bridget lived in a village in Northern Ireland not far from the border with the Republic of Ireland. In her village everyone knew everyone, and it had always been that way. When she was eighteen, Bridget married Seamus. Seamus was a hardworking young man and all seemed well in the early years of the marriage. They had three children, and as a result of their joint efforts they were close to completing the building of a house, when one night he didn't come home. Though his wife had known nothing of it Seamus had been an active member of the Provisional IRA for some time. He had been involved in terrorist activity and now the authorities had evidence and the police were after him. He had gone "on the run" and from now on he spent most of his time south of the border. Bridget was profoundly upset. All her plans for a quiet happy home were in disarray, but worse was to come. Seamus and Bridget had from time to time employed a young local girl to look after the children. Some months after Seamus went on the run it became apparent that this young girl was pregnant, and Bridget's husband Seamus was the father of the child. The authorities in the south caught up with Seamus and he was jailed in the Republic, but for many people in the local village, Seamus was a hero. Bridget sought help from her friends and neighbors and from the church. They were all, in their own ways, very supportive of her, encouraging her to visit Seamus regularly and remain faithful to him and look forward to his release from the prison which was many miles away in the south of Ireland. Despite the support she became depressed. She couldn't sleep properly at night, but was too tired to function properly during the day. She found no joy in her children. She stopped cooking properly and began to feel suicidal. She showed all the symptoms of depression and so the local family physician put her on a course of anti-depressants. Weeks passed but she simply sank lower. The family physician became increasingly concerned for Bridget's welfare and referred her to the psychiatrist.

Since the clinic was at some distance and Bridget was not at all well the psychiatrist agreed to visit her at home. Sitting down with Bridget he asked her to describe how she felt. She slowly recounted all the symptoms. "I wonder why you are so dreadfully unhappy?" said the psychiatrist. Slowly and with some hesitation Bridget began to tell the story. After listening for an hour or more the doctor said, "I can understand why you are so miserable. This has wrecked your life. You knew nothing of all this, and you feel angry and betrayed, but you are trapped by how everyone else sees the situation." Bridget began to talk some more about how she felt. After a little more time the psychiatrist intervened again. "This is a terrible position for you" he said. "but you are not mentally ill, and I don't think that medication will be any help. Indeed I really don't think that there is anything that I can do to help." "But you have helped," said Bridget. "What do you mean?" asked the doctor. "You have told me that I am not mad," she said. "That's right," said the psychiatrist. "Then," said Bridget, "I know what I need to do. Until now I have not been able to talk to anyone about this, but now that I have talked to you about it, and thought about it, I actually know what I have to do. I will take my children and leave this village and go to England. My children, when they are grown, may come to understand that this was the only solution; but whether they understand or not, this is what I must do."

To leave the husband who had so completely betrayed her was socially, religiously, politically and culturally problematic in the extreme, but the alternative was to be paralyzed by depression. She was deciding to choose health.

A police officer had been married for forty-five years. It was now time for him to retire, and his wife was delighted. Their early married life had been happy. They were married before the outbreak of the Troubles and within a year their first child was on the way. More children followed, as did success and promotion for the policeman. With the outbreak of the Troubles everything changed. He was no longer a local community police officer. Now he was in the front line of the defense of his community against a terrorist campaign. He lost colleagues who were murdered by the Provisional IRA, and he and his wife narrowly escaped assassination one night on the way into their golf club. In spite of all the risks and tragedies he survived and now he had just embarked on a well-earned retirement. Better still there was a peace process under way, and a lot of positive things were being said about the future.

Soon after retiring, he became restless and depressed. His wife urged him to find a hobby. The golf club needed help and so he offered to spend a few days a week helping out. It didn't help. People might be talking about better futures but that was not how he felt about his own life. His wife and he now had all the time they had always promised each other but night after long passionless night he lay beside his sleeping wife feeling dreadful. For the first time in his life he experienced a sense of hopelessness and despair. He went to see his family doctor who started him on medication but without success and so he referred the retired police officer to a psychiatrist. It did not take long before the man began to speak, and it was in angry tones. He began to question bitterly what his life had meant. The enormous commitment to his work, and the sense of enthusiasm he had once had for it and for his colleagues— what of it? The world was still the same. Worse still, those who had led the terrorist campaign that he and his colleagues had risked their lives to defeat were now being feted and glorified around the world and were taking up ministerial positions in government. What had his life's work accomplished? His contribution to the police force itself, while meritorious, had changed nothing. They might as well have given in to the terrorist campaign a quarter of a century earlier and saved a lot of lives. There was a deep and bitter sense that for all he had done with his time on earth, he had done nothing. Anything he had tried to do in his life to help his country was for nothing. He now had time for his wife, but his utter despair left him no space for her. His questions and bitterness could not be assuaged by helping at the golf club. The loss of his job left him victim to an onslaught of existential despair and personal regret that came packaged with a gift of too much time. The intensity of his anger and despondency was destroying his marriage. The future seemed hollow and meaningless.

The psychiatrist invited the retired police officer and his wife to attend separately, and then later together. The man soon began to speak about the loss of his former thrilling and dangerous work and how much it had meant to him to be doing something important for his country. Gradually he began also to see how this excitement had relieved him of the need to address the more pedestrian needs of a marital relationship, and the struggles of family life. His low spirits were not improved by beginning to realize how much he had missed of his children's growing up. Fortunately his wife still wanted to make something of their life and slowly it became possible to put the larger picture of the community to the side and focus on making the best of their remaining time together. It would not be right to say that he became a happy man, but he and his wife found a way to build some shared life and to relieve the existential pain he brought along to the first session.

The request was a common one. The psychiatrist had received a letter from a lawyer asking for a medico-legal report, and the subject of the report now sat in the psychiatrist's chair. He was no great upstanding citizen. A young man in his twenties, he was overweight with a shaved head but looking surprisingly timorous and uncertain. The reason for the referral was that the young man was making a financial claim against the government for mental debility caused by a bad experience he had had as a result of the Troubles. The government legal case was that there was no evidence of serious psychiatric disorder and, in essence, that he was malingering.

The man claimed to be suffering from panic attacks, which he said started just after an assault some years previously. The question for the psychiatrist in such circumstances is how to judge the veracity or otherwise of the claim. Was the man genuinely unwell or was he trying to fool the justice system by malingering and play acting?

The man was anxious, but when asked he described in some detail the episode which he believed had triggered his symptoms. He was sitting in a house with a friend, whom he knew to be involved in drug dealing. He himself was not involved, nor was he a user, though he had a history of alcohol problems. Suddenly a number of masked men burst into the room. They announced that they were from the PIRA and demanded that the men lie down on the floor immediately with their faces to the ground. Terrified, the men obeyed immediately. A man stood over them holding a gun first to the prisoner's friend whom he then shot. The prisoner then heard the click of the revolver and assumed he would be next. He screamed out that he hadn't done anything and then a sort of shutter came down over his eyes and he didn't remember anything more, until he recalled finding himself lying on the floor of the room shaking, but not physically injured. Since that time he had suffered from regular panic attacks.

His story was interesting particularly because of the account of the dissociative episode of the "shutters coming down," and so the man was asked to speak about this in more detail and in particular whether he had ever experienced anything like this before. What emerged was as follows.

He had grown up in rather poor circumstances laced with domestic violence and alcohol abuse. His father would come home and beat his wife (the young man's mother) and if the boy had been disobedient his father would beat him too. On one occasion he recalled his father had accused him of something he had not done. The boy fled to his room, but the father followed. Once in his bedroom the father locked the door, slowly took off his leather belt, and started to beat the boy unmercifully. The boy became terrified for his very life and then suddenly he experienced the same phenomenon—the shutters came down over his eyes and remembered nothing more.

The man was not very sophisticated. There was no reason to believe that this story was manufactured. He did not himself immediately see any connection between these two experiences and his panic attacks, but the description was striking. The experience of terror at the hands of the IRA had brought back to his mind the experience(s) at the hands of his drunken, abusive father. The panic attacks were an expression of the feelings which these emotionally powerful memories engendered. It seemed highly unlikely that this man was play-acting. On the contrary this account was evidence that his symptoms were real. It was appropriate on this basis to file a report to the courts giving a fairly confident assertion that the patient was indeed suffering from an anxiety neurosis to which he had been made vulnerable by some very specific episodes of childhood trauma, and which had been triggered by the terrorist attack.

All three patients had symptoms which were clearly related to their very different experiences of terrorism at close quarters. If the therapist is to understand how trauma and emotional conflict convert such experiences into psychiatric symptoms it is necessary to set aside one's own presuppositions and experience the patient's internal world, finding the connections that were expressed in the symptoms and with the possibility of helping the patient to make connections that can make sense of their predicament and may lead to symptom relief.

The Frame and the Psychoanalytic Space in the Face of War and Terror

MORDECHAI BENYAKAR

as written and reported by Danielle Knafo

DR. BENYAKAR'S WORKSHOP WAS VERY RELAXED AND comfortable, considering the subject matter at hand. He was a laid back speaker who shared some of his views on terrorism and reactions to it from a wealth of experience that derives from having participated in five Israeli wars as well as terrorist events in Israel and Argentina (e.g., the 1994 attack on the Jewish Community Center). To me, the highlight of the workshop consisted of Dr. Benyakar's clarification of several relevant concepts and making clear distinctions between concepts that are not usually well differentiated.

Disruptive situations, a designation outlined by Benyakar and his colleagues, refers to actual external events that implode the psyche, violent irruptions in social environments that threaten the inner world of its inhabitants. These changes turn a familiar surrounding into a threatening and alienated one, full of unknown, unde-tectable and omnipresent menaces, and may result in mental disorders. Benyakar is opposed to labeling situations as traumatic because he believes we cannot qualify sit-uations. Rather, we can say that a situation is disruptive and one's experience of that disruptive situation may or may not be a traumatic one. The word "trauma" is reserved for internal processes, in this case, the breakdown of the articulation between affect and psychic representation.

Benyakar proposes a diagnostic category, *Anxiety by Disruption Syndrome (AbD)*, to address the disorder caused not by an inner conflict or dynamic but, rather, by deterioration and/or collapse of the external environment. He is sensitive to the use of the word "victim" when speaking of those affected by disruptive situations. In his view, victims lose their subjectivity when they are needed by society to repre-sent its memory of an event. Benyakar emphasizes the necessity of recognizing not only those who are directly injured by the impact of such an event but, also, the larg-er threatened group.

Because reactions to such catastrophic events may be *either* stressful or traumat-ic, Benyakar believes that the designation of Post Traumatic Stress Disorder (PTSD), which combines both, is a misnomer and should not be used. Rather he suggests that we pay attention to the ways in which persons react to environmental disruptions and that treatment approaches will follow such a differentiation.

When the disruptive event is experienced as a threat, the psyche may process it in one of two ways. On one hand, it erects defense mechanisms, the result of signal anxiety, that produce a *stress experience*. On the other hand, feelings of helplessness emerge, as a result of autonomic anxiety and unsymbolized affect, that lead to a *trau-matic experience*. Benyakar labels experiences as stressogenic when a person reacts by mobilizing defensive structures that nonetheless may contribute to phobic or anxiety symptoms. Conversely, experiences become traumatic when affect emerges with no concomitant representation. When speaking about traumatic experiences, Benyakar refers to a defenseless and helpless psyche. Stress and traumatic experiences represent ways the psyche establishes its relationship to the outside world.

Yet, the traumatized individual is one who is incapable of putting his or her experience into words. Although the person has already achieved symbolization through language, the traumatic experience is one that remains unstructured. This distinguishes it from psychosis, for example, in which a de-structuring process takes place. The trauma, on the other hand, was not structured to begin with. In treatment, therefore, the traumatized person needs help to transform his or her nameless pain into suffering that can be communicated, thereby bringing about an emotional metabolic process.

Benyakar opposes the DSM category of PTSD not only for its lack of distinction between trauma and stress but, also, because it focuses on a set of symptoms in a cause and effect manner—that is, a specific event, depending on its intensity and duration, is thought to directly cause a set of symptoms. Benyakar, on the other hand, understands the traumatic experience as rooted where there are no words, where it cannot be verbalized or explained, since it cannot be represented. Therefore, the so-called "symptom" is that which conceals the trauma which was never symbolized in the first place.

Benyakar wished to clarify the concept of *experience* (*erlebnis*), which he relates to a subjective component rather than an external, objective fact. More specifically, experience is the articulation between affect and representation. Some languages do not have two different words for experience and therefore the subjective and the objective often become confused. Not everyone who experiences an objective disruption in his or her environment responds with a subjective traumatic reaction. The English language employs the word "experience" to denote both subjective and objective occurrences, even though "happening" and "experience" might better distinguish them from one another. Other languages do possess words that specifically denote the subjective connotation of experience: in Hebrew, the word *chavaya*, in Spanish, *vivencia*, in German, *erlebnis*. In French, although the same word is generally used, Jean Paul Sartre proposed the expression *fait vecu* when referring to the subjective component of what has been experienced by the individual. When Benyakar employs the term "traumatic experience," he is referring solely to its subjective connotation.

The "traumatic experience," then, is one of the ways in which the Negative (à la Andre Green) arises in the psyche. Benyakar appreciates the paradox in trauma because, for him, the traumatic, because it is unsymbolized and unstructured, is the experience of non-experience and therefore precisely what renders it so traumatic.

Benyakar also emphasized the difference between aggression and violence, a difference that parallels that between stress and trauma. With *aggression*, one is aware of one's opponent, and this awareness allows one to prepare and defend oneself accordingly, both psychologically and concretely. A good example of this is war. Soldiers go into combat knowing who their enemy is and what they need to do in order to protect themselves. The situation is different when we speak of violence. In this case, one is taken by surprise and therefore cannot defend oneself properly. One does not know when and from where the harm will come, a situation that leaves a person feeling both helpless and frightened. Terrorism, unlike combat situations in war, has created a violent world, a world in which the enemy can be anywhere and might attack at any time. The defenselessness that results from this situation is what leads to trauma.

Finally, Benyakar spoke of the necessity to maintain the psychoanalytic frame when treating those who suffer from disruptive situations. In a world of violence, a world that lacks stability and predictability, it is all the more critical for the therapeutic setting to remain stable and constant without becoming dogmatic or rigid. The frame provides *containment* for the patient's most malignant thoughts and feelings; *holding* so that the patient does not feel alone in his or her encounter with violence; and *figurative interpretations* to aid in the translation of affects into symbolic verbal representation. In this manner, the frame and setting of the treatment impart stability and a sense of safety to the therapeutic relationship and the patient's inner world, all of which help bolster the self that has no choice but to survive in a society that has lost its sense.

Perspectives from Ground Zero: Snapshots of Coping (or not) from High School and College Students

BETH HART & HERBERT H. KRAUSS

ON DECEMBER 7TH, 1940, ABOUT 3,000 AMERICANS died in the attack on Pearl Harbor. Almost all served in the Armed Forces. On September 11, 2001, nearly 3,000 were murdered in New York City alone in a coordinated set of terrorist attacks directed against New York City and Washington, D.C. All of those killed in New York City in what has come to be termed the "World Trade Center Disaster" (WTCD) were, by any generally agreed upon standard, non-combatants.

While the attack on Pearl Harbor was unanticipated at the highest reaches of the American government, it was understood that at any time war might be declared against the United States by the government of Japan. In fact, that the attack took place before a declaration of war was delivered to the government of the United States was inadvertent. Of course, the attack on Pearl Harbor was designed and intended to initiate hostilities in a manner advantageous to the Japanese Empire.

In retrospect, as was the case for Pearl Harbor, there were signs in the last decades that acts of terror were being planned against the American homeland by groups with roots in foreign lands, in foreign nations, with an aim to striking, not only at the foreign policy of the United States, but at the root values which are its reason for existence. Even were there not, there were ample examples worldwide that dissident groups in Northern Ireland, in Israel, in Kashmir, in Sri Lanka, to cite but a few examples, would direct terror attacks against the public. And, were this evidence not compelling, the previous deadly assault against the World Trade Center in 1992 and the 1995 bombing of the Alfred P. Murrah Federal Building in Oklahoma City that killed 168 should have dispelled the average American's or New Yorker's belief that it could not happen again, here. Why it did not do so is an apt focus for psychoanalytic investigation in itself, but that it did not is palpably evident in the recollections of the WTCD presented by this workshop's participants.

With but one exception, T., he being a student at nearby Stuyvesant High School, all those scheduled to speak at the workshop were associated with Pace University's campus in New York City. Located in Lower Manhattan with an enrollment of approximately 7,500 undergraduate and graduate students, Pace's Civic Center Campus is about three blocks from the site of the World Trade Center. Its World Trade Institute was located on Floor 55 of 1 World Trade Center; none from the World Trade Institute died; it was successfully evacuated. However, the Pace community lost four students and over 25 alumni/ae in the WTCD; a great many more suffered injuries.

While those in the immediate area who fortunately survived the WTCD apprehended the tragedy individually, there was considerable overlap in their early experience of it. There were the explosions and subsequent concussions as the planes hit the towers, each in its turn. Then came the flames, smoke, falling debris, and jumpers. When the towers came down, blinding, choking smoke, more debris, and a 300-foot tower of ash and dust engulfed all of Lower Manhattan. "In a moment it went from being a perfectly blue, crystalline late summer morning into a dusk-like nuclear winter filled with particles of pulverized buildings, souls, plastic and steel floating and swirling like a blown blizzard" (Raskin, Fenichel, Kellerhouse & Shadick, 2002, p. 23). And, of course, there were the sirens, the injured, the dead, the panicked and islands of help givers organized or not. By any acceptable definition, for those at the scene the WTCD was indeed a traumatic event. It produced catastrophic conditions which evoked "uneconomical" reactions of anxiety because of external threat, the inability to cope with it, and the breakdown of the capacity for abstraction (Goldstein, 1943). It was "an event that involve[d] actual or threatened death or serious injury, or other threat to one's physical integrity; or witnessing an event that involve[d] death, injury or a threat to the physical integrity of another person (*DSMIV*, 1994, p. 424). It had each of the three features that define traumatic events—(1) a lack of control, (2) a highly negative experience, and (3) unpreparedness. Almost all there who were interviewed reported being flooded by a succession of intense sensory impressions and existential shocks of overwhelming force. Almost all experienced emotional overload. Their behavior and emotions surprised them. Few could believe that what was happening was happening. Almost all sensed they had lost two things of fundamental importance: their sense of sureness about themselves and what might happen, and their sense of safety in the world.

Expectably, as the immediate threat to life and limb diminished and the commitments of past circumstances and the demands of reality gained traction, the life trajectories and, hence, the experiences of those who were there diverged increasingly. But not before injury and scarring had been initiated or had taken place in a high percentage of those present. Five months after the event, investigators found that, of a convenience sample of 271 Pace students, 50 per cent met the criterion for Post-Traumatic Stress Disorder (Rothman, Krauss & Armeli, 2002), a proportion well within that which might be expected on the basis of previous research on traumatic events (e.g., McNally, 1999).

This workshop, which was held approximately eight months after the WTCD, focused upon the personal testimonies, the autobiographical memories of one high school and six college students who were nearby when the planes struck the towers and the towers came down. They saw people jump out of windows and crash to the street. They felt the ground shake beneath them as smoke and dust filled their lungs and bits of debris hit their faces. They heard rumors of poison gas, germ warfare, and approaching attack planes. In an environment characterized by both a dearth of information and a chaos of misinformation they and many around them believed they were living the last minutes of their lives. And, in September 11's aftermath, all returned to the scene of the all too visible crime, smelled for months the pervasive odors of the charnel house, and tried to get on with their lives. From their rememberances, from their life stories, the intent of the workshop was to discern something of the impact the WTCD had upon the persons who were present, and, it is hoped, to a degree on those who experienced it from a greater physical distance. For, besides our own experience, every American lost something particular to our individual lives before September 11, something based on our personal histories, our ideals and world view. The autobiographical particulars provide the context within which the meaning of the WTCD may be understood.

As viewed currently (e.g., Young, 1995), the therapeutic action for the treatment of trauma, just as Freud described it over a century ago, entails mourning and remembering. Remembering, retelling, gives words to images and sensations, transforming them into affects and meaning. Interpretation links the present to the past, to one's life, ideals and assumptions before the trauma occurred. Interpretation deepens awareness of meaning structures that have been deformed or lost and seeks to rebuild them. Recovery requires courage. Mourning requires the ability to bear painful trauma. Without mourning, trauma leads to continued dissociation and, worse, to destructive defensive operations mounted against oneself and others.

What ought to impress researchers and therapists perhaps more than the signs and symptoms of trauma is people's remarkable resilience, their capacity to restore what was broken and lost in themselves, and to carry on productively. The testimony of the panel attests to that capacity as well as to the individuality of reactions to an event that was, in more ways than not, common to all who were there.

Unfortunately, for a number of reasons—the difficulty that inheres in accurately transforming human performances into prose, the lack of space to attempt to do so here, to cite but two—the synopses of the testimony given by the workshop's participants do not do justice to the wealth of information they contained, or the power with which they were presented or to the impact they had on listeners. Thus, these synopses cannot fully stand on their own. Undoubtedly, their most significant deficiency is their failure to convey the extent to which the panel members, without exception, but some more than others, seemed to relive their memories of the WTCD, seemed reabsorbed into them, during their presentations. The impression given was that these remembrances remained green, powerful, and not fully integrated into the weft of everyday memory. Consistent with this interpretation was the characteristic surprise participants displayed when their "loss of distance" was pointed out to them.

W. self-identified as an Arab. He is a resident assistant in the Pace dorms and a man who expresses himself vividly. He remained in class after the first tower was hit because he felt sheltered there; the class was talking about how everything would be all right. He saw the first tower collapse on CNN and went to the street feeling guilty for being grateful that he wasn't in those buildings. Later in the day he tried to donate clothing at a collection point set up by the fire department. The firemen there declined his donation; nothing was wanted from an Arab. Like so many Arab-Americans, who became victims perceived as perpetrators, he felt awful, alienated, and betrayed. Nevertheless, he spent the next several weeks subsequent to September 11 in the dorms attending to students who had nowhere else to go. During this period the air outside, and inside as well, was rancid and the neighborhood as still as a ghost town but for the sirens and sounds of the rescue workers sorting through debris looking for body parts.

A high school student, T., was on the ninth floor of Stuyvesant High School when the first tower was hit. He watched "200" ambulances and fire trucks speed down the West Side Highway. He watched the first tower burn and saw a plane hit the second tower. Before anyone dismissed the students, he ran down the stairs and started walking up the West Side Highway. When he reached Fiftieth Street he felt he was in another world that was totally surreal. What bothered him was that the events he lived through were being told and retold in the street as an abstraction as portrayed through the media and that this account seemed to have more meaning to people than his own concrete experience.

His pain at the lack of attentive, empathetic listening was palpable. It emphatically told how much victims needed to be listened to and validated and how much an intellectualized response felt like an intrusion, an empathetic failure, and a trauma in itself.

C., a young woman from Sweden, coming to her first practicum at the psychology clinic, stepped out of the subway and saw a cloud of black smoke and a crowd of people coming toward her. "So this is what rush hour is like in Manhattan," she thought, managing to deny for a moment that people were hysterical and those sitting on the sidewalk were being led away by friends and police officers. As she saw that one of the towers was on fire, a woman came up to her screaming, "They are jumping from the towers, can't you see they are all jumping." C. stood for 10 minutes watching fire trucks coming from Brooklyn, thinking the firemen wouldn't survive the inferno, for the towers were now so enveloped in black smoke they could not be seen. She did not want to be late for class and walked toward the clinic wondering about a friend who worked at Windows on the World. Only then did it occur to her that thousands of people must be trapped; she felt nauseous.

When she arrived at the clinic, she was told that the Pentagon was also hit; this is war. Someone screamed, "They're back, I hear more planes coming." She went down the stairs with many others and got locked in the basement. Someone knew another way out and led them through a dark corridor to the door. As she opened it, thick black smoke, dust and debris hit her and those she was with in their faces. They engaged in tortured deliberation about whether to stay in the dark basement where they could not see, or to go outside where they could not breathe. Once out, she and a classmate debated about whether to run uptown or cross a bridge to get out of Manhattan. Police officers had no advice to offer. Denied access to the Brooklyn Bridge, she made her way over the Manhattan Bridge fully expecting that the planes overhead would destroy it. Then the second tower collapsed. She recalls all the people on the other side of the bridge looking at Manhattan, and a mother pleading with a police officer to let her cross the bridge to look for her child who had been in school on the other side. During the hours and hours of walking, with rumors that the dust was filled with asbestos and bio-hazardous agents, she felt many times that she would not survive. Nine hours later she arrived home.

C.'s testimony, abbreviated here, was a riveting account of how difficult it was to process what was happening and how quickly denial translates signs of catastrophic danger into an ordinary event—a usual Manhattan rush hour. In telling it, she relived every moment of her experience, which although eight months past, was as if it were happening here and now.

L., C.'s classmate, also saw the plane hit the tower. She headed for class. Although she saw people jumping from the towers, she couldn't believe there were actually people in the building. She knew this was war and believed she would be "bombed out of existence" and had no idea "if my fingers and toes would be attached to me anymore." L. doesn't like to tell her story because she feels that so many people who were not there suffered just as greatly and received no attention. She mentioned a woman who passed out when she was told what had happened. She thought of her mother who hadn't heard from her for so many hours that she must assume that her daughter was dead. She felt guilty about speaking on the panel because "what others went through was as horrible as actually being there." Her predominant response was guilt and a feeling that she was "on a pedestal" taking something away from others whose suffering may go unrecognized.

As she spoke, the alternation between a logical incomprehension and reality, dissociation and conscious awareness were evident. Today she suffers from Post-Traumatic Stress Disorder and is receiving counseling.

J., another student on the way to practicum, got off the E-train at the World Trade Center. Someone told her that the towers were hit; she didn't believe it. When she got to the street she saw fire and "things" flying from the windows. She too headed for the clinic where she tried to reach her fiancé, a policeman, who advised her not to go outside because there might be poison gas. Several times she counted the messages on her cell phone as if consoled by the evidence people cared. She spoke to a clinic director about what to do and held onto her as they went down the stairs. When they got outside, they were so overcome by smoke they stopped at the lobby of the next building to reconsider their plan to walk uptown. Despite having an asthma attack, J. had little choice but to walk up the East side with the director stopping first at a hospital to get gas masks. She recalled the feeling of "stunned disbelief" when the second tower collapsed. She reported that the greatest trauma she experienced was that inflicted by a colleague and neighbor who took off in his car over the Brooklyn Bridge leaving her and the director to fend for themselves. After five hours they reached the director's office. J. heard from her fiancé, the policeman, who was called to work: she did not hear from him again until the next evening.

After her initial denial, the things that stood out in J.'s testimony were her need to reach out and establish connection and her feeling of betrayal.

J. and E. were resident assistants in the Pace dormitories. Both felt they had to stay strong and get to work helping students and responding to parental phone calls. They were late-adolescents with responsibilities and self-expectations perhaps no one could fulfill. Weeks later both became anxious and relived their experiences in nightmares and waking states. They were unable to do school work that semester and their grades dropped. They never asked institutional authorities for accommodation or understanding.

In their thoughtful consideration of how to think about psychiatric disorders and, by extension, health, McHugh and Slavney (1998; Slavney, 1990) propose that there are currently four conceptually distinct perspectives in use; these center on (1)

Disease, (2) Dimensions of Personality, (3) Goal Directed Behavior, and (4) Life Stories. Each perspective generates a particular way of looking at, assessing, and intervening with persons and their circumstances. Because each is, in its own realm, persuasive, but each provides data, albeit important data, about only certain components of human functioning, and because, at times these components interact or complement each other to form a coherent and meaningful picture of an individual's conjuncture, it may be necessary to make use of more than one. For example, "Huntington's disease," as Slavney (1990) points out,

> is a genetic disorder . . . reasoning from the disease perspective has pride of place when one considers *the etiology* of the condition. In *caring* for patients with Huntington's disease, however, that perspective alone is insufficient . . . Patients with Huntington's disease often wish to have children of their own, despite the knowledge that these children will be at risk to inherit the disorder. The anguish they experience cannot be described in terms of the disease construct . . . but it is easily appreciated through the life-story method, which deals with "broken hearts." . . . What is illuminated through one perspective is invisible from the other.

The signs and symptoms of the trauma these panelists experienced in the aftermath of the WTCD ran the gamut of those reported in the literature (McNally, 1999). Among them were breakdowns in the capacity for abstraction, sensory and emotional over-arousal, feelings of helplessness, fear, horror, and depression, episodes of derealization, depersonalization, or other dissociative phenomena. Nearly all reported later flashbacks triggered variously by loud noises or sirens, stalled subway cars or groups of police officers congregating in a place they were not expected to be. Many developed reoccurring headaches or hives, became depressed, anxious or weepy, found themselves anxious when traversing bridges, riding subways or entering tunnels. And, one or two developed full-blown Post-Traumatic Stress Disorders.

While some may attempt to understand these sequelae of the WTCD in terms of the "broken parts" of the disease model, or the personality traits of the panelists, or some two-factor learning theory, it seems plausible, at least, that any comprehensive understanding of the impact of the events of September 11, 2001 must necessarily take into account the significance they held for the life stories of the individuals experiencing them. While their lives go on, they do so in an existentially different world.

REFERENCES

American Psychiatric Association (1994). *DSMIV: Diagnostic and statistical manual of mental disorders*. Washington, DC: American Psychiatric Association.
Goldstein, K. (1943). On so-called war neuroses. *Psychosomatic Medicine, 5,* 376.
McHugh, P. R. & Slavney, P. R. (1983). *The perspectives of psychology*. Baltimore, MD: Johns Hopkins University Press.
McNally, R. J. (1999). Traumatic stress disorder. In T. Millon, P. H. Blaney & R. D. Davis (Eds.). *Oxford textbook of psychopathology*. New York: Oxford University Press.

Raskin, R. H., Fenichel, A., Kellerhouse, B. & Shadick, R. N. (2002). In the shadow of the World Trade Center: A view from a college counseling center. *Journal of College Student Psychotherapy, 17*, 17-38.

Rothman, P., Krauss, H. H. & Armeli, S. (2002). The influence of quality of adult attachment and degree of exposure on post-traumatic stress symptoms after the World Trade Center Disaster. Unpublished Manuscript.

Slavney, P. R. (1990). *Perspectives on "hysteria."* Baltimore, MD: Johns Hopkins University Press.

Young, A. (1995*). The harmony of illusions: Inventing post-traumatic stress disorder.* Princeton, NJ: Princeton University Press.

In the Aftermath of September 11: The Analyst as Container for the Parents in the Real or Imagined Threat to a Child

PHYLLIS BEREN & CORLISS PARKER

PHYLLIS BEREN AND CORLISS PARKER BEGAN WITH A discussion of how the analyst and psychotherapist act as containers for parents' anxieties about their own and their children's safety. How parents handle their own fears plays a crucial role in how effective they will be in helping their children manage their anxieties. The younger child, for example, will scrutinize her parent's face and will note changes in body language and voice. We know both from clinical experience and theory that a parent's anxiety is often transmitted to her child in a variety of ways. Even under normal circumstances, the propensity for parents to project thoughts and feelings onto their children is high, and in crises, the tendency not to differentiate between their own and their children's feelings and fantasies is understandably heightened. Therefore, it is extremely important to encourage parents to express their own fears to us, both to help them articulate their specific questions and anxieties and to learn how they view and understand their children's reactions to disturbing events. Our experience after 9/11, both with adult patients who are parents and with parents of our child patients, was that the more we were able to listen to the parents' anxieties, both spoken and implied, the more they were able to soothe and calm their children.

Phyllis Beren described how during the bombing of London in World War II, Anna Freud and her colleagues found that small children did not seem to display the anticipated trauma when they came into contact with the horrors of war, as long as they were not separated from their mothers or a familiar caretaker. It was different for those children separated from their parents or who had lost a parent. Therapists working in London observed, as did we, that the more the parent remained calm and soothing, the more the child could go on with play and activities in a normal fashion.

People attending our workshop described a variety of experiences in their work with parents, adolescents and children after 9/11. One participant living in a suburb of New York reported that people in her psychotherapy practice often didn't speak directly about the World Trade Center attacks and terrorism, but appeared overall more anxious and complained of more somatic symptoms. She felt that many people needed to deny that they had been affected by 9/11. Another participant from Ontario, Canada, reported that adolescents who called a hotline he staffed after the WTC attacks had expressed fears of being attacked by terrorists (in Canada); they also said they were glad they could speak to someone privately about fears they were reluctant to share with their family and friends. A third participant in our workshop described running groups for parents of elementary age children. She said that these parents were almost totally focused on their own symptoms and fears after the WTC attacks, rather than their children's. We discussed the very significant need for clinicians to provide a space for parents to address their particular concerns and worries.

Then when these are contained well enough, the parents can provide a space for their children to express thoughts and feelings.

Phyllis Beren described her work with a boy of nine who had been in treatment for two years when the attacks on the World Trade Center occurred. The parents and John came for their regular appointment a day after the terrorist attack on the WTC. The parents did not discuss the event until it was brought up with them. While they spoke in a calm manner about their fears, their body language was far from contained. They felt that John seemed OK, he was not exhibiting any unusual anxiety, and they were maintaining their routines. Father, who would normally have been in his office in a building at Ground Zero was not there on that day, and the building suffered considerable structural damage and had to be evacuated. As they were able to talk a bit more about their anxieties, some suggestions were offered about how they could talk about the event and the displacement of father's office. They were also told of the possibility that John might revert to old behavior and become more demanding.

John, in session, was clearly more anxious, more motoric and exhibiting earlier tic-like symptoms. As was typical of John, he kept busy so as not to talk about anything disturbing. Toward the end of the session, he conveyed what was on his mind. He stood a box of Kleenex upright, called it the twin towers and then proceeded to attack it again and again with a paper airplane. In the next session, he created a board game that had spaces for landing on volcanoes and the WTC. Later in that same session, he created a game by laying out a maze with Legos and adding five marbles, representing five lives to be used in the play. The object of the game was to roll the marble through this maze to an opening at the end. Managing to accomplish this by only losing two marbles, John suddenly began to talk. He reported that his father had told him that the US had a bomb that could explode and put the world to sleep for 10,000 years. On inquiring whether there really could be such a bomb, he assured me that his father had said so. He was visibly anxious about this, but also wanted to believe his father. The parents might indeed be talking to him in ways that were not very useful, or he might be distorting what he had heard them say. John was clearly in a dilemma, since he wanted to view what he thought his father had said as protective but at the same time it made him anxious, because it mirrored his own aggressive impulses and his grandiose fantasies.

When it was time to leave, both parents were waiting to pick him up. John went into the waiting room and said to his father: "Didn't you tell me that we had a bomb that could destroy the world and put it to sleep for 10,000 years?" The next ten minutes were spent in the waiting room talking together, while John sat in his father's lap. The father explained that we did not have such a bomb, and the conversation moved to talking about various neutral things. The parents saw more clearly that their son did in fact think about these things and became anxious, and they realized they had to be more careful about what they said in front of him.

Subsequent sessions with John and the parents indicated that they were all trying to get on with their lives and to do more things together during this period. John, who had regressed during this time to his earlier tic-like symptoms, seemed to get better with each session where he had the opportunity to play out what was on his mind. John's treatment and the sessions with the parents seemed to help calm everyone down. John reported a dream for the first time. This is the dream:

> The kids at school were going on a field trip to Osama's Zoo. Osama bin Laden was
> the tour leader. The children were lined up and John looked behind him and saw a
> girl with shoes that had screws in them. He realized it was a bomb. He told all the
> children to press a button on their body that would allow things to go through them.
> When Osama found out that his bomb was discovered, he hit himself in the head
> with it and died. The police came and gave the children a 25 million dollar reward.

After inquiring if there were any adults in the dream, John remembered: "Oh yes, three adults got captured and put in a tank of water in one of the cages and they would have to be there for 1000 years." He could admit to being frightened in the dream but also happy about the reward.

Obviously there is a lot to analyze in this dream having to do with John's own unconscious conflicts and dynamics and, of course, the bomb spoken of in an earlier session appeared in this dream. But what is equally important was John's wish to conquer his own anxieties. Furthermore, he was able for the first time to fully own up to his aggressive and sadistic impulses. He graphically described what he would do to Osama if he captured him. He was for the first time comfortable with his own aggressive impulses and also visibly less anxious.

Corliss Parker described working with a woman who began psychotherapy weeks after September 11, when she found herself "losing control," including shouting at and criticizing her four-year-old daughter. This woman lives two blocks from the World Trade Center site, and, along with her husband and daughter, had seen the towers fall and then been relocated uptown for four months. When her daughter "whined" about living uptown and about the "smelly air" and her "smelly school" downtown, the patient would become suddenly furious: "I wanted everything to be normal; I hated her reminding me that it wasn't." When asked about her particular experience of 9/11, this very accomplished woman was eventually able to say that she'd felt terrified of dying as the towers fell and darkness and ash surrounded her family and her home. When asked about her own early history, she gradually remembered being terrified of her mother's voice and hands and raging temper, and I learned that the patient's mother had routinely hit and punished her whenever she expressed negative and independent feelings and thoughts. As she gradually felt safe enough to explore, in a psychotherapeutic context, some of her own very specific feelings about being in danger (near the Twin Towers, and in the presence of her mother and the therapist, in transference), the patient has become less frightened of her own aggressive, angry emotions and impulses. She has also become significantly better able to listen to and tolerate her daughter's experiences of frustration, anger, and loss.

In summary, we all felt that we were in a very privileged position to help parents and children deal with the traumas unleashed by the events of September 11. Some of us also experienced our own fears and anxieties as being contained, as we struggled to contain the fears of our patients. We were comforted when we were able to witness the capacity of our child, adolescent and adult patients to get on with their lives, even as they integrated aspects of this crisis in the contexts of their own personal histories.

The Destabilization of Attachment Processes in Children and Adolescents: Clinical Material from the Oklahoma City Bombing

ANNE EARLY & KAY LUDWIG

Kay Ludwig

PRIOR TO 9/11, THE OKLAHOMA CITY BOMBING ON April 19, 1995, was the worst terrorist attack on American soil in the history of the United States. One hundred sixty-eight people were killed when a truck bomb exploded, destroying the downtown Federal Building. The building also housed a daycare center, and 19 infants and toddlers also perished in the explosion.

The following information comes from published articles and reports from area health agencies and hospitals treating bombing survivors. In Oklahoma City, the rescue endeavor involved over 12,000 individuals (Whittlesley, Allen, et. al., 1999). Mental health professionals organized to provide services for approximately 1,500 requests for crisis intervention in coping with this tragedy. A FEMA funded agency opened within a week, and, within two years, 9,000 persons received services including support groups, crisis intervention, outreach, consultation and referral.

The Oklahoma Department of Health reported that of 341 survivors, 6.5% were off work for more than one year, and an additional 13.8% never returned to work. It is assumed that much of the disability related to psychological aftereffects had complicated the known physical injuries. An additional report surveyed 914 direct survivors of the blast; of these, 92% reported being injured in the bombing. The more severe the physical injury, the higher the reported rate of anxiety, depression, and PTSD. The most common problems associated with exposure to the bombing were auditory damage, depression and PTSD. Of these 914 survivors, 2/3 received psychological counseling and 1/2 required audiology services.

In the following clinical vignettes, there is a recurrent countertransference theme. In all four treatments, I experienced an ongoing, nagging feeling that I was unable to engage these patients in the work—that is, the work I assumed was appropriate and necessary to work through a trauma of this magnitude.

Patient #1, a Red Cross referral, was a woman whose father had been nearly killed in the blast and whose photo was flashed on television in the media for months. This patient canceled numerous sessions, was out of control with alcohol and drugs, and could not deal directly with the reality of the bombing. It was necessary to terminate her from the counseling sessions due to non-compliance with treatment. Two years later, I learned that she committed suicide.

Patient #2, also a Red Cross referral, was a man whose sister had been killed in the bombing. The focus of the nearly one year of psychotherapy was on marital problems, and difficulties in self-care functioning (i.e., paying bills, managing money, etc.). Only a few times, and only when I directed his attention to the bombing and loss of his sister, was he interested in or able to deal with anything related to the event. His affect remained constricted and he seemed extremely uncomfortable during these attempts to address the bombing. During treatment with him, I frequently felt frustrated and confused about what I would later come to understand as a difference in expectations between patient and therapist. I thought my role—especially since the fee was being paid by the Red Cross—was to focus on the trauma and help him recover from expected PTSD and loss issues. I felt some degree of guilt cashing checks when I didn't feel I was accomplishing treatment goals.

Patient #3 was referred as a private patient one year after the bombing. As a high level administrator within a government agency housed within the federal building, he lost 19 employees in the blast. He was out of town on business at the time of the bombing. The stated reason for coming in, however, had to do with an increasing depression related to a sudden and humiliating demotion in the workplace. He was angry yet unable to mobilize his aggression, resulting in a severe depression. Regarding the bombing, he rarely brought it up. He said he got through it by being helpful to those employees who survived. He stated he felt angry towards survivors who were not returning to work after a few months, or who were "taking advantage of the government and not returning to work."

This experience, too, left me with a nagging sense of failure that we were not dealing with issues related to the bombing. Many months later, after termination, I began to understand that avoidance and displacement were used as a necessary protection against the onslaught of overwhelming grief, helplessness and survivor guilt that may have lurked inside. When he began to mobilize his anger regarding the demotion and decided to fight back, his depression lifted. He filed a lawsuit, won, and decided to retire from his career. He left a much happier man who felt empowered and vindicated. I now believe we were doing bombing-related work indirectly.

In reading papers written by other professionals at the local university hospital who treated survivors, I found confirmation of my suspicions and answers to nagging questions. Dr. Jim Allen and his colleagues (1999) in their paper on avoidance in trauma described my own clinical experience accurately. What was expected to be an onslaught of requests for long-term psychiatric care in actuality turned out to be parents and children scheduling appointments, then canceling or not showing up at all. Of the children and parents who did come, most were unwilling to speak of their losses, the bombing or the aftereffects. Dr. Allen's group concluded that avoidance was the primary coping strategy used by these children and their families. Family members turned to each other for support, oftentimes viewing mental health providers as unwelcome outsiders. Some survivors only found comfort in receiving support from other survivors and felt that no one else could understand their devastating internal experience. Henry Krystal (1978) speaks to this issue when he writes about "counterfeit nurturance."

I learned a great deal from my work with bombing survivors, but not what I had thought I would learn. It would be several years before I would completely understand that I had entered my work with survivors with fixed ideas on what would help and what these patients would need. Working with victims of terrorism creates an extremely complicated space between patient and therapist. When therapists have also experienced the reign of terror, we unknowingly lose a degree of objectivity more readily when our own experience is untouched by the atrocity. Displacement is a common defense mechanism needed to cope with the unbearable reality. We learned that brief therapy will more frequently be chosen than long-term therapy.

Patient #4, Dorothy, was also a Red Cross referral. I was contacted about Dorothy in August, 2002, 6 ½ years post bombing. Her two year old grandson, Michael, who was in the day care center of the Federal Building, perished in the blast. Having functioned as the boy's mother since his birth, Dorothy regarded herself as his mother. I was Dorothy's fifth therapist since the bombing. I saw her only five visits, two being telephone sessions when she couldn't get out of bed to come. There was one visit after 9/11 and after that I never saw her again.

After the bombing, Dorothy could not return to her job one block from the Federal Building. After 16 months of leave, she was terminated from her employment after 20 years. In the first session, she spoke hesitantly, looked scared and intimidated, and complained of her many physical ailments. At 53, she had a serious heart condition, thyroid disease, migraines and high blood pressure. She was on a multitude of medications. Her memory, she claimed, was terrible since the ordeal and she was very forgetful and chronically tired. She described several years of uncontrollable angry outbursts, only mediated by heavy doses of medication. She described the "day from hell" in the following terms: Chaos and mass confusion after the explosion as people began running toward the building, screaming for their children and loved ones. She remembers little, but stated that she would never forget the thick black smoke and putrid smell filling the air. As she wandered aimlessly, a volunteer guided her to the makeshift compassion center to await news of her grandson. It would be four days before the remains of his body would be recovered.

One of the most disturbing aspects of the experience of losing Michael was having no body to bury. Most mothers and grandmothers were advised not to view the remains of the bodies or read the medical examiner's report. All wished they had not received this information. Since the condition of many of the bodies was so poor, mothers were denied the important ritual of dressing the body for funeral.

The story of Dorothy is tragically sad. She told me in the first session that she would never get over this. I believe for her that is true. Caring for another grandson, faith in God and an ongoing trusting relationship with her primary physician seemed to be the strongest stabilizing factors in her life since the bombing. She lived a very isolated life, trying each day not to be overwhelmed by the experience of living. The attack on 9/11 was a terrible blow to an already fragile person. I saw her only once after 9/11 and she could hardly speak. Her main concern was for a particular New York firefighter who had come to Oklahoma City after the bombing and who had been extremely kind to survivors. She could hardly tolerate the possibility that he had died in 9/11.

Seven years later, the people of Oklahoma City continue to feel the effects and bear the scars of the bombing. 9/11 rekindled fears, memories, and stirred great compassion for a city affected so much more intensely than ours. Many people directly involved remain affected, forever changed. The "Dorothys" of the world continue struggling to live each day and not be overwhelmed by ordinary life. Many individuals have moved on, finding strength to rebuild their lives and live as fully as possible.

Anne Early

Due to the limited space, the focus will be on the clinical process that took place in the play therapy of a three and a half year old boy named Jimmy. On April 19, 1995, Timothy McVeigh bombed the A. P. Murrah Federal Building in Oklahoma City. Jimmy was across the street in daycare. He was two and a half years old at the time of the bombing. Jimmy's back, neck and the sides of his face were peppered with tiny dagger-like knives of glass; fortunately his eyes were left untouched. He was left with no physical abnormalities, but the emotional scarring was deep.

His parents sought treatment for him after the first anniversary of the bombing. Jimmy's symptoms included periods of time when he dissociated to being a dog. At night he had difficulty sleeping because of nightmares. He had regressed in his toilet habits and his behavior had become more aggressive. Since the bombing, Jimmy's attempts at bedtime to provide himself with the safe and comforting internal representations of his parents, was no longer possible. His mother reported that the only way Jimmy could sleep was to make himself a cocoon-like bed of mattresses, pillows and blankets in the middle of the room on the floor (away from all the windows). In a way, Jimmy was creating a boundary that had been blown apart by the bombing. He wrapped himself up in a sheet and wiggled in between the pillows and blankets to form a protective skin-like covering. His parents took turns lying down with him until he fell asleep.

Jimmy shared his experience of one of his nightmares. "It's too boring being Jimmy. I don't want to be Jimmy. Jimmy is four years old and he is scared of the dark. Joey [his friend] isn't. Jimmy sees monsters that are made out of dark. The monsters eat kids for dinner. I almost got bit by a shark at Pete's castle [a play area at the day care center he attended]. The monsters are invisible. Joey can take care of the monsters. My daddy can do anything but get the monsters to stop." The monsters had become part of his self experience (Boulanger, 2002).

I decided to include Jimmy's parents in his play therapy sessions for the following reasons. Both Jimmy and his parents were having a difficult time being separated from each other, so I thought that being together would give Jimmy and his parents a feeling of safety. By watching the play therapy unfold, the parents would learn to interact with their son in ways consistent with what was occurring in the play therapy. With the parents in the room, I would have immediate access to the history of the events that occurred with Jimmy on the day of the bombing. I thought the history would help me to assist Jimmy in integrating and resolving his unbearable experience.

The following session was the last time I worked with Jimmy. Jimmy began the session at the sand table with a male doll and a big plastic bug he had brought from home. He buried the male doll in the sand. Jimmy said, "He got killed. Somebody powed him." He asked me to help cover the doll with sand, and I did. Then Jimmy decided to get some farm animals out and made a barnyard scene with the animals and placed a fence on top of the man he had buried under the sand. Jimmy said, "These animals are hungry, they are looking for something to eat under the snow." Jimmy exploded the man out of the sand in a tumultuous fashion and everything was in disarray.

I said, "It looks like there has been an explosion." Jimmy said, "Yeah." Jimmy proceeded to put a noose around the man doll's head and hooked the doll on to the back of the trailer and pulled it off of the sand table and left the doll dangling by its neck. Jimmy laughed, and with that he let go of the doll and the tractor and they both fell to the ground. Jimmy went over to the animals and picked up a pig and said, "This pig is going potty." He picked up several animals and repeated that they were going potty. Jimmy strolled over to the dollhouse and selected a toilet from the house and brought it back to the sand table. He retrieved the man doll from the floor and sat the doll on the toilet and said, "There is a bug on the potty." He put the doll down and left the sand table. He walked over to some shelves and chose a baby bottle and put it in his mouth to suckle. He crawled to his mother and she picked him up and cradled him in her arms. She rocked him and pretended to feed him and said to Jimmy, "This is how I used to feed you when you were a baby." She burped him and he delighted in expressing a generous burping sound. After he finished pretending to burp he continued crawling around the room. He seemed to enjoy pretending to be a baby. I said to Jimmy, "When you were a baby, you felt safe and your parents took care of you and fed you. It seems like you are having fun pretending to be a baby today." Jimmy smiled at me and said, "Yeah." He crawled a little longer then placed the bottle back on the shelf. It was important for Jimmy to feel safe so he could risk the re-enactment (Greenberg, 1991).

Jimmy then retrieved the doll from the sand table and took him over to the doll house and placed the doll on top of the chimney. He pushed the doll off of the house and said, "This man is hurt." Next, he built a structure with blocks next to the doll house; he knocked it down and said, "This building is exploded." Jimmy picked up the doll and took it to the hospital. He got some Kleenex and wrapped the man in a Kleenex blanket. Jimmy said, "He is cut all over and he is bleeding." I handed Jimmy a red magic marker (Gaensbauer, 1995) and he made dots of blood all over the Kleenex blanket.

Jimmy said, "He is bleeding." I said, this is what happened to you when you were at the doctors—you were bleeding and they wrapped you in a sheet." Jimmy replied, "Yeah, he's hurt." He found the doctor's bag and took out a stethoscope and pretended to listen to the doll's heart. His mother said, "Thump-tha-thump," making heart sounds and Jimmy laughed. Jimmy picked up the red magic marker again and made more dots on the Kleenex sheet. I said, "This sheet must have looked like the sheet they wrapped you in after the bombing." Jimmy said, "Yeah, he needs a shot." Taking my cue his mother followed by saying, "Jimmy had to have a shot and he was brave when they gave him the shot." Jimmy smiled at his mother and listened to the doll's heart. By now, his affect had changed and he was tenderly nurturing his patient. Jimmy said in a somewhat repetitive and blunted voice (Terr, 1994), "This man's face is cut, this man's legs are cut and his feet are hurt. He has something in his ear." Jimmy got the tweezers and pretended to pull something out of the doll's ears. Jimmy's mother said, "Jimmy had to have something pulled out of his ear."

Jimmy replied, "Yeah." Then Jimmy responded, "Oh it hurts, I'm hurt." He picked up the doll and carefully wrapped it again in a Kleenex sheet. He pretended to give the doll another injection, and then, another. This continued for some time until he said, "I'm well."

Jimmy placed the man doll on the roof of the dollhouse and knocked him off again. Then he took the doll over to the exploded building and buried the doll in the rubble. Jimmy said, "I can't get out." Finally, he helped the doll out of the debris. He took the doll back to the doctor and the doctor fixed the doll again then took the doll over to the dollhouse to rest. Jimmy said, "I worry about my Daddy because I'm afraid his building will explode and my Daddy will get hurt." I responded by saying, "Your Daddy drives a van and is not in a building. You don't want anything to happen to your Daddy." The session was over.

Jimmy's father was working as a dispatcher. The jeeps and tanks in Jimmy's play, the van his father drove, and Timothy McVeigh's Ryder truck may unconsciously represent Jimmy's fantasy of blowing up what was blown up inside of them. Jimmy's father had been unable to reach him after the bombing, whereas Jimmy's mother had gotten to Jimmy shortly after the bombing. His father had a very difficult time because he thought Jimmy had been killed.

Part of Jimmy's de-structuring experience was his own regression, which involved learning how to regulate and control his feces. The toilet training added another complication in working through the trauma of the bombing. It possibly left him feeling like there was something internally destructive inside that was not only represented by the monstrous images that haunted him at night, but also, by destructive feces that made plop sounds. The plop sound may have been similar to the "pow" word he used to describe killing a GI Joe action figure in the repetitive play he had been involved in throughout his treatment.

Jimmy had identified with the role of the aggressor in order to control the aggressive monsters from within. He bombed and destroyed things during play in an attempt to make his world a safer place. When Jimmy did not feel safe, he utilized the process of dissociation (Bromberg, 1994) to disavow his fear of being eaten by the monster bomb.

In play therapy and at home, he re-enacted the trauma through sensorial (feeling) memories. In this last session he added another dimension to his past play sessions. In this session, he was able to bring together the split between the good doctor/healer and the bad destroyer/ bomber (Mahler, 1972b). It seemed like he was able to integrate these opposing sides and his identification had enlarged to include himself as a healer. The negative side of this organization was the turning passive into active because it left him feeling omnipotent, powerful and in control.

His mother played a crucial role: her ability to be with Jimmy when he re-enacted the trauma of the bombing helped him to realize both she and I could tolerate his fears and destructive urges. I believe we acted as stimulus barriers to regulate and prevent further trauma as he revisited through play the devastation of his sense of safety, the shattering of his attachment to those he loved and the de-structuralization of his inner self. His mother and I put into words what had happened to him as he showed us through play.

In play, Jimmy directed a doll through the rubble of the explosion as his mother had done with him. In play he pretended to take the doll for medical treatment, as his mother had done for Jimmy. During play, Jimmy talked about the doll and his wounds. Several times during the re-enactment Jimmy referred to himself as he began to connect his feelings to the events he had the doll portray. He transferred his feelings from the doll to himself and ended the play with the comment, "I'm well."

The verdict is out for the long-term results. Jimmy is at risk developmentally to continue his fears in sublimated ways as described by Henry Krystal (1978), John Bowlby (1980), and more recently by Ghislaine Boulanger (2002) who suggests that, "in childhood trauma becomes part of the self experience."

In conclusion, we learned that patients' and parents' expectations of what is entailed in a therapeutic process is dramatically different than the therapists'/analysts'. In every case, the therapy ended abruptly. In the case of Jimmy, I believe his parents were waiting for the re-enactment. When that occurred the therapy was over. It appeared to me that the need on the part of the parents was for a brief, short term, focused re-enactment of the trauma, whereas as a therapist, I wanted to work through the trauma toward stabilization and a reintegration of what had been shattered. I can only hope, as Donald Winnicott (1965) has said, that my work with Jimmy was "good enough."

REFERENCES

Allen, J., Whittlesey, S., Pfefferbaum, B., Ondersma, M. (1999 February). Community and coping of mothers and grandmothers of children killed in a human-caused disaster. *Psychiatric Annals 29, 2.*

Allen, J. and Allen, B. (1998 July). Transactional analysis notes from Oklahoma City: After the bombing *Transactional Analysis Journal 28, 3.*

Allen, S., Dlugokinski, E., Cohen, L., Walker, J. (1999 February). Assessing the impact of a traumatic community event on children and assisting with their healing. *Psychiatric Annals 29, 2.*

Bowlby, John. (1980). *Attachment and loss. Vol. III* New York: Basic Books.

Boulanger, G. (2002). Wounded by reality: The collapse of the self in adult onset trauma. *Contemporary Psychoanalysis 38, 1.*

Bromberg, Phillip M. (1994). Speak! that I may see you. Some reflections on dissociation, reality and psychoanalytic listening. *Psychoanalytic Dialogues. 4, 4.*

Gaensbauer, Theodore J. (1995). Therapeutic approaches to posttraumatic stress disorder in infants and toddlers. *Infant Mental Health Journal 16, 4.*

Greenberg, Jay R. (1991). *Oedipus and beyond: A clinical theory.* Cambridge/London: Harvard University Press.

Krystal, Henry (1978). Trauma and affects. *Psychoanalytic Study of the Child, 33.*

Mahler, M.S. (1972b). Rapproachment subphase of the separation individuation process. *Psychoanalytic Quarterly 41.*

Terr, L. (1994). *Unchained memories. True stories of traumatic memories lost and found.* New York: Basic Books.

Tucker, P., Pfefferbaum, B., Nixon, S., Foy, D. (1999 February). Trauma and recovery among adults exposed to a community disaster. *Psychiatric Annals 29,* 2.

Whittlesey, S., Allen, J., Bell, B., Lindsey, E., Speed, L., Lucas, A., Ware, M., Allen, S., Pfefferbaum, B. (1999). Avoidance in trauma: conscious and unconscious defense, pathology and health. *Psychiatry 62,* 1.

Winnicott, D. (1965). *Maturational processes and the facilitating environment.* New York: International Universities Press.

Thinking Analytically About the Unthinkable: Framing Crisis Management in a Psychoanalytic Paradigm with Special Emphasis on "Debriefing" and the Importance of "Forbidden" Affect

ABBY ADAMS-SILVAN

THE AIM OF THIS WORKSHOP WAS TO EXPLORE the possibility that reactions to terrorism and terrorist events can be understood—at least in some significant part—within the framework of psychoanalytic theory and psychoanalytically informed practice. Thinking in this professional mode may help clinicians to maintain their unique identity and to offer their special services in times that in the past we would have thought unthinkable.

That is, we would hope in times of realistic stress or tragedy to think in terms not only of a fundamental conscious empathic response that characterizes many important human interactions, but also to retain a clear conviction of our particular and unique approach to understanding human behavior and dynamics under any conditions. It is in the latter mode, essentially the maintenance of our specific professional identity while meeting the needs of crisis management, that we may function most productively and to our own greatest satisfaction. It is to those ends that the following issues are suggested for thought and discussion.

The practical significance of a strong internal maintenance of our professional identity would affect a number of aspects of response to such events. Of these, three seem primary: (1) immediate clinical services; (2) subsequent clinical services related to what has been diagnostically categorized as PTSD; and (3) the nature and technique of meeting the therapeutic needs of the caregivers ("debriefing").

I Immediate Clinical Services

With reference to immediate clinical services, it is generally understood and accepted that crisis management requires different skills than those in which the psychoanalyst has been trained. Is this, however, accurate? Is it not, in fact, possible that most of these skills are already fundamental to the analytic armamentarium? If not, where and how do they differ; if so, how might it be most useful to find their application? Can we formulate these differences and equivalents in terms of our theoretical model?

For example, crisis management stresses "normalization" of functionally disruptive psychological reactions; we help the patient to understand that she is experiencing a normal reaction to an abnormal experience. Is this not a clinical application of the reality principle that can be likened to distinguishing between grief and depression, or anxiety and fear? In structural terms we would conceptualize this as strengthening the ego in the face of extra pressure exerted on the id by events outside the self that tend to lower superego controls and exert a regressive pull on ego defenses.

It is also true that crisis management stresses ventilation and catharsis which requires the therapist to use careful and very, very patient listening skills. The crucial importance of these skills may, in fact, always be in need of re-emphasis in the consulting room.

While crisis management certainly emphasizes the importance of avoiding personal over-involvement, is it perhaps especially helpful in particularly tragic circumstances to be able to think psychodynamically about the reasons for limiting identification with the sufferer beyond what may be necessary to achieve the necessary empathy. This might be formulated as allowing a clear adult/protector object transference (not a narcissistic one). This in turn allows the worker to serve as an identificatory object in the maintenance of ego control and in the optimal function of superego controls.

II Subsequent Clinical Services

As we know, many of those who had particularly strong reactions to the potential trauma of 9/11(albeit sometimes defended against by various defense mechanisms such as denial) have found themselves unable subsequently to work through, process, and/or erect effective and positive defenses. Generally speaking they develop the symptoms of PTSD, and when they present themselves for treatment it is in the belief that their suffering is caused only by the traumatic events which they have recently experienced.

Psychoanalytic theory and experience, however, suggest strongly that an event suffered in adult life cannot of itself and in isolation from earlier (usually childhood) events truly function as a trauma. While the behavioral manifestations of a true trauma usually do not manifest themselves until adolescence, nevertheless very often the event or events (cumulative trauma) probably were suffered early and in the relative absence of effective internal or external defensive measures.

In that context the question arises as to whether the diagnosis of PTSD is actually a useful one, or whether the syndrome would better be considered as a particular symptomatic picture that has emerged in response to a situation rearousing or exacerbating already existing neurotic and /or character traits. If so, it is important to consider how the initial emergency treatment stance and the subsequent dynamic exploration may be oriented.

A particularly salient question arises regarding the guilt resulting from conscious or unconscious pleasure and/or narcissistic gratification inherent in traumatic situations. Such pleasures arise from bonding, a sense of superiority, having "escaped" at someone else's expense (which would be associated with death wishes towards another: "better him than me") etc. PTSD seems often to be associated not only with fear, but with conflict around pleasurable components.

III Meeting the Therapeutic Needs of the Caregivers

Psychoanalytic theory posits that all human beings sustain—consciously, preconsciously or unconsciously—forbidden wishes. Many emotional disturbances are thought to be related in significant part to the unresolved conflict and subsequent guilt arising from those wishes. The wishes are strong and push for satisfaction, but their gratification is usually indirect, involves inappropriate defenses and may be said almost always to provide a combination of disguised fulfillment and punishment, which is pathogenic. All this is manifested either in symptoms or characterological problems. When by one means or another the conflict has been resolved, sublimation has ordinarily become the dominant successful defense.

Psychoanalysts and other "healers" are usually said to have accomplished the task of sublimating destructive or other normal but negative impulses into their professional activities. Perhaps their participation as workers able to be active in the process of helping others who have been trapped in a passive stance may function to stimulate unconscious pleasure in those who have been able to function as caregivers where activity is the preferred mode. Other pleasures, such as those mentioned above with respect to the patients may also function, in addition to such narcissistic gratifications as a sense of superiority, exhibitionism, etc.

If we accept this hypothesis, even in part, then it will be important to discuss in debriefing sessions, as well as to give an opportunity to ventilate and share the more "acceptable" emotions evoked by the experience of working with those who are in one way or another victims. It is also important in working either with both survivors and/or caregivers to remember that the defense mechanism of identification with the aggressor may lead to considerable guilt.

Group Discussion

Although limited by time, the group discussion ranged over the issues suggested, leading to the overall impression that indeed maintaining one's professional identity, rather than "re-specializing" as a crisis manager, was critically important to a sense of effectiveness. Re-casting dominant experiences into a psychodynamic frame is very important.

Some specific clinical issues were addressed as well. One participant spoke strongly to the point that even though a crisis may stimulate unconscious conflicts and drive states, one must put the pathogenic importance of failure by the patient to deal with reality first. He suggested that the patient be helped to assess the traumatic threat, and having done so, to articulate what specific changes he/she would like to make in his/her own life. Then the clinical task is to evaluate if the patient is behaving appropriately to his own level of threat assessment and to explore emerging contradictions. The neurotic mechanism is the failure of the patient to deal with reality, and this is more important than exploring conflicted drive states. For example, if a patient worries intensely and chronically about another attack, and still maintains that such an attack will not occur, this is the neurotic failure to deal with reality.

A participant from Israel noted that Israeli government officials are more available to discuss psychological issues, and that some are even directly involved in the analytic community, attending meetings and workshops. This accessibility makes it easier to convey professional opinions about terrorism, trauma, and so forth to the policy makers, and therefore less frustrating to the professionals. Another participant who has a personal connection to a United States official noted that for her the problem is not so much gaining access, but what actually can be said that might be definitive and helpful.

The group felt that a number of salient issues had been brought up, and hoped to continue thinking about them within the analytic frame.

Terrorism Comes to the Analytic Consulting Room: Methods and Techniques of Coping Based on Diagnostic Assessments

MARIA BERGMANN

BEFORE THE EVENTS OF SEPTEMBER 11, A TRAUMATIC reliving in transference would have been linked only to a patient's own traumatic events from the past. The attack of September 11 was traumatic by creating a social trauma; the sudden onslaught and experience of destructiveness shared by everyone, and its violence mutilated America's self-image as an invulnerable world power; it created a hitherto unknown feeling of vulnerability and a personal sense of insecurity in its population. As is well known, an unexpected terrorist attack, by virtue of the uncertainty of its potential repetitiveness, creates an additional powerful psychological weapon against its victims and constitutes a social trauma.

When Freud discovered the impact of trauma on psychic structure and development, he had only personal trauma in mind. Freud had thought that libido and aggression were in balance. In psychoanalytic work, we have been used to dealing only with internal psychic conflicts and personal traumata even if they contained social traumata of major proportions. We have been used to establishing connections between past and current internal conflicts: psychoanalysis connects issues that were previously separated. A trauma disrupts these connections and isolates psychic continuity; it makes "false connections." The social trauma of September 11, shared by both analyst and patient, created a new social and psychic reality and a need for different psychological techniques to modulate anxiety and enhance coping mechanisms within each person.

Under the impact of the present danger of a terrorist attack, we face a new psychoanalytic situation: our focus needs to address first the patient's capacity to function in the present and in current relationships—work or any other capacity, where psychic cohesion has been impaired as a result of the current crisis. Once the conscious self is re-involved in reality-oriented thought and action, anxiety diminishes and appropriate self protection becomes possible again. Differentiating between realistic fear related to current traumatizing external events versus reliving of past traumata with attendant anxiety then becomes possible. Otherwise, earlier traumata that have persevered surface again and burden current experiences. This is likely to be the case, because traumata have a quality of repetitiveness that tend to fuse previously experienced traumatizing states with present dangers.

A fear of dangers related to the current social reality may become fused with personal traumatic reactions from the past and not be differentiated when re-experiencing pain that actually stems from the past. As an analyst cannot protect the patient from current social danger, or from reliving traumatic reactions (which may have occurred with a parent who did not protect the child, and which may be relived in the analytic situation), the patient may feel unprotected now by the analyst in mastering *external* dangers.

When differentiation between past and present and between internal and external dangers cannot be kept apart affectively and cognitively, a crisis may occur in the analytic situation. Narcissistic hurt may attach itself to a current traumatic feeling-state, and produce anger and a feeling of having been left helpless and unprotected. This may be experienced by the patient in transference and expressed in various affective ways: silence, anger, or in a general state of feeling wanting, and in need of comfort. In order to diminish suffering and avoid a massive negative therapeutic reaction and lack of trust, the specific fantasy content and meaning of retraumatization in treatment is critical. By retraumatization, I understand that a previous trauma is being relived in a new form, not just as an experience of reliving, but with the affect of anxiety and shock of a new trauma. The experiences of September 11 created a new trauma, but for many it revived old traumata as well, and thereby fusion of past and present comprised an experience of retraumatization.

September 11 and the Holocaust have taught us how sudden massive destructiveness can temporarily wipe out or mute a belief in one's own libidinal capacities and those of others. Since the Holocaust we have been aware that a massive onslaught that is traumatic may lead to a denial or numbing of affect or to excessive affective overstimulation, which may be discharged by acting out, by performing symbolic acts that have unconscious meaning and aid in discharging affect. Feelings of personal helplessness may cause narcissistic rage and not be differentiated from past dangers. After Holocaust survivors became patients, psychoanalysts learned to assist in coping with social trauma. When Holocaust trauma was related in analysis either as having happened to parents, grandparents, or to patients as small children, these could be worked with as traumatic impacts that affected a person's personal past which could be linked to a reliving in the present.

For many, particularly persons with traumatic Holocaust or other past experiences of persecution, anxiety became overwhelming and there was no sense of social communality. Such persons do not feel better when an opportunity is presented to help others, because their anxiety is not connected to the realistic fears of a new social reality, but primarily to internal private traumata from the past. When retraumatization occurs, it isolates the person from a sense of sharing. Distress and anxiety have to be discharged, but no comfort can reach the person under the impact of reliving trauma or phobic anxieties. When private trauma is understood, social trauma remains. In the current situation, awareness of the unknown and living with it are not liberating: a real danger shared by everyone cannot be diminished. An unforeseen attack of terrorism is shared by patient and analyst alike. Such an event creates a psychoanalytic situation in which we are as helpless and as frightened as our patients.

When we can admit that we are as affected by the current trauma as are our patients, it becomes more acceptable for them to express fantasies of destruction and socially unacceptable affects, which may have been unleashed by witnessing massive public destructiveness: such an admission on the part of the analyst may act as a permission for the patient to express feelings and fantasies of a forbidden nature.

Witnessing massive destructiveness in the outside world reawakens unconscious hostile conflicts and attendant pain, rage, and anxiety, which then becomes attached to current experiences and invades personal, private relationships with hostility.

We have known from clinical work that witnessing a terrorist attack may unleash socially unacceptable affects, which have previously been repressed, and wishes to be destructive. The violence of the current trauma may cause regression and undo psychic integration, allowing the emergence of socially unacceptable affects and unconscious hostile fantasies of massive destructiveness. When these unacceptable fantasies are expressed in a civilized society, they create an internal pressure on the psychic capacities of individuals who are socially at odds with societal safety. Feelings of anxiety or potentially self-destructive or destructive acts may surface and create social fears in those who do not share in socially sanctioned wishes and aims.

Once the dangers of our current external reality have been acknowledged in the analytic setting, it will become easier for a patient to deal with personal anxieties and frightening fantasies: both analyst and patient have faced together that internal psychic conflicts coexist with external pressures that have created a new social reality. When, in one analytic situation, I helped a patient separate her private trauma from the current social trauma, she said: "The way you put it is sobering rather than reassuring, but it is true."

There are some experiences that immediately evoke themes from past conflicts, particularly in patients who have grown up with parents who were not protective and could not be trusted to shield a child from danger or even prevent its occurrence when this would have been possible. Such memories are likely to awaken anxieties and retraumatization from the past. These memories become amalgamated with burdens imposed upon the current life situation and its uncertainties.

Until September 11, we had not been called upon to assist patients to differentiate current personal fears from phobic anxieties, which originated not only in internal psychic conflicts related to the personal past, but also in a social fear which was shared by everyone. In the atmosphere of the current shared social uncertainty, this task has become more difficult, particularly for people who have been unable to master traumatic dangers in their past. Such persons are likely to fuse past unmastered and current traumatic themes. Such fusion creates states of retraumatization. A patient's emergency responses, initiated by September 11, may initially be differentiated from genetic reconstructions of traumata. The meaning of previously internalized events and symptoms as the result of traumatic experiences from the past may eventually become integrated and shed light on the manner in which the terror of September 11 was experienced. As a rule unconscious meanings are not immediately apparent.

Re-establishing the capacity to experience an anxiety signal with the help of treatment and to anticipate danger, which may have been lost during a sudden traumatic onslaught, facilitates establishing some of the groundwork for being able to treat people who have been traumatized in the past and are now being retraumatized. Understanding the difference between reliving a past trauma with affective memory, or being retraumatized by it, is an important differentiation.

It has been a recurrent experience in analytic work to witness how the attack on the World Trade Center and its aftermath have led many patients in treatment back to core traumatic experiences from earlier life, and even traumatic experiences remembered currently for the first time. Once a differentiation between the current social reality and a personal traumatic experience have been accepted and internalized, many patients experience resurfacing of early memories and freedom to discuss core traumatic experiences from childhood that can now be remembered. Most patients linked the physical, social, and psychological attack of September 11 to traumata in their own childhood.

September 11 created a new American social trauma by which patients and analysts were equally affected. The interaction between public trauma and personal traumatic events, and how to keep both in focus, presents a linkage that calls for help with mastery and management of anxiety in the face of massive external destructiveness, which constitute new challenges to therapeutic technique.

I have found that new coping strategies for management of anxiety vis-à-vis massive destructiveness in the *external* world are needed. It helps in many instances if the analyst asserts that the current traumatic reaction to terrorism is shared by both patient and analyst.

I believe it is necessary to develop totally new techniques of helping with the current social situation that has never before occurred in just this way on American soil. Psychoanalytic technique can assist in separating reliving anxiety of traumatic internal dangers from fears arising as a reaction to the current external world. When this differentiation is made, analytic strategies of helping with acute internal anxieties are possible, but helping with the external situation is necessarily very limited or impossible in a terrorist attack.

The totally unexpected aspect of this attack created a new trauma. On the other hand, for many, it represented aspects of retraumatization, which became amalgamated with new events. For some, it brought about a lifting of repression and an experiencing of the affect of anxiety and horror about events in the external world for the first time. For others, it was a completely new experience, which was not linked to the past. The aura of certainty is gone not only from American soil, but also from the analytic situation which hitherto remained related to internal anxieties caused by internal conflict only.

From the Loss of the Leader to the Leader of the Lost: The Patient Escorts the Therapist on a Guided Tour of Hell

K. WILLIAM FRIED

DR. WILLIAM FRIED PRESENTED A WORKSHOP ENTITLED, "From the Loss of the Leader to the Leader of the Lost." The title was predictive of what would follow—a perceptive, intriguing presentation of considerable depth. In retrospect, I now see that it was a summary of horrible, unbelievable, terrifying events which he would be describing. I have not forgotten a detail of what he told us.

His presentation can be divided into pre-9/11, the events of 9/11, and some brief comments about post-9/11. The patient he described is a thirty-year old, single college graduate who is an emergency medical technician. He is the youngest of three sons in an Italian family. They have lived in this country for over forty years but are very tied to the mores and behavior of the old country. This man sought treatment four and a half months before these events because he was concerned about his anxiety, distractibility, forgetfulness, and that he was not accomplishing what he wanted in life. The family did not approve of his seeking treatment.

Seven years previously, his older brother, whom he admired but for whom he also felt bitterness, came out of a local club when a woman unknown to him asked for help starting her car. While he was examining the engine, a mugger appeared, accosted the woman, and the brother was murdered in his attempt to protect this woman. She refused to testify at the court hearing. Ever since that time, the family has visited the gravesite weekly.

On September 11, the patient was asked to report to work and was told to accompany a number of firemen whose task it was to find victims and bring them to safety. The group was extremely cautious and palpably anxious. They took the elevator to the nineteenth floor, where they sensed impending danger and decided to leave. The patient was first in line and reached for the doorknob as the floor below them crumbled. Fifteen of the twenty-two fell to their death. If the patient had not had his hand on the doorknob he never could have found it because of the mass of debris. The remainder of the group went to the eighth floor because one man thought there was a ballroom there. Upon arrival, this floor collapsed, and the patient balled up in a fetal position near a doorway. Heavy drapes fell on him and he survived. When he stood up, he was all alone. When he reached the third floor he surmised that all the floors were collapsing in sequence so he let himself fall from a collapsing balustrade. He had immediate pain in his back, neck and legs. Smoke and dust prevented visibility. In the dimness of it all, he came close to another EMT person who said that he could not help because no one knew where to go or what to do. Eventually he saw a red flashing light of an emergency vehicle which helped him get out of the area. He saw a fire chief surrounded by men to whom he was giving work assignments. The patient warned him of the danger in the spot where they were standing. The chief waved him away dismissively, and the patient walked on. He had gone about fifty yards, when a gas main split open and ignited. They were all killed immediately.

The patient was taken to St. Vincent's Hospital and was discharged the next day. Physically he had ruptured two spinal discs. He disavowed his hero status and would not allow himself to be bribed by reporters to give his story. When he returned to treatment he told his story in a very matter of fact manner.

Prior to 9/11, the treatment focussed on the ways in which the patient's unconscious identification with his brother—the eponymous "Lost Leader"—had made it almost impossible for him to transcend the rigid, stultifying limits of his current and historical family. One discovery was that there was a distinct and highly significant difference between his idealized picture of the brother, on the one hand, and the impression that emerged from a closer examination of the brother's actual behavior, on the other. Although the brother had been a dutiful son, he had also defied his parents' wishes by purchasing an apartment and living there, unmarried, with a woman. So gross had his distortion been of his brother, that he had been unable to recognize even the quite obvious contradictions just described.

Another theme early in his treatment was a dramatic change in his personality that had occurred at about the age of 11, when his father had suffered what he termed "a massive coronary." Before this event, he had been something of a neighborhood celebrity, as a brash, tough, "show-off" who was a leader among his friends and had excelled in sports. After his father's attack, he became introverted, shy, cautious, and critical of anyone resembling his former self. The Oedipal guilt that contributed to this transformation was analyzed to the degree possible in therapy as opposed to analysis.

Subsequent to 9/11, there was a period of several weeks in which the therapeutic work involved rehearsal of the traumatic events in which he'd participated, but this period ended relatively quickly and successfully. He then expressed a great deal of bitterness about those of his colleagues who seemed to exploit the tragic events for their own profit. This attitude was extended to politicians, the press and the City administration. Gradually, the therapy sessions resumed their pre-9/11 character, with more emphasis on problems in his intimate relationships and his efforts to separate from his family. At termination, he was involved with a suitable, supportive woman and thinking seriously of changing his career. In some sense, his pre-9/11 treatment may be regarded as a sort of innoculation that allowed him to handle the later trauma more resourcefully.

Dr. Fried feels that the major trauma of this patient's life remains the murder of his brother. The fact that the patient was currently in treatment when the horrors of September 11 occurred has been of immeasurable help to the patient in coping with the traumas he has endured, past and present.

Discussion in this workshop was lively and drew upon other traumas, like Oklahoma, as well as alternate theories to approach the treatment process for victims. We were appreciative of Dr. Fried's sharing this meaningful but painful experience.

Marginalized Groups: Challenges to Healthy Identity

*GILEAD NACHMANI

TERRORISM IS HORRIFIC AND STARTLING, BUT IT IS not a strange state of affairs. Its elements are knowable and reproducible and these elements are not new. People can be educated to terrorize. Terrorism and religious fundamentalisms are also not recent. What is new is the capacity for mass destruction of a non-warring, non-combatant *civilian* population by means of weapons of mass destruction. Terrorism is a type of warfare directed at civilians not armies. Throughout history, however, warring armies have attacked civilians, and this constitutes terrorism.

Terror is a state of mind in which both fear and anxiety are present without the possibility of being reduced or diminished by the self or by others. As a result, victims are helpless and continue to feel terrified. It is a state of being in which one cannot depend on others for safety or protection. Unconscious regressions into earlier more dependent modes of *external* relatedness fail, and as a result basic trust is betrayed, and panic and confusion result as well. In response to the loss of trust, further regression toward more primitive *inner* object relations occur. With this, experiences of paranoid anxieties and dread predominate. Terror eliminates psychoanalytic space, the claustrum. Even before injury or atrocity occur, it is the sudden helplessness that instills trauma. In terrorist acts, the trauma is deliberately caused by others for the purpose of killing, harming, and creating helplessness, shame, and humiliation. It is the inability to be assertive and self-protecting that causes the shame and humiliation. When fear cannot be reduced, the source of the fear remains present either in external reality or internal reality. Others are of no help in reducing the fear or taking away the danger. Fight, flight and delayed reactions to the danger do not work. With regard to internal reality, there is a progressive failure of defense where projective identification fails, causing even greater splitting into bizarre part objects. Magical thinking can then act as a fundamental organizing principle. There is no person in the victim's life who can introject and detoxify the persecutory dread and anxiety.

To intentionally create this state of mind in others, terrorists-to-be cannot think of their victims as fellow human beings for whom empathy and morality apply, but as inhuman or less-than-human, foreign, and as enemies against whom all violence is justified. For the terrorist, violence is worthy of reward by the moral authority of the group that sponsors the terrorism. Terrorism itself is not an ideology or political doctrine, but a *method*. It is justified by an ideology like a religious fundamentalism that has a type of primitive morality. In order for terror to occur, the terrorist must be created. How can this be done? In any culture there usually are individuals for whom violence comes with ease, and for whom empathy and concern for others exist marginally, if at all.

*From the presentation by Avram Bornstein, Elizabeth Hegeman, Gilead Nachmani, and Alan Grey

Paranoid experiences play a role in terrorism insofar as the justification for acts by terrorists lie in conspiracies by hostile groups against their group. There is an inclination to blame outsiders, not-us, or foreign enemies for the misery that they and their group suffer. Resentment and hatred emerge in families or cultures where there is a type of absence of social justice, where one group reaps rewards and another suffers deprivation, where poverty, crowding, hunger, and inadequate employment create social oppression, and, needless to say, where there is military oppression. This can be perceived as "protective environmental failures" to borrow a term from Winnicott. This refers to the child's expectation that parents protect, and that this function of parenting is called "the holding environment." It also refers to the near total dependency of young children on their parents, and the harm that they can suffer if their parents are not holding or protecting them. Children who are not protected from the dangers that only adults can protect them from, experience a premature sense of aloneness long before they are mature enough to know what to do with it. This is sometimes called *despair*. They experience dread and persecutory anxiety and their only means of addressing dread is with massive projective identification: They precariously locate the dread "outside" of themselves and feel persecuted by it. This leads to even more projective identification, and they feel emptied and despairing. Such children are vulnerable to feeling hatred, but confusion can obscure who the betrayer is. Usually it is a parental figure, but it can be toward parental surrogates like teachers, social institutions like a school or orphanages, or a government that cannot protect. While such hatred may be projected outward, this is precarious and a confusional state results. *A cynical agitator or agent knows how to take advantage of confusional states by being seductive, promising protection and false certainty.*

Vamik Volkan (1997) has studied religious fundamentalism and terrorism and has defined a protracted process from which an individual or small group can move from trauma to fundamentalist terrorism. I will briefly summarize and discuss his rich contribution.

Regression is a response to trauma. Unconsciously, one moves toward former dependency relationships, rallying behind a composite mother-father-leader who in some fashion promises to meet those dependency needs. In dealing with groups that are larger than families, we call them "leaders" not parents. The leader insists that an "us versus them" mentality accounts for the trauma: Enemies (they) caused the trauma. This bold distinction between "us and them," good and bad, friend and foe, establishes the crude but clear categories of a new morality that will be cultivated. This helps to displace helpless rage onto the foreigners (them). This is cunning. New external objects begin to become the foundation of a new superego under a new leader. In order for so bold a structural change to occur, replacing one older "bad" morality with a new "good" morality, magical thinking and the blurring of reality must occur and be taken advantage of by a leader. Given states of mind in which reality is blurred and magical thinking exists, where traumatized people are dependent and gullible, a revisionist history establishes the new "good" and new "evil" distinctions. This is cynical exploitation. Good and evil did not just occur in the mind of a group leader, but the leader cynically reveals or demonstrates pseudo-historical precedents. Past traumas and past glories are selected as the new narrative text.

156

Selecting a trauma is necessary. In choosing a trauma, a very critical message is conveyed: Something horrible happened to the group and the victims cannot mourn what happened and reverse the helplessness or change the humiliation. Forbidding mourning, generally by the stirring up of rage by an *agent provocateur,* insures that the new pseudo-history remains part of the group's mythology. As a result, feelings of humiliation and helplessness remain an intrusive part of the group's consciousness, and this is passed on to the next generation. The next generation then shares the same images of the event and these images become part of the group's identity: The transgenerational transmission of trauma. When this happens, symbols become fixed, and lose their ability to change for different shades of meaning. Multiple determinants of meaning cease to exist and rhetoric replaces meaning. This is instrumental in the creation of certain symbols which convey group identity, and which overtly distinguish the group from another group, such as a mode of dress like a uniform, or a particular slogan or greeting (e.g., *Sieg Heil!*). It provides a further touch of magical thinking to the group identity. Volkan calls this "border psychology" because it can literally mean a real physical border like a demarcation on a map such as a national boundary. It denotes where you are safe and where you are threatened. As such it can also be like the notion of psychological boundary.

This border psychology facilitates noting how different one group is from another. Minor differences assume great importance because it is a last ditch effort of protection. When a border psychology is established, basic trust within the family disappears. The "us" is the "in" group, led by the composite charismatic leader, and no longer the family of origin. Basic trust is founded in the early mother-child relationship. As such it is a bedrock of relatedness. A successful cynical leader knows that you cannot just destroy something without creating needs, and he will use political or religious ideology to replace what is destroyed. This is important, because morality comes from early relationships that become aspects of identity. A new identity is needed if the leader is to remain in control and not be in conflict with the original parents.

Furthermore, for a new identity and morality to exist, the pseudo-revisionist must blame the former generation as well as the outsiders who caused the traumas, helplessness, and humiliation. Who better to blame than the family. They represent the generation that failed to prepare and protect their children from trauma. An example can be found in the Nazi injunctions to children to spy on their parents for the security of the leader and the state. The destruction of basic trust creates instability such that there can be bold mood changes from a manic triumphant omnipotence to states of unrelenting persecutory anxiety. There appears to be a new history based on rhetoric not relatedness. In fact, relatedness will be blamed for the traumas and suffering. By discrediting and discarding relationships, the enemy ceases to be seen as people but as aspects of abject waste material—feces, urine, vomit, destroyed body parts. The symbolism that is projected onto the enemy becomes bodily waste material. You will not be killing a person if you murder your enemy. You will be killing excrement.

Groups that undergo such a malignant regression then become very preoccupied with blood. In part this has to do with blood as stain, and as female. Female is no longer mother, but waste, and blood is proof of it. When this occurs one cannot differentiate between what is beautiful (relatedness) and what is ugly (abject waste material). With the destruction of basic trust, there is a loss of the sense of simple beauty such as love. The apprehension of beauty and aesthetics are part of the formation of the superego. Destroying old values does not readily recreate love, and a state of mind is achieved where violent acts can be committed against family or the self. With so much contaminated, one needs to get involved in purification rituals that get rid of unwanted parts. These rituals concretely involve purifying the language such that certain words or phrases become unmentionable, or more violently, ethnic cleansing.

This condensed summary traces the progression from group trauma to hatred. It involves regression, identity reformation, and a social force that forbids grieving. Creativity and symbol formation are forbidden as well, and are replaced by rhetoric. It is a study of cynicism and violence where atrocity becomes justified by a new pseudo-morality.

REFERENCES

Volkan, V. (1997). *Blood lines: From ethnic pride to ethnic terrorism.* Boulder, Colorado: Westview Press.

The Aftermath of Survival: Effects on Survivors, Perpetrators, and the Next Generation

DEENA HARRIS

THIS WORKSHOP WAS GIVEN AS AN EXPERIENTIAL seminar, using the model described in this paper. The group told their stories after watching a fifty-minute video made by the BBC, "Children of the Third Reich."

The aftermath of any event refers to time, place, and conditions for those remaining. We are referring to the time from the acute period, to the first two weeks, to years and essentially the rest of one's life. Obviously, there are differences in how we treat the immediate phase after survival, the long term, chronic sequelae, and the issues that come up for the next generation; the intrapsychic conflicts and resolutions that are aroused by the trauma and effects on healing. The aftermath refers to future as well, how a group will consolidate a new identity around the trauma that has occurred. Usually, when we talk about this topic, we are talking about the victims. Little attention has been paid to the perpetrators and their motivation, behavior, and then equally as important, the transmission of their trauma to their subsequent generations. Every conflict involves two sides, whether it be intrapsychic, interpersonal, territorial, political, or, at the extreme, war. Terrorism is a subset of all of these—it is the manner in which a more desperate side decides to fight its battle. Terrorism goes beyond the conventional rules of warfare, meaning innocent civilians are at risk, the hurt inflicted is gratuitous, it is unpredictable, it is outside the realm of governments, and daily life is not allowed to proceed.

My work in this area began formally in 1992. I had, before then, been treating patients who were Holocaust survivors and children of survivors. Fortuitously, I was treating a German patient in analysis who was a child of a Nazi (I say child, yet he was now a grown man in his 50s.) Before then, I had not considered the legacy of the Holocaust for the perpetrators and their offspring.

Unfortunately, we have had too many opportunities throughout history to observe the effects of war, terrorism and oppression from the side of the victims and the persecutors. As analysts, we have become increasingly sophisticated in our theories of the psychology of perpetrators, terrorists, victims, sadism, martyrdom, etc. What we have also discovered is that applying this knowledge to prevention and treatment is more difficult. Often, it is only years later, or in the subsequent generations, that we learn of the breadth of psychological effects of trauma, torture, natural disaster, war.

The Holocaust is a particular example of mass killing where there is probably unanimous world agreement as to who were the victims and the persecutors. One of the differences between persecution and war is that the power is determined in the beginning, and there is less symmetrical enmity with an uncertain outcome (Sofsky, 1997). If we use the Holocaust as one specific prototype, where the definition of victim and perpetrator are generally agreed upon, we see that even there it has taken fifty years to begin to address all the complexities of the legacy. These include symptoms and adaptations in survivors, survivor guilt, mourning, and meaning. In the next generation, we see issues and symptoms, transmission of trauma, issues of memory, memorialization, witnessing, reparations, restoration of relationships, mainstreaming into the culture, art, movies, etc. There are also stories of displacement, immigration, and refugees. These experiences affect one's sense of rootedness, language, socioeconomic status, etc. For those who remain in their native country, there are issues of representation in government, politics, truth commissions. There are also conflicts about identity, identification with the transgressor, masochistic submission, and alienation from the larger group. One usually thinks of adaptation for the victims when considering the above mentioned issues. It is more difficult to consider the effects on perpetrators and their families. The reasons for this are both obvious and not so obvious.

For both sides, victims and perpetrators, a sense of identity and cohesiveness within one's group makes it difficult to give up entrenched positions. For example, the fear of peace, which may sound like an irrational position, can be a very powerful force perpetuating violence and hatred, and the need to keep sides known to be good and bad. The reasons for this are complex and have to do with identity, solidarity, excitement and purpose. The righteous position of the victim can also be very hard to give up. Very often, the claim to victimization becomes a core identity that is passed on transgenerationally.

I am going to present one approach to conflict resolution and healing that originated in the specific context of the Holocaust. The aim was to see if meeting together could break down any fixed stereotypes and identifications. This included the fairly common feeling on both sides of "we don't talk to the other side." We had some other questions in mind which I mention later. The group did not begin with a formal idea which was then operationalized. Rather, in an organic way, the group evolved a pattern and method that we had to step back from in order to describe and replicate what we were doing. The essence of the work involved bringing people from two (or more) sides of the conflict into a group where they told their stories to each other. Freud wrote in "Why War" (1932), anything that encourages the growth of emotional ties between men must operate against war. He goes on to talk of the two types of emotional ties—those as toward a love object, and those based on identification. Emotional ties do develop among group members which may develop empathy for the other and help shift entrenched positions ever so slightly.

Many unanticipated issues came up such as how does one take the experience back to one's tribal group? Can one be a multiplier and set up other such groups? Must one do such work outside the group? How does the experience of the groups enable us to work differently in our governments and policy making, that is, does peace-building from the bottom up have an effect on the peace-makers who are working from the top down? Are we betraying our parents, those who have died? Where will these meetings lead to?

The group, now called TRT, was an outgrowth of work done by Dan Bar-On in the 80s. At the time the group first met in 1992, the German component had been meeting on their own for some time. Also at that time, there were many second generation Holocaust Jewish groups discovering their identities as an entity and meeting in the US and Israel. Much was written about the effects of the Holocaust and the transmission of trauma with the focus on the group of second-generation children of survivors (Kestenberg, Epstein, Danielli, etc.). Most of these subjects had never met with their German counterparts. Bar-On was one of the first people to have written about the Germans' transgenerational issues.

The first meeting between the two sides took place in 1992 in Germany. We met for four days, and what started out as going around the room to make introductions turned into a four day marathon of story-telling. It took that long to get around the room. That has become the essence of the format that we use in all other groups. Some of the questions that we had when we came to the experience were the following:

1. Could the two sides face each other in a genuine way?
2. Would it help work through aspects for each side that could not be worked out in the setting of the tribal ego?
3. Through such an encounter, could any common agenda emerge, would there be any common ground?

Key to success was storytelling. This enabled us to see each other as human, beyond a stereotype. Since that group was not involved in a current conflict, it was more possible to genuinely listen to each other. I am going to jump ahead in the story to get to the video. The group has continued to meet every one or two years since 1992. We rotated between Germany, Israel and the U.S. It was actually during our second meeting in Israel that the BBC video was made.

At our sixth meeting, it was clear that our group was at a juncture in deciding its future. Many of the members were working on their own projects, fueled by the group experience. The group served as a mother ship to which we could come back for reconnection, refueling, etc., but the issues had changed and we had changed. The opportunity presented itself (thanks to generous funding from the Koerber Foundation) to take our model and try to apply it to groups in conflict. It was clear that at this point we would either take the challenge, or disband. In a way, it was a blessing that we were so naive, or we would have been scared off. We chose three conflicts: The Israeli/Palestinian (this was obvious since the Israelis in the original group were already putting a great deal of energy there). It was this expansion that forced us to incorporate, so to speak. We needed a name, we had to define a mission, we had to have a theory and method, and describe the model we were going to test. We were one group now, a testimony to the success of the original idea. We were not so naive as to think it would be the same for people living in conditions of war, violence, ongoing threat. We didn't know how those differences would play out and need accommodation. We were moving into new territory that was much more dependent on political processes, governments and policy. We were going to be working with people who were living in the midst of insecurity, pain and suffering. We were prepared to adapt our model as needed to see what worked for the culture and conflict we were dealing with.

This process is described in *Bridging the Gap* (Bar-On, 2000), published after our first meeting in Hamburg with the additional conflict groups. Since then, we have met with the Palestinians, Israelis, Northern Irish and South African groups in Bethlehem, U.S, and Northern Ireland. Now it is an international group with a very different mission. The role of the Americans and the Germans is very interesting as facilitators and resources in a group in which we do not directly belong to any conflict. Many interesting lessons have come from hearing the stories of others, and watching the process of peace building firsthand. The need for government and grassroots to be in phase with each other, the delicate issues of attending to the needs of victims and perpetrators, indeed, recognizing the fluidity of such labels as each storyteller and listener can gradually find both sides within himself have influenced our work every step of the way. The differences and similarities between conflicts and cultures guide us in terms of what can be generalized and where we need to be flexible. We have become convinced in the value of storytelling and listening, not just for personal healing, but for peace processes and healing on a community or national level. Social and economic concerns affect the public, and people want to have a voice. Providing opportunities is a challenge and then constructively allowing the public voice to be represented in a participatory way is something we can learn from every culture and conflict.

In every situation of victim and perpetrator there is a point in which the victim is seen as other than human to be other than the victimizer. Whether there is a split that takes place in the perpetrator, a systematic degradation to turn the other into non-human by a political machine, or the subtle transmission of racism and hatred of the other through generations, the differences become intolerable and ultimately lead to the need to destroy the other. By putting a human relationship and face on the other, one has to confront one's own split, recognize empathy, and move from an intransigent position. It becomes harder to kill a real person rather than a devalued, stereotyped, non-human. It has been described in print, media, interviews, how killers need to numb themselves with alcohol, drugs, sex, splitting and compartmentalizing in order to carry out their tasks.

There is a risk in becoming involved in this process, as it threatens to separate the group member from his main group of origin and identity. Indeed, the notion of "reentry" is something the group members of both sides can share and can understand. We have begun to answer some of the questions posed in the beginning, and new questions emerge. It is clear that we have a very powerful tool in the work toward peace, yet like any process, it is slow, fraught with resistance, and can only occur when the frame is safe. Essentially, we have laid the groundwork for the frame, and provide some models and tools, and we are repeatedly amazed with the resilience, strength and humanity of all people. When we see it in each other, and locate that inside of the other as well as the hateful persecutor in the other, there is some hope.

REFERENCES

Bar-On, D. (1989). *Legacy of silence*. Cambridge: Harvard University Press.
Bar-On, D. (2000). *Bridging the gap*. Hamburg: Koerber-Stiftung.
Browning, C. (1992). *Ordinary men*. New York: Harper Collins.
Freud, S. (1933). "Why War?" Standard Edition, London: Hogarth Press.
Sofsky, W. (1997). *The order of terror*. New Jersey: Princeton University Press.
Volkan, V. (1990). *The psychodynamics of international relationships*. Lexington, MA: Lexington Books.

Instances of Genocide in the Modern World: The Bosnian and the Jewish Holocausts

VALENTINA VRTIKAPA & LEON ANISFELD

The Bosnian Holocaust

Valentina Vrtikapa

I WAS WORKING AS A MEDICAL DOCTOR IN BOSNIA from 1992-1995 during the war in which every twenty-fifth person got killed and every third person was displaced. Over three years I was in charge of treating refugees, people who lost loved ones, people who witnessed murders, terrorist attacks and other horrors of war. Witnessing murders, daily bombings, losing loved ones puts extreme stress on everybody involved, physician as well as patient.

Children were often taken from the safe environments of their homes, sometimes separated from their siblings or parents. They were no longer members of the same family: they could not choose their clothes, toys or schools. They lived with people they most likely had never met before. Sudden change in life style and anticipation of an uncertain future exerted a profound effect in their psychological functioning.

Children responded to traumatic experiences in many different ways. Some had reactions soon after they experienced a traumatic event, others were doing fine for weeks or months, or even years before they began to show behavioral changes. I observed marked regressions in young pre-school children. Older children usually presented with vague physical complaints. They tended to become restless, refused to do schoolwork, resisted authority or experimented with drugs or alcohol. Some were haunted by memories of seeing bombings, injured or dead people and suffered from recurrent nightmares, flashbacks. In adolescents, feelings of helplessness and guilt were common perhaps due to the fact that they were unable to assume adult responsibilities or because they were forced to leave their families behind.

In order to illustrate some of those issues I have chosen two cases, a brother A (15 years old) and sister L (7 years old). A and L were separated from their parents at the beginning of the war. He and his sister left the city for few days and stayed away for three years. A had the opportunity to talk to his parents with the help of radio amateurs but he did not show any special interest in this contact. In his words, "the first part of the day I am grateful to them [parents] because they took care of us, the second part of the day I hate them because this is not a life I want or chose…" A had sudden grown up responsibilities, having to take care of his younger sister L while he was still a child himself. He felt as if he didn't belong to anybody any more. Refusing to talk to his parents was easier than admitting his resentment.

L experienced the beginning of the war with immense fear. She witnessed the bombings and saw dead people lying on the street. She became afraid of sudden noise and complained of having vivid images of the people lying on the street. For months she was nauseous at the sight of meat. She shared with me that she had been eating meat when the bombing started.

Women had strong responses to traumatic loss, although they expressed it in different ways. Some were showing signs of depression and anxiety for months. Some had feelings of rage, wanting to find who was responsible for their suffering. Some cope by becoming very active, trying to assist others. A woman declared that being of help to others "keeps me sane, I have no time to think what I will eat tomorrow, or if I ever would see my husband again."

Some women seem to dissociate themselves from reality pretending that life was normal, that nothing unusual was happening. A twenty-five year old pregnant woman who left her hometown when she found out she was pregnant, used to come for her regular prenatal visits, refusing to talk about the atrocities she had witnessed in the past. "Did you bring anything with you?" I asked on one occasion. She replied: "My wedding pictures and keys." I went on asking about the reasons she brought the keys. I learned that when homes were destroyed people never left their keys behind.

The workers, doctors, nurses were themselves victims of war. Some lost their families, some had loved ones on the war front, and some were refugees themselves. They were tired, afraid, anxious and as everybody else they asked, "Why is this happening to me?" They were both grateful and angry at international organizations. Foreign aid workers were coming and going, they led a normal life somewhere else, while people in Bosnia had no choice.

The Jewish Holocaust

Leon Anisfeld

I sat before my television set on September 11, 2001, watching a news program with no particular thought in mind, when suddenly, with absolutely no introduction, the staff of *The Today Show* announced that something had happened at the World Trade Center. An airplane was shown crashing into one of the towers, a scene that was telecast repeatedly over the subsequent hours and then days, much like the mesmerizing, incomprehensible, recycling footage of the assassination of President Kennedy in 1963. At first exposure, I imagined that this was a fantasy simulation of a science fiction nightmare or horrific prediction, but then thought it would be too horrible a tragedy to "play with," that the portrayal of such a thing would frighten too many people in so large a city as New York, that a "War of the Worlds" in a nuclear age might tempt some unbalanced soul to create an unthinkable situation.

My mind trailed off for some seconds, until the announcement of a second airplane striking a second building. Then I saw the confusion and the reality too horrible to be anything but real. People were running in the streets. Newscasters were themselves horrified. It was only an infinitesimal mental leap to then imagine that this was a visual depiction of the Jews scattering in the streets of Europe during Kristallnacht, which had announced the plans of those who hated the Jews to rid Europe of the "Jewish Problem." I wonder whether any of those fleeing Jews could have guessed that it was in preparation for their deaths that the glass was broken, that before long uniformed young men in suits bearing swastikas would intrude into their homes to take away their own young men. Was the attack I was witnessing, virtually live, another intrusion of the Nazis into the homes of American Jews, the dreaded possibility we had come to believe could happen "never again"? I had heard many warnings recently about the resurgence of Nazism in America and in Europe. I had grown up in the shadow of that terror as the child of Holocaust survivors, my life, literally, beginning in a displaced persons camp in Germany. The destruction of the World Trade Towers gave gruesome credibility to those fears, as every loud siren, ambulance, or other street noise rattled my composure and undid my complacent certainty that we were safe from any such danger.

One workshop participant, a psychiatrist who had recently immigrated to the United States subsequent to witnessing the genocide in her native Bosnia-Herzegovina, also reported the reactivation of traumatic prior experiences as a result of the attacks on America. It became clear that PTSD was not simply an individual phenomenon but, in these instances, a collective one.

The Treatment Of Traumatized Refugees

SVERRE VARVIN

MY BASIC HYPOTHESIS IS THAT A CONSEQUENCE of extreme traumatization is a defect in symbolization and mentalization of the traumatizing events, leading to more or less permanent defects in later mentalization, especially of emotionally stressful experiences. There are several ways of coping with these effects some of which are described in the diagnostic categories of PTSD, dissociation syndrome, somatization syndrome, drug abuse, etc. The after-effects of traumatization, are, however, more complex and can only be understood in the context of the underlying mental and neurobiological processes as well the social context in which they emerge. Especially for refugees, the social context of being exiled and living in exile is important. Generally, diagnostic categories may be misleading as they fail to convey these complexities.

In this workshop, I discussed psychotherapy of a severely traumatized woman who arrived as a refugee in Norway in her late thirties with two children, joining her husband, also heavily traumatized, who had been living in Norway for some years. The aim of presenting this case was to allow for a discussion of the complexities of the interaction of the bodily-emotional, identity formative group related, and, the social-cultural levels of the traumatized person in exile.

Pain was a main problem of this woman. The therapy process represented a journey where the bodily pain was gradually translated into mental images and representations of increasing complexity and where the ability to deal with what they referred to and represented was increasingly improved. These two processes are referred to as symbolization and mentalization, respectively.

Pain is a prime example where the communication of the content of the distress fails. It is by its nature invisible to the other even though its presence is most real for the person who suffers. However, what is even more troublesome is the inexpressibility in language of the experience of having pain—hence, the distance from the suffering person that the listener may experience. Elaine Scarry expresses this phenomenon in the following way:

> So, for the person in pain, so incontestably and unnegotiably present is it that "having pain" may be thought of as the vibrant example of what it is to "have certainty," while for the other person it is so elusive that "hearing about pain" may exist as the primary model of what it is to "have doubt." Thus pain comes unsharably into our midst as at once that which cannot be denied and that which cannot be confirmed. (Scarry, 1985 p.4)

This may also explain the apparent ease with which the torturer can inflict pain on the victim, aware that he is inflicting pain but not knowing or denying its implications for the other human being. One is also reminded of some of the problems met in the countertransference with patients in pain; the wordless suffering of the patient in pain also evades mental representation and makes the internal work of the therapist strenuous.

However, the problem is more complicated. Having pain may be communicated in different ways. Certain bodily pains seen in traumatized patients are mute in a special way. They may be reported, but the emotional significance of having the pain, not to mention the emotional significance of the pain itself, tends to evade the listener. In terms of countertransference, one would speak of a certain unresponsiveness or stifling of emotional response.

The Patient *(Elena)*

She was a thin, slightly bent woman, dressed in ordinary clothes and wearing a traditional Muslim scarf covering her hair. At the first meeting, she was pale and talked in a low voice. Her eyes were much of the time fixed on the table or the floor, and from time to time she looked with a very direct gaze at the therapist. She gave an alarming impression of being not only very depressed, but a person who had almost given up life.

She came from a middle-class family in a large city as the only girl with three brothers with whom she had a good relationship and who took good care of her. Her mother was somewhat modern and supported her in her struggle to get an education. She was raised in the crossfire of the apparent conflict between the mother's and the father's view of what was appropriate for a girl. According to tradition, said her father, she should be subservient to the men in the family and to men in general. Early on she felt this to be most unjust, but became accustomed to being quiet about her feelings while nevertheless pursuing her goals with a determined stubbornness (of which her father, no doubt, was a good example). She had two episodes she described as very frightening between the ages of eight and ten years. She did not reveal the content of these episodes, but indicated that they were an intrusion of some sort from a male neighbor.

Her father died when she was fourteen years old. In spite of the conflicts she had with her father, she maintains that she had a good childhood, experiencing much warmth and care. She was, however, the listener, the one who took care of other people's problems, and she was extremely afraid of offending or hurting others. This was probably associated with her sensitivity for the same problems that afflicted her. She had few friends.

After high school she was educated as an assistant nurse, and worked for several years in the poorer part of the city. Through this work she became aware of the enormous poverty and suffering in her country. While working in a legal political organization, she met her husband. He was a university teacher and held a leading position in the political movement. They had two children who were 11 and 13 years old respectively at the start of therapy.

The political climate deteriorated, and mass arrests began to take place shortly after her children were born. Her husband and several members of his extended family were arrested. Eight of them were soon killed or executed. Her husband survived but was severely traumatized in prison.

Soon afterwards, she was arrested with her two small children, then 4 months and 2 years old. Elena and her two children spent two years in prison, and some of their experiences are beyond human understanding and, for her, beyond words to describe. She was able to talk about them during therapy, but she gave the impression that a good deal of them were too difficult to recount.

Trauma story

The following presents a summary of what the therapist heard: First, they were in a prison in a small town for about a year. Elena and her two children had to live in a small cell, less than one square metre in size. As it was impossible to stretch out when sleeping, she developed a technique of bending her legs backwards in order to rest and to give the children more room. At the beginning of therapy (about ten years later), she was still obliged to sleep in that position to get some rest. Food was scarce and hygienic conditions were poor. At a time when her youngest child was about to die of hunger and thirst, the guard brought milk that contained a noxious substance that almost instantly made the child extremely sick and brought him nearer to death. For days, she had to stand, hooded, against the wall, not allowed to sit or take care of the children, who had to crawl on the floor. They could hear the screams of people being tortured, and the mother was hit while the children watched.

They were then moved to a larger prison in a central city. Here they were placed in a large, over-crowded cell. She had to curl up to give space to the children and to her fellow prisoners. The fellow prisoners were regularly tortured, and bleeding and maltreated persons were a common sight. Many had their toes or fingers cut off, some became lame, and some were killed in front of her and the children. In her own words: "Yes, because there we have seen so much, too much, we had never expected that human beings could do things like that" (session 1).

The effects for herself and her children were devastating. She lived for years in her country afterwards in constant terror and terrorized by the police. She emerged from this living in total fright, to the extent that she did not know it was fright. It was only after years of therapy that she began recognizing and differentiating emotional states including her fright. She said during follow-up: "Before I was afraid of everything, all the time. Now it is totally changed."

The Therapy

The psychotherapy was conducted face-to-face with a total of 165 sessions. The focus of the psychotherapy was formulated by the therapist in the following way: "...to find what happens in you when you get pain, when you become sad or dreary, and if there can be ways you can work with yourself to feel better in your body without having to take medicine" (which she didn't want).

The instruction given at the beginning of therapy was an invitation "to try to say whatever came into her mind," with an additional explanation of the meaning of this as it related to her cultural beliefs.[1] This seemed to be, as could be expected, a rather difficult task for her. Having been in prison and interrogated numerous times, this invitation naturally evoked resistance, and the therapist was rather active throughout

[1]Even though psychotherapy was alien to her, there was room in her culture for the privileged dialogue. The doctor held a central place, but other persons could also be approached.

the therapy. One main aim was to help her to talk in general and in particular about difficulties regarding both the current situation and her past experiences. She often behaved in a passive way, expecting to "get treatment."

This was understandable in relation to cultural traditions and also in relation to the helplessness she experienced towards her rather disabling symptoms and problems. It was also a defense to avoid painful themes, and was also due to a deficient mentalizing capacity (Krystal, 2001).

She often regressed into a passive-aggressive position, demanding her therapist to "make her well." "When will I be well, doctor?" and "When will the pains go away?" were recurrent questions. The transference implications of this demand, putting the therapist in the difficult position of being the helpless helper, and thereby preparing the ground for disappointment, were obvious, but proved difficult to clarify.

She sought a variety of somatic treatments while in therapy (when disappointed by or mistrusting the therapist) and even managed on one occasion to persuade a surgeon to perform an operation, which had no positive effect.

The therapy process could be divided into three phases:

1. *The rapprochement phase* (sessions 1-18): the first verbalization of traumatic memories and the establishment of a preliminary alliance. The immediate effect was a spontaneous improvement in her depression and some of her somatic problems.

2. *Resistance and mistrust* (sessions 19-90). In this phase she had many somatic complaints, very often openly distrusted the therapist and even quit therapy twice.

3. *Phase of autonomy* (5-6 years). Here she was able to make mental connections on her own and work with what frightened her in her daily life, and thus gained considerable autonomy.

She saw the psychotherapy as an integral part of the health services she was offered and often blamed the psychotherapist for wrongdoings committed by other doctors. This undifferentiated view subsided markedly towards the end of therapy.

The stories about her traumas had a strong impact on the therapist, causing a range of feeling including anger, sadness, despair and helplessness. They also provoked a desire to help and not to hurt, which, it seems, influenced the conduct of the therapy. It seemed that the therapist was often supportive and reluctant to interpret negative transference and distrust/hopelessness. The following themes were important for Elena during therapy:

—Bodily problems, especially pain as described above.
—Her relation to traumatic experiences.
—Being able to speak to others about her thoughts and feelings.

A basic underlying theme was her difficulty in trusting others, including the therapist (she was, in fact, terrified of most people). This made it difficult for her to believe that psychological treatment might help, and to trust the psychiatrist. In the therapist's evaluation, this was related to four factors:

1. Her culturally based belief that psychiatric treatment was for the "mad."

2. Her background as the quiet girl and an upbringing where there was little scope for talking about emotions.

3 The pain she experienced when talking about her extreme experiences.

4. The damage to her trust in herself and others as a result of her extreme experiences.

The last seemed to be the overriding problem affecting the other themes.

Discussion

The discussion in the workshop focused on the nature of trauma and the need to go beyond the PTSD paradigm to get a deeper understanding of the posttraumatic process and to identify what aspects of the therapeutic process and therapeutic technique could be helpful. There was considerable agreement that the problems caused by extreme traumatization such as torture were complex and longstanding and that there exist no simple therapeutic solutions. The reference here was to the many short-term therapies on the market. Moreover, it became obvious during the discussion that the acknowledgement and reflection in society at large was necessary for these victims/survivors in their struggle to find a place and reintegrate into society.

REFERENCES

Krystal, H. (2001). Trauma und affekte. posttraumatizche folgerscheinungen und ihre konsequenzen für die psychoanalytische technik. In *Die Gegenwart der Psychoanalyse-die Psychoanalyse der Gegenwart*. W. Bohleber & S. Drews, eds., Klett-Cotta, Stuttgart, pp. 197-207.

Scarry, E. (1985). *The body in pain. The making and unmaking of the world*. NY: Oxford University Press.

Subjectivity Under Extreme Conditions

MARCELO VINAR

as written and reported by Isaac Tylim

THE MEMORY OF TRAUMATIC EVENTS IS OFTEN threatened by a tendency to take refuge in theoretical, that is to say, detached reflections on that which either horrifies or fascinates us. Regarding experiences of terror, there is no room for objectivity and neutrality. We either react with the intensity of blinding political passion, or try hard to make sense of the fragmentation of reality whose complexity and over-determination always over-powers us.

We must therefore abandon the fallacy that only an objective outlook could bring us to the truth. This objective, sought-after outlook may actually be at the service of the status quo. I believe that every perception of reality is just a fragment that builds and interprets the reality in question, and the grasp of reality in its totality is not possible.

Terror may co-exist with the spectacle of apparent normality. Human tragedies become degraded and trivialized by being the object of journalistic news inspiring a fleeting commotion or an impotent indifference. Under these circumstances it becomes imperative to restitute the tragedies' human dimension and significance through a human narration. To surpass the cathartic effect offered by the media is indeed a challenge. Ordinary narrative can't convey the magnitude of certain types of events, and the result is a story that easily deteriorates into a succession of horrifying scenes that leave us speechless, without articulate words or logical discourse.

The experience of terror creates the need for a different and demanding narrative texture. Horror only produces silence. It requires long and hard work to be able to represent or to narrate it. We must avoid quantifying these experiences, and confuse horror with the narration of horror. Horror has its own dimension of time and logic. The timing of horror brings convulsion, a state that betrays calm reflection or thought. Horror elicits combat or escape, withdrawal being the most frequent and serious form of escape. The impossibility to rationalize the new and terrible circumstances generates bewilderment and paralysis.

Treating horror as a show or as a hypocritical or mercantile object to be consumed is as harmful as silence. It creates the illusion that one has found the way to deal with it. I believe that the challenge does not consist of achieving a theatrical, dramatized exorcism of terror, but in examining the human race regarding its capacity to generate those political spaces of abjection.

In this century of "mega-dead," from the Holocaust to the risk of the atomic bomb, the quantification of phenomena is unavoidable. Yet it is risky to deal with these matters only in terms of numbers. Statistics promote anonymity, and enhance the transformation of singularity into generalizations. The relation between the single case and the whole is not a problem of scale but a problem of changing perspective in the narrative of horror.

In regard to the memory of terror it seems to me that it is impossible to conceive a connection between these two terms—memory and terror. They are incompatible, and cannot be related. The reason for this incompatibility is that memory is built upon words and representations, while terror is the result of destructive forces that overwhelms and paralyzes human metaphors. Yet we have an ethical responsibility to construct a narration of terror in order to promote the learning of history.

To tell what cannot be named requires hard work. Human groups must represent their existence through what we call Social History. This becomes the source of Social Memory, an area of conflict and controversy between generations, between social layers, and between groups. In this respect Social Memory is a contradictory human construction, a peculiar mixture of old, durable, ancestral matters, and new, recent, burning painful issues.

When we are working on collective memory of horror, it is not the question of reconstructing the past or reformulating it according to present utopias, but of rebirth, of restitution of missing pieces. Social Memory lies on the ridge of two slopes: the political one, which is always loaded with strong interests and passions, and the hidden perpetual sphere of intimacy which includes a permanence of genealogy and belonging, and which is bound to touch the very essence of being.

IPTAR: Origins, Structure and Functions

THE INSTITUTE FOR PSYCHOANALYTIC TRAINING AND RESEARCH (IPTAR) was founded in 1958 as a membership society for non-medical analysts sharing an interest in
Freud's theory and technique. It provided a congenial setting for the exchange of
ideas and the discussion of cases and theory. In 1960, the Membership Society established the IPTAR Training Institute to offer what was as yet unavailable in this country: rigorous and thorough training in Freudian theory and technique for serious,
qualified students from a variety of academic and professional backgrounds.

In 1989, IPTAR became a provisional component society of the International
Psychoanalytical Association (IPA) and a full component society of the IPA in 1991.
IPTAR has the distinction of being one of the first non-medical societies in the
United States to become affiliated with the international psychoanalytic community.

IPTAR is both a Membership Society and a Training Institute. It is a community committed to the lifelong study of psychoanalysis. IPTAR offers its membership
a rich variety of programs and opportunities for study, discussion, and the continuing interchange of ideas. As Training Institute, it offers a carefully planned curricu-
lum governed by a contemporary Freudian perspective. Rooted in the original
Freudian text, it also includes important elaboration and transformations of the original concepts that have led to today's expanded understanding of psychopathology,
development, technique, and application. Teaching is done in the context of clinical
illustration, making theoretical learning relevant to actual practice.

Three boards carry out all of the functions of IPTAR. The Board of Directors of
the Society consists of Fellows and Members elected by the full membership. It is
responsible, through committees, for carrying out the program of scientific meetings, membership selection, education, ethics and research programs. It is also
responsible for electing the Board of Administrators of the Institute, and the Board
of the IPTAR Clinical Center (ICC). The Board of Administrators of the Institute
carries out all the training functions. The ICC is the clinical component of IPTAR:
Candidates and Members provide the community with affordable mental health
services. IPTAR has its own headquarters on the Upper East Side of Manhattan,
which houses the Edward Frankel Memorial Library, a conference room, and facili-
ties for IPTAR Clinical Center practice as well as for private practice.

THE IPTAR CLINICAL CENTER (ICC)
IPTAR'S Unique Commitment to the Community.

The ICC is a not-for-profit community resource dedicated to providing low-cost
psychoanalytic psychotherapy and psychoanalysis to adults, adolescents and chil-

dren in the Metropolitan New York area. While maintaining a reasonable fee scale, it offers psychoanalytic psychotherapy, as well as psycho-diagnostic assessment and psychiatric consultation and medication when necessary, to a population that often is not able to afford quality mental health services on a regular and long-term basis. The ICC is committed to maintaining the treatment of each patient until its natural completion regardless of changes in economic circumstances.

The ICC's community presence is through its bi-annual newsletter, community outreach programs in schools and organizations, and in workshops and conferences held for professionals and the general public. Ongoing research on the effectiveness of the treatment offered at the ICC is an integral part of our program.

NOTES ON CONTRIBUTORS

Abby Adams-Silvan, Ph.D., received her psychoanalytic training at the NYU post-doctoral Program where she is now a clinical professor, faculty, supervisor and training analyst. She is a past president of the NY Freudian Society, where she is a training analyst and supervisor, and a member of the faculty; a member of the Institute for Psychoanalytic Training and Research; a member of the International Psychoanalytical Association; Associate Editor for North America for the News Magazine of the IPA. Dr. Adams-Silvan has published on a number of different subjects: the role of excited discharge in PTSD, the nature of trauma in hysteria, treating a dying patient, the dynamics of acrophobia, the nature of teaching of psychoanalytic listening, etc. She was a volunteer for the Red Cross in the days immediately following 9/11 and is in the private practice of psychoanalysis and psychotherapy in New York.

Lord John Alderdice, FRCPsych MLA, Speaker of the Northern Ireland Assembly and a practicing Consultant Psychiatrist, was born in Northern Ireland in 1955, graduated in medicine in 1978 and qualified as a member of the Royal College of Psychiatrists in 1983. After training in psychoanalysis he was appointed Ireland's first Consultant Psychotherapist in 1988. He has been a Senior Lecturer at Queen's University Belfast, Director of the Northern Ireland Institute of Human Relations, and Executive Medical Director of South and East Belfast Health & Social Services Trust, one of Northern Ireland's largest health and social care providers. He is an Honorary Fellow of the Royal College of Physicians of Ireland, an Honorary Fellow of the Royal College of Psychiatrists, an Honorary Affiliate of the British Psychoanalytical Society and an Honorary Professor in the Faculty of Medicine, University of San Marcos, Lima. He has substantial experience of living with terrorism because from 1987 to 1998 he was Leader of Northern Ireland's cross-community Alliance Party and played a significant role in the Irish Peace Process, being one of the key negotiators of the Belfast Agreement signed on Good Friday 1998. After his election to the new Northern Ireland Assembly in 1998 he was appointed the first Speaker of the new Assembly.

Leon Anisfield, DSW, is a graduate and member of the Institute for Psychoanalytic Training and Research; a member of the New York Freudian Society and the International Psychoanalytic Association. He earned a DSW, MA (in political science) and certificate (in Latin American Studies) at Columbia University, and an MA degree (psychology) at the New School for Social Research. His mother and father were both survivors of the Holocaust. Dr. Anisfield has co-led groups for Holocaust survivors at Mt. Sinai Medical Center in New York City.

Mordechai Benyakar, M.D., is a psychoanalyst, school teacher, psychologist, and psychiatrist, member of the International Psychoanalytical Association (IPA), the Israel Psychoanalytic Association, and Training Analyst of the Argentinean Psychoanalytic Association (APA). He is an Honorary Member of the World

Psychiatric Association (WPA), and currently serves as President of the Section of Military Psychiatry and Disaster Interventions of the WPA. Dr. Benyakar is also International Director of the Training Program on Stress, Trauma and Disaster Intervention, and related Masters' Programs at the University of Paris, University of Complutense in Spain, Tel-Aviv University, and the University of Buenos Aires. He is professor, Sakler Medical School, Tel-Aviv University, and the Medical School and Psychology Faculty of the University of Buenos Aires. He directed mental health programs in Israel during the Gulf War, and in Argentina following the terrorist attack on the Jewish community of Buenos Aires. His main academic and research interests and publications are in the areas of stress and trauma, mental health in disasters, psychic impact of disease, therapeutic approaches for children, adolescents and families, and primary process, therapeutic experience, and the therapeutic frame and space in psychoanalysis. He lived in Israel for thirty years, including eleven years on a kibbutz; he currently resides in Buenos Aires as an active clinician and member of the APA.

Phyllis Beren, Ph.D., is Past-President, Fellow, Supervising Analyst and Faculty of the Institute for Psychoanalytic Training and Research (IPTAR). She is also Training and Supervising Analyst at The New York Freudian Society, Member of the IPA, and Editor of *Narcissistic Disorders in Children and Adolescents.*

Maria V. Bergmann is a practicing psychoanalyst in New York. She is a training and supervising analyst of the New York Freudian Society and the International Psychoanalytical Association; faculty and member of the Institute for Psychoanalytic Training and Research; and member of the American Psychological Association, Division of Psychoanalysis and the American Psychoanalytic Association.

Martha Bragin, Ph.D., is a consultant on the psychosocial reintegration of women and young people affected by war and community violence in the United States and abroad. Recent postings include Afghanistan, the Sudan, and Sierra Leone, as well as Central America and Southeast Asia. She has served as consultant in social work to the government of Vietnam, to UNICEF, the United States Office of Juvenile Justice and Delinquency Prevention and to a number of international and national non-governmental organizations. She has focused on the creation of programs that address developmental and intrapsychic needs while meeting urgent practical ones. Dr. Bragin writes and speaks extensively about the cross-cultural derivation and application of psychodynamic principles. Her most recent publications are "The uses of aggression: healing the wounds of war in communities around the world" and "Evaluating psychosocial programs for children: a community based approach." Dr. Bragin is a member of the committee on Psychoanalysis in the Community of the American Psychoanalytic Association, of the Clinical Advisory Board of the International Trauma Studies Program at New York University, of the Advisory Board of the International Social Work program at New York University, and a candidate at IPTAR.

Joseph A. Cancelmo, Psy.D., is a graduate and member of the Institute for Psychoanalytic Training and Research (IPTAR) and member of the International Psychoanalytical Association (IPA). He is the Coordinator of Training Programs for the IPTAR Society, past Coordinator of Adult Clinical Services for the IPTAR Clinical Center (ICC), and supervisor for the ICC and Pace University Center for Psychological Services. He has published work on the application of psychoanalytic thinking to: the parent-child caregiver relationship (*Child Care for Love or Money? A Guide to Navigating the Parent-Caregiver Relationship*), on pregnancy decisions, on major depression, and on Munchausen Syndrome. He is actively involved in research studies of the outcome of psychoanalytically oriented psychotherapy for children and adolescents, and the impact of chronic anxiety related to terrorism. He co-chaired the conference and is an editor of these conference proceedings.

Ann Early, M.S.W., is in private practice in Oklahoma City; member, Psychoanalytic Institute of N. California

Shmuel Erlich, Ph.D., is immediate past president of the Israel Psychoanalytic Society; a training analyst on the faculty of the Israel Psychoanalytic Institute; a Sigmund Freud Professor of Psychoanalysis and Director of the Sigmund Freud Center at the Hebrew University of Jerusalem. He is in private psychoanalytic practice with adolescents and adults. His publications include: adolescent development and treatment; psychoanalytic theory, especially experimental factors; and psychoanalytic-systemic studies of group and organizational processes.

K. William Fried, Ph.D., is a psychoanalyst in private practice in New York City. For thirty-two years, he was Associate Director of Psychiatry Residency Training at Maimonides Medical Center In Brooklyn. He is an Emeritus Associate Professor of Psychiatry at the SUNY Health Sciences Center in Brooklyn, The New York College of Osteopathic Medicine, and the St. Georges College of Medicine in Grenada, West Indies. In 2000, he was named "Teacher of the Year" by the Association for Academic Psychiatry, the first non-physician to receive this award. His interests lie in the interface of aesthetics and psychoanalysis. He has published, taught and presented on the subjects of film, imaginative literature, the psychology of the creative process and the training and education of mental health professionals. In April 2002, his photographs were displayed in a one-man show at the Amacord Gallery in Beacon, New York. Dr. Fried has presented several workshops under the auspices of IPTAR and is currently conducting one on the process of supervision

Myrna Gannagé was born in Beirut and earned her Ph.D. in Clinical Psychology from the University of Paris-V Sorbonne in 1995. With her thesis on "The psychological consequences of war on children and their families," she was the recipient of the first thesis award of the Human Sciences Department of the University of Paris-V. In 1996, she founded three psychological consultation centers for the welfare of war children in Lebanon, the first specialized outpatient units for children who had suffered from the war, for which she serves as Director. In 2001, she was appoint-

suffered from the war, for which she serves as Director. In 2001, she was appointed Professor of Clinical Psychology at Saint Joseph's University in Beirut. She has authored numerous scientific publications in the field of trauma and is a member of the scientific committee of the European Association for Child and Adolescent Psychopathology. She is also member of the French Society for Child and Adolescent Psychiatry and Allied Professions and member of the International Society for Traumatic Stress Studies.

Caroline Garland, Ph.D., is a consultant Clinical Psychologist and Psychoanalyst, working in the adult department of the Tavistock Clinic in London. Following a degree in Literature from Cambridge University, her early work concerned the study of social behavior in chimpanzees. In the Tavistock, she has been head of the Unit for the Study of Trauma and its aftermath since 1987, engaging in clinical work, teaching, training and research on the nature of trauma and its long-term outcome. The Unit's work has been published in the volume *Understanding Trauma* (Ed. Garland, London: Karnac, 2003), in which Dr. Garland has written several chapters. Her other professional interests include the use of heterogeneous therapy groups for the treatment of trauma, and the use of psychoanalytic therapy in the treatment of chronic depression.

Deena Harris, M.D., is an Assistant Clinical Professor of Psychiatry at Columbia College of Physicians and Surgeons and The New York State Psychiatric Institute. She is also a faculty analyst at The Columbia Center for Psychoanalytic Study and Research. She has an interest in transmission of trauma, Holocaust studies, and treatment of trauma, PTSD, and conflict resolution. She has been part of a group, TRT, which began working with descendants of victims and perpetrators from the Holocaust and has extended their work to include victims and perpetrators of conflicts in Northern Ireland, South Africa and Palestine/Israel. She is interested in applying analytic principles to her work with groups to establish paradigms for peace and rebuilding in the aftermath of conflict. This includes exploration of memory, memorializing, witnessing, story-telling on a grass roots level, and questions of truth commissions, reparations, policies, and programs on a political level.

Beth Hart, Ph.D., is Professor in the Psychology Department of Pace University and Director of the McShane Center for Psychological Services. She has conducted a six-year longitudinal study of adolescent depression and development that has provided data for over 65 doctoral projects. For the past several years she has published numerous articles in the *Opera Quarterly* on how women have been represented in opera. One will appear in the Berlioz Centennial issue this summer, "The Loves of Hector Berlioz in his life and in *Les Troyens*." She received a postdoctoral certificate in psychoanalysis at NYU Postdoctoral Program for Psychoanalysis and Psychotherapy and is a member of The Institute for Psychoanalytic Training and Research, The International Psychoanalytic Association, The American Psychological Association, and The New York State Psychological Association. She maintains a small private practice.

Joan Hoffenberg, Ph.D., is Member and Faculty, IPTAR; Co-Director, IPTAR Clinical Center; Supervisor, IPTAR Clinical Center; Clinical Assistant Professor, Downstate Medical Center, SUNY, Psychology Dept.; Assistant Editor, *Journal of the International Psychoanalytic Association*; and a Psychologist/Psychoanalyst in private practice in New York City.

Laura Kleinerman, MS, is Director, Child and Adolescent Psychotherapy Training Program, Institute for Psychoanalytic Training and Research; Faculty and Supervisor, Columbia University Institute for Psychoanalytic Training and Research; Parent Infant Program, IPTAR. She is in private practice in New York, NY.

Herbert Krauss, Ph.D., is Chair of the Psychology Department, Pace University, NY. He has been Director of Rehabilitation Research and Outcomes Management at the International Center for the Disabled in New York; adjunct faculty Cornell Medical School; associate Attending Psychologist Payne Whitney Clinic; co-editor of *International Journal of Group Tensions*; consulting editor *Journal of Individual Psychology*. Among his publications are *Living with Anxiety and Depression*; *Between Survival and Suicide*; *A Provider's Guide to Psychiatric Services in the General Hospital*; *The Aging Workforce: A Guide for University Administrators*.

Naama Kushnir-Barash, Ph.D., Fellow (Training and Control Analyst), Institute of Psychoanalytic Training and Research, Training and Supervising Analyst, Israel Psychoanalytic Society, Senior Member, National Psychological Association for Psychoanalysis. In private practice, New York City.

Kay Ludwig is a licensed clinical social worker and Board Certified Diplomate in social work. She is a graduate of the University of Oklahoma (1979), where she received both a Bachelors' and Masters' degree in Social Work. Post-graduate training includes a certificate from Menninger in the Postgraduate Psychotherapy Program (1988), and a Certificate of Psychoanalysis from the Colorado Center for Psychological Studies (1997). Ms. Ludwig is in private practice in Oklahoma City, OK, and provides psychotherapy and psychoanalysis to adolescents and adults. She is also a member of the Psychoanalytic Institute of Northern California and currently teaches students interested in psychoanalytic psychotherapy as part of PINC's regional training program.

Hattie Myers, Ph.D., is a member and faculty of the Institute for Psychoanalytic Training and Research (IPTAR); member, the International Psychoanalytical Association (IPA); Co-Director of the IPTAR Clinical Center (ICC); and faculty, National Institute for the Psychotherapies (NIP).

Gilead Nachmani, Ph.D., William Alanson White Institute.

Corliss Parker, Ph.D., Fellow (Training and Supervising Analyst) and Faculty, Adult Psychoanalytic and Child Psychotherapy Training Programs, IPTAR; Supervisor, Clinical Psychology Doctoral Program, City University of New York; in private practice with adults and children; co-lead a study group, The psychology of Adoption and Foster Care (sponsored by IPTAR); Member, IPA.

Karen Komisar Proner, MA, is a child and adult psychoanalyst who was trained in England at the Tavistock. She is a member of IPTAR and a faculty member of the child and adult training programs. She is also a senior faculty member of the Centro Studi Martha Harris Child Training in Florence, Italy

Maribeth Rourke C.S.W., is a graduate and member of the Institute for Psychoanalytic Training and Research, and an Advanced Candidate in the New York Freudian Society's Child Analytic Program. She currently teaches and supervises in IPTAR's Child and Adolescent Psychotherapy Program. She has a private practice in New York City treating children, adolescents and adults, and supervising.

Edith Schwartz, Ph.D., is on the faculty, New York Freudian Society; Institute for Psychoanalytic Training and Research (IPTAR), and National Psychological Association for Psychoanalysis (NPAP).

Ruth Stein, Ph.D., is a training analyst, Israel Psychoanalytic Society; Member, Institute for Psychoanalytic Training and Research (IPTAR), and member International Psychoanalytic Association (IPA); Associate Clinical Professor, New York University Postdoctoral Program for Psychotherapy and Psychoanalysis; Member of the Advisory Board of the International Association for Relational Psychoanalysis and Psychotherapy (IARPP); Associate Editor, *Psychoanalytic Dialogues* & *Israel Journal of Psychoanalysis* ; International Editor, *Studies in Gender and Psychoanalysis* ; Editorial Board, *American Journal of Psychotherapy.* She is the author of *Psychoanalytic Theories of Affect* (reprinted by Karnac, 1999), and of a forthcoming book on the mind of the religious terrorist. She has published extensively on affects, sexuality, perversion, and the philosophy of psychoanalysis. She is in private practice in NYC.

Irving Steingart, Ph.D., is Faculty and Fellow (Training and Control Analyst), Institute for Psychoanalytic Training and Research; Clinical Professor of Psychology and Supervising Analyst, New York University Post-doctoral program in Psychotherapy and Psychoanalysis; and Member, Association for Child Psychoanalysis and International Psychoanalytical Association.

Isaac Tylim, Psy.D., is a Training Analyst, International Psychoanalytic Association (IPA); Secretary of the International Psychoanalytic Association, Committee on the United Nations; Faculty, Training and Supervising Analyst, Institute for Psychoanalytic Training and Research (IPTAR); former Chair of Scientific Programs, Faculty and Supervisor, New York University Postdoctoral Program in Psychoanalysis and Psychotherapy; Faculty and Supervisor, Institute for Child, Adolescents, and Family Studies; Assistant Professor of Psychiatry, Downstate Medical Center; Coordinator Inpatient Psychology, Maimonides Medical Center. Dr. Tylim has published numerous papers in professional journals on topics ranging from applied psychoanalysis to arts and politics, multilingualism, and transference. He has traveled extensively, lecturing in the USA and abroad. He is a psychoanalyst in private practice in New York City.

Sverre Varvin, M.D., Ph.D., is a Training and Supervising analyst; Member of the Norwegian Psychoanalytic Society; Vice-president of the International Psychoanalytic Association; Senior Consultant Psychiatrist, Department Group of Psychiatry, Psychosocial Centre for Refugees; University of Oslo Faculty of Medicine; Chair of the Committee on Human Rights, Norwegian Medical Association.

Marcelo N. Vinar, M.D., graduated from Medical School in 1965 and completed his psychoanalytic training in 1969. From 1968 to 1973 he was the coordinator of Medical Education at the Uruguayan School of Medicine. When the military dictatorship took over, he went into exile in Paris. While in France, he commuted between Paris and Bois and was appointed director of L'Ecole de Psychiatrie Institutionelle de la Chesnai. In 1985, when democracy was reinstated in Uruguay, Dr. Vinar returned to his homeland and founded the first interdisciplinary group to study the effects of terrorism. Sponsored by the French Embassy and the Paris College of Philosophy, he organized the first colloquium on Historical Trauma and Violence. He is the co-author with his wife, Dr. Maren Ulriksen de Vinar, of *Fracturas de Memoria* (*Memory Fractures*). A psychoanalyst in private practice, Dr. Vinar is at the Uruguayan School of Medicine, Psychology, and Psychoanalytic Institute. He is involved in a variety of research projects including working with marginalized adolescents and neglected infants.

Valentina Vrtikapa, M.D., Graduate of the University of Sarajevo, is currently a third year Resident in Psychiatry, Department of Psychiatry, Maimonides Medical Center, Brooklyn, NY.

INDEX